ON TARZAN

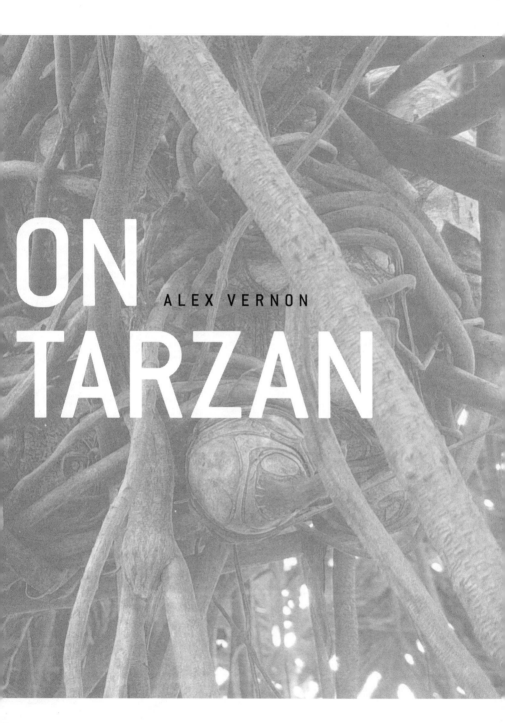

ON

ALEX VERNON

TARZAN

THE UNIVERSITY OF GEORGIA PRESS   ATHENS AND LONDON

Designed by Mindy Basinger Hill

Set in 10.5 / 14 Adobe Caslon Pro

Printed and bound by Thomson-Shore

The paper in this book meets the guidelines for
permanence and durability of the Committee on
Production Guidelines for Book Longevity of the
Council on Library Resources.

Printed in the United States of America

12 11 10 09 08 C 5 4 3 2 1

12 11 10 09 08 P 5 4 3 2 1

Library of Congress Cataloging-in-Publication Data

Vernon, Alex, 1967–

On Tarzan / Alex Vernon.

          p.   cm.

Includes bibliographical references and index.

ISBN-13: 978-0-8203-3183-6 (hardcover : alk. paper)

ISBN-10: 0-8203-3183-X (hardcover : alk. paper)

ISBN-13: 978-0-8203-3205-5 (pbk. : alk. paper)

ISBN-10: 0-8203-3205-4 (pbk. : alk. paper)

1. Tarzan (fictitious character) in mass media.

2. Burroughs, Edgar Rice, 1875–1950—Characters—Tarzan. I. Title.

P96.T37.V47 2008

813'.52—dc22   2008028665

British Library Cataloging-in-Publication Data available

Image on title page © Fotolia / Angela Köhler

*To Walter and Ruth, Walt and Barbara, Chip and Rick,
our dogs, Rick's gerbils, and the fish.*

*And in memory of Bryant Jensen (1940–2006),
who was also larger than life.*

The experience of a work of art is, as everyone seems willing to grant without pondering the implications, unique and untranslatable; to suggest that one has captured it in an analysis is, therefore, to falsify and mislead. The best criticism can hope to do is to set the work in as many illuminating contexts as possible. . . . The contextual critic desires only to locate the work of art, to point toward the place where his contextual circles overlap, the place in which the work exists in all its ambiguity and plentitude.

LESLIE FIEDLER, *LOVE AND DEATH IN THE AMERICAN NOVEL* (1960)

Thus did the scent of Numa, the lion, transform the boy into a beast.

EDGAR RICE BURROUGHS, *THE SON OF TARZAN* (1915)

It is, more than almost anything, African in its essence. There is everything in it. Let him who would envision the soul of this ancient continent, eat lion sperm.

PHILIP JOSÉ FARMER, *A FEAST UNKNOWN* (1969)

CONTENTS

ACKNOWLEDGMENTS

My appreciation goes to a number of people who fielded email inquiries: George McWhorter of the Burroughs Memorial Collection; Bill Hillman of ERBzine.com; Philip Melling of the University of Wales, Swansea; the anonymous researcher from the Chicago Historical Society; the members of the American Studies list-serv; and those cited in the notes. I am also grateful for the prompt and positive responses from Edgar Rice Burroughs, Inc.

I also must thank Dan and Simon Green for their tenacity. This book is better for their effort. Joanna Hildebrand Craig's professional counsel and her friendship, ever since my first book, have been invaluable. The editors, staff, and readers for the University of Georgia Press ensured this book achieved its potential on its own terms.

The Hendrix College community deserves special gratitude: the Provost's Office for its professional and modest financial support; the library staff, Peggy Morrison in particular, and the English Department's student workers, Kelley Melhorn, Keeley Murray, and Russell Moore, for their many hours of labor on my behalf; Matt Stinson for his translation assistance; Jay Barth and Duff Campbell for saving me those extraneous trips to campus (Sister Earth thanks you, too), not to mention their abiding friendship; and, most important, my students for their constant inspiration. Class preparation and discussion yielded any number of insights. They are this book's true collaborators.

Finally, I need to recognize the many Tarzan fans who over the decades have devoted themselves to collecting, creating, and preserving Tarzan lore and miscellany. They are the aficionados; I am the hack.

ON TARZAN

Tarzan (Elmo Lincoln) cradles his dead mother Kala.
From *Tarzan of the Apes* (1918).

I had this story from one who had no business to tell it to me, or to any other. I may credit the seductive influence of an old vintage upon the narrator for the beginning of it, and my own skeptical incredulity during the days that followed for the balance of the strange tale.

NARRATOR, "TARZAN OF THE APES" (1912)

ONE

OUT TO SEA

Hurtling from tree to tree, page to screen, crying his unspellable cry, Tarzan enthralled us for a century. He arrived in our world in October 1912, in *All-Story* magazine, and matured into full bookhood in 1914. In 1918 we apotheosized him, the silent film the perfect medium for his brand of brawn.

By 1926, Tarzan books were already being sold in at least twenty-one foreign countries; by 1953, they had been translated into fifty-six languages.[1] According to Robert Fenton's 1967 *The Big Swingers*, Sol Lesser's production company, which stopped making Tarzan films in 1958, estimated that Tarzan films had "been seen by more than two billion people."[2] Lesser himself, who produced seventeen Tarzan films starting in 1933, liked to boast that "there is always a Tarzan picture playing within a radius of 50 miles of any given spot in the world"—"in Arab village theatres, African bush theatres and in pampa settlements down Argentine way."[3] Imagine: Edgar Rice Burroughs, a failed businessman many times over, had created Tarzan simply to put food on the table. By 1975, according to his grandson Danton, Tarzan had become "next to Coca-Cola . . . the best-known name in the world."[4]

I write this book from Little Rock, the capital of the self-monikered "Natural State," Arkansas, where Elmo Lincoln, the Tarzan of that 1918 film, once worked as a state trooper. But I met Tarzan in the 1970s, the decade of my childhood. Those black-and-white movies on television on weekend afternoons. That safari play set one Christmas, the vanilla-wafer-colored white men, the chocolate-kiss-colored natives, the jeeps and assorted jungle creatures, and the soft plastic fold-up mat for the hard plastic cliffs and huts, just a generic safari play set, not a Tarzan product, but I always think of him when I think of it. In the backyard of our Dallas home we had a fort built around a tree, where my brothers and I played cowboys and Indians, and where we must have played Tarzan, too—until we moved to Kansas City, lost the fort, and *Star Wars* came along.

A few years out of college, I noted a blurb in a movie video catalog for *Tarzan Finds a Son!* Astonishing: the lord of the apes, the epitome of pure animal manhood, couldn't even, in 1939 America, beget a child. Tarzan and Jane find the baby near a crashed plane, the only survivor, having been thrown from the plane (through a window?) and landing, ever so gently, on the soft jungle floor—this being the filmmakers' way of dodging possible censorship and definite public outcry over having a child born to an unwed couple. The topper I wouldn't discover until researching this book: Maureen O'Sullivan playing Jane was herself pregnant during the filming. Watching her hide her pooch behind flowers, laundry, a water pitcher, and the family's pet baby elephant is a little like watching Mike Myers hide his willy behind various suggestive objects in the Austin Powers films. O'Sullivan gave birth ten days after filming ended. No wonder she didn't swim in this one.

Around the same time I discovered Tarzan's impotence, I caught the opening of an old Tarzan film on a cable station, most likely *Tarzan and the Huntress* (1947). Jane, looking out the window of her well-appointed tree house kitchen, sees her man returning from his long hard day hunting and cavorting in the jungle. She calls out to Boy, presently occupied making a fishing rod and reel, to come home and get ready for Tarzan's arrival. *Leave It to Beaver* in the jungle.

A few years later still, I decided to teach the original novel in a college course on literature and the environment. My students, born in the early

1980s, had never read a Tarzan novel or seen a Tarzan movie other than the Disney animated version that came out during their teen years. We tackled *Tarzan of the Apes* after some readings in Darwin and Thoreau, including this passage from *The Descent of Man* that captures the racist spirit of Burroughs's novel:

> For my own part, I would as soon be descended from that heroic little
> monkey, who braved his dreaded enemy in order to save the life of his keeper,
> or from that old baboon, who descending from the mountains, carried away
> in triumph his young comrade from a crowd of astonished dogs—as from
> a savage who delights to torture his enemies, offers up bloody sacrifices,
> practices infanticide without remorse, treats his wives like slaves, knows no
> decency, and is haunted by the grossest superstitions.[5]

Thoreau's essay "Walking" celebrates the human "yearning for the Wild," for "absolute freedom and wildness" as "all good things are wild and free."[6] Jane's presence in the Tarzan books and films is secondary; our primary image of Tarzan is of the man alone. Much to their surprise, my students discovered that *Tarzan of the Apes* ends with Tarzan leaving Jane behind (Burroughs with no plans for a sequel). You can walk in the wild, Thoreau writes, when "you are ready to leave father and mother, and brother and sister, and wife and child and friends, and never see them again."[7] Ironically, Tarzan's and this essay's calls to uncivilized wildness rely upon the refinement and inheritance of high culture—Tarzan's blue blood and Thoreau's literary steeping.

Even more to my students' surprise, *Tarzan of the Apes* ends on a Wisconsin dairy farm. Who knew?

Alongside novels such as Ernest Hemingway's *The Old Man and the Sea* and Margaret Atwood's *Surfacing*, Ed Burroughs's *Tarzan of the Apes* helped the class explore the tenuous (and gendered) relationship between the human world and the natural world. I speculated that *Tarzan*'s popularity in his day stemmed as much as anything else from the book's radical divergence from American literary naturalism. In those tales—think of Jack London's "To Build a Fire"—the environment, be it Mother Nature or the big city, always won. What a breath of fresh air Tarzan's sentimental self-determination would have been to those dispirited readers!

The first Tarzan novel became for us a convenient window into the era that produced and embraced it, as turn-of-the-century America transitioned from a rural economy and lifestyle to urban ones and yearned nostalgically for the good old days, as Darwin and Freud cast out human consciousness from the divine center of the universe, and as emancipation increased white racial anxiety and white racist hostility. When Tarzan in darkest Africa kills the black natives by catching them in a vine-fashioned noose and yanking them into the trees, white readers can't help but have images of lynching close by—there were sixty-one lynchings that year.[8] Gail Bederman, in *Manliness and Civilization*, calls Tarzan a "one-man lynch mob."[9] When he takes aim with poisoned arrow at the first civilized blacks he encounters, white readers are supposed to appreciate his instinctive reasoning—"They are black. . . . I do not know why I should kill the blacks back there in my jungle, yet not kill them here"[10]—while also (grudgingly) appreciating his civilized comrade's restraint of that instinct. And in one of the many coincidences that fill the universe of Tarzan phenomena I have come to call Tarzania, Elmo Lincoln, the first screen Tarzan, had earlier played in that epic film about the Ku Klux Klan, *The Birth of a Nation*.

Outside of class, I began catching references and making connections. In 1939 America, twenty-five years before the sexual revolution, of course Tarzan and Jane had to find their son. Ten years later that tree house scene of Jane's imploring Boy to come home to meet Tarzan, and the other films' scenes of Boy helping set the table and clean the tree house, would have been quite familiar to the movie's youthful audience, as it mimicked the hundreds of social guidance films, such as the ten-minute *A Date with Your Family* (1950), that American schools inflicted on their charges between 1945 and 1960. What an odd moment in that tree house scene of behavioral instruction in the context of Tarzan, our great fantasy figure of liberation from unnatural, civilizing restrictions. Yet such mixed messages fill Tarzania. They are the heart and soul of the oxymoronic ape-man.

~~~~~

A complete cultural biography of Tarzan would require ten years and several volumes. I would have to read every Tarzan novel, every possible source, and every obvious spawn. I would have to digest every Tarzan movie and television episode (live and animated), the radio series, the decades of comics, and the legions of rip-offs, unauthorized versions, imitations, parodies, and fan fiction in book, film, and comic form. Kaspa the Lion Man, anyone? I would have to review every article I could track down, every old hardcopy fanzine and the new online ones, every piece of scholarship. I would need to cull through the boxes and boxes of unpublished Burroughs material. I would need to get my hands on every Tarzan-related toy and product, on every Tarzan-inspired song by performers like Baltimora and Tina Turner, on every cartoon or remembrance that references him—in short, on every scrap of anything. And ask you to digest it all, too.

Life is too short.

So not an exhaustive cultural biography or thorough scholarly accounting, but an essay, an idiosyncratic consideration. A memoir even. Our Tarzan—my Tarzan—is and isn't Burroughs's Tarzan; he only started there.

On Tarzan offers a density of curiosities, discoveries, observations, suppositions, and associations; it appeals to breadth of material examined and approaches explored, while respecting brevity; it writes to nonspecialized readers even as it hopes to offer provocative perspectives to readers and scholars already well acquainted with Tarzan's place in cultural history; it sometimes acknowledges the self that is its source. The book touches on childhood, adolescence, and adulthood, especially for the male of the species; on colonialism and nationhood; on Hollywood and commerce, race and gender, sex and death, Darwin and Freud. On nature—is Tarzan eco-friend or eco-foe? On imagination and identity.

Touches on. For example, the differences in genre, audience, and commodification among the novels, films, and comics—not to mention the differences within each medium—are plenty, are overplenty. Although this book observes some of them, it instead focuses on the patterns of meaning that emerge from joint consideration, on the messages shared by, created in concert by, the various guises and texts and artifacts. My method, as captured in the epigraph from Leslie Fiedler at the beginning of the book, is to toss up as many contexts as possible, watch them cross paths as they cut their circles, and see which ones drop and thud, which ones keep the air.

~~~~~

Another challenge lies in the very act of taking seriously a subject as silly as Tarzan. Burroughs often condemned those commentators who took Tarzan as anything other than mindless entertainment.[11] He expressed his distaste for academics well before the highbrow weighed in on his works. In *Tarzan of the Apes,* Jane's father, Professor Archimedes Q. Porter, acts the perfect part of the bumbling intellectual whose book-filled head spares only a small space for reality. And in a story of 1913, "The Cave Girl," Burroughs was, in his own words, "having a little fun with higher education." In the story, as he summarized it to an editor, a young intellectual from "Bosting" finds himself "cast ashore somewhere" where he "[f]alls in with a bunch of cliff dwellers—aboriginal men and women. Accident throws him with a young female. She is strong, husky and intellectual as a she ape. He is a physical weakling filled with the knowledge of an encyclopedia."[12] He names his bookworm protagonist Waldo Emerson (Smith-Jones), after university-ridden Boston's most famous armchair naturalist.

Burroughs's savaging of literary critics partly involved his own insecurities as a writer. He never graduated from college, and he knew that he was a hack lucky to enjoy as much success as he did. But his dismissal of any significance to his own work was also just plain honest. Early in the second Tarzan book, *The Return of Tarzan* (1913), Burroughs already alerted his readers to the triteness of the Tarzan stories he dimly saw stretching into his future. Tarzan saunters past two characters who turn out to be the chief villains of this book and the next two. "They reminded Tarzan of melodramatic villains he had seen at the theaters in Paris. Both were very dark, and this, in connection with the shrugs and stealthy glances that accompanied their palpable intriguing, lent still greater force to the similarity."[13] Burroughs ends the next book with this choice bit of self-consciousness about some minor characters: "Possibly we shall see them all there amid the savage romance of the grim jungle and the great planes where Tarzan of the Apes loves to be. Who knows?"[14] There's something almost vaudevillian about the Tarzan series in its absurd and repetitive plot devices, its comic playfulness with exaggerated character types, and its moments of delightful self-consciousness.

Burroughs's most playful moments occur when he toys with Hollywood, such as when a character named Shrimp meets our hero in *Tarzan and the Foreign Legion* and asks, "'Is dat Johnny Weissmuller?'"—Weissmuller being to Tarzan what Sean Connery is to James Bond, the one and only.[15] *Tarzan and the Lion Man* winds up in Hollywood, during the production of a Tarzan picture. When the casting director recommends Tarzan to play Tarzan, not knowing he is Tarzan, the production manager looks him up and down and declares him "'Not the type. . . . Not the type, at all.'"[16] A week later Tarzan finds himself playing "'the part of the white hunter that Tarzan rescues from the lion'" when said lion charges the actor playing Tarzan. The real Tarzan intercepts the beast and saves the day only to be fired for killing the studio's expensive lion.[17]

Even more amusing is the novel's opening scene, in which a producer and his team hash over a jungle adventure movie they are preparing to film on location:

> "Joe's written a great story—it's goin' to be a knock-out. You see, this fellow's born in the jungle and brought up by a lioness. He pals around with the lions all his life—doesn't know any other friends. The lion is king of beasts; when the boy grows up he's king of the lions; so he bosses the whole menagerie. See? Big shot of the jungle."
>
> "Sounds familiar," commented Orman.
>
> "And then the girl comes in, and here's a great shot! She doesn't know anyone's around, and she's bathing in a jungle pool. Along comes the Lion Man. He ain't ever seen a woman before. Can't you see the possibilities, Tom? It's goin' to knock 'em cold." . . .
>
> "Joe always was an original guy," said Orman.[18]

Add to the unoriginal story a famous hunky athlete with a long European name who doesn't need to act and the sexpot starlet—the scene doesn't miss a thing. Such passages certainly take shots at the film industry's usurpation of Burroughs's creation, but they also recognize the synergy between his Tarzan and Hollywood's, and they even let Burroughs belittle the unoriginality and senselessness of his own stories. In this scene not even Burroughs escapes Burroughs's humor. When *Tarzan of the Apes* came out, it received harsh criticism for employing tigers when tigers aren't indigenous to Africa. So in *Lion Man* Burroughs has the producer pitch "'a great tiger sequence'" that's "'goin' to yank 'em right out of their seats,'" only to have the director explain, "'They're ain't any tigers in Africa.'" To which the producer replies, "'Oh, what's the difference? We'll make it a crocodile sequence.'"[19] There's a crocodile sequence in nearly every movie version from 1932 on, and hardly a croc in all twenty-four books.

Burroughs never cared much for the Tarzan movies. More Batman than Superman, his Tarzan was possessed of a darkness and ferocity unknown to his screen self. In the novels, Tarzan's victory cry is blood-curdling howl; in the movies, it's a warbling yodel. In the novels, Tarzan has a lust for violence that gives these stories their edge; in the movies, Tarzan fights like the reluctant soldier doing his duty. There's also a fantasy element to the Tarzan novels, with voluptuous dagger-armed priestesses overseeing lost civilizations. The films that attempt this element never pull it off. How can a single film include a femme fatale and a slapstick chimp?

The films do manage, on occasion, to step lightly, to throw a knowing wink to the audience about the ridiculousness of it all. "Why do I have to waste my time on *Treasure Island?* . . . Whoever calls this exciting should write a story about the jungle. That would be something,"[20] Boy tells Jane in *Tarzan and the Trappers*, after we have suffered a glutting, for nearly fifty years, of jungle stories and films. As Jane replies: "*Treasure Island* is a classic. There's more to this world than just the jungle." The classic Tarzan films of Johnny Weissmuller especially, from 1932 to 1948, have their share of fun, such as when Maureen O'Sullivan's Jane tells Boy in *Tarzan's Secret Treasure* (1941) to just "forget about civilization. Our world here is far more lovely and far more exciting than the outside world I promise you. Now you run and get the caviar from the refrigerator." How else could we possibly read such dialogue except as camp? At least one contemporary reviewer recognized the well-appointed tree house, with its refrigerator, stove, and elevator, as a "[delectable] parody of the mechanized American living and cooking comforts,"[21] though he did not see the film as a parody of the sanitized cinema demanded by middle American propriety, or as a self-parody of the entire Tarzan cinematic oeuvre. Julian Lesser's carping that MGM's last Tarzan film, *Tarzan's New York Adventure* (1942), "turned the Tarzan figure into a joke," missed the point.[22] Tarzan had nearly always been something of a farce.

When RKO took over from MGM a year later (under the production of Julian's father Sol), the films became even campier. *Tarzan's Desert Mystery* of 1943 looked like a typical Western with horse chases across a desert vista, campfire cooking with a girl in pants and a button-down shirt, and, in a lonely town, a jailbreak followed by the rescue, amid a stampede of horses called by a whistle from Tarzan, of a damsel from the hangman's noose—just like a Western, that is, until Tarzan and gang discover a jungle inhabited by battling dinosaurs and crawling prehistoric lizards. RKO's talent for musicals apparently leaked over into the staginess of some of these Tarzan numbers—

all those veritable chorus lines of extras parading about in *Tarzan and the Mermaids, Tarzan and the Leopard Woman*, and *Tarzan and the Amazons*. The later Weissmuller Tarzan films have the same effect on me as Tim Burton's *Planet of the Apes* remake of 2001—it's as if the filmmakers have dared us to deny our skepticism, pushing the limits of our susceptibility and laughing their way to the bank. Many of the Tarzan books have that effect as well: *Tarzan and the Lion Man* features a group of apes who were genetically engineered to possess human intelligence and whose society has been fashioned by their creator—a mad British scientist who calls himself God—after the British court. There's an ape-creature named Buckingham, a Suffolk, and a Henry the Eighth, as the entire mock-London scene perverts the very aristocratic structure on which Tarzan's superiority depends. In *Tarzan at the Earth's Core*, Tarzan travels to Pellucidar, a land fitted to the inner wall of the earth and surrounding a single light source at the very center. Pellucidar stars the Mahars, a species of flying reptiles with mind control powers, and Horibs, a race of snake-men with generally human torsos covered in scales and sporting horned snake heads.

Indeed, we have claimed for Tarzan mythical, archetypal status, even though his own creator dismissed him. Burroughs classified the story as belonging to the "'damphool' species of narrative" and lumped himself "in the same class with the aerial artist, the tap dancer, and the clown."[23] Hollywood's Walk of Fame perhaps testifies to the film industry's regard for Tarzan: Big Bird, Bugs Bunny, Donald Duck, Mickey Mouse, the Rugrats, the Simpsons, Kermit the Frog, Rin Tin Tin, Lassie, Woody Woodpecker, and Godzilla all have stars. Not Tarzan.[24] There's a certain irony that just as the literary, art, music, and film scene was moving into postmodern self-consciousness and parody in the 1960s and 1970s, Tarzan foundered. In 1984, *Greystoke: The Legend of Tarzan* made a notable effort at a realistic Tarzan film, but for all of its lofty posturing about restoring Tarzan to the original, the film lost Burroughs's light-hearted spirit in the process. The WB's strenuously updated *Tarzan* television show of 2003 also failed, in part I think, because of its absolute refusal to admit its own cheesiness.

One relatively late Tarzan production, however, didn't just acknowledge its own silliness. It reveled in it. It positively sloped about. Burroughs probably would have hated Bo and John Dereks' *Tarzan, the Ape Man* (1981)—she produced and starred, and he directed—even though the film took full advantage of his own tradition of self-bemused senselessness. Most Tarzan fans hated it; it is one of the (if not *the*) most maligned of the Tarzan films.

I discovered the film's farcicality late in the story, when a chimp we presume to be named Cheta must warn Tarzan that Jane requires saving. Whereas Weissmuller's chimps on similar missions would scuttle along the jungle floor in real time, this chimp speeds through the jungle on a vine Tarzan-style in the high drama of super-slow-mo. By my watch, the camera holds him to an agonizing on-screen swing time of 5.6 seconds. The scene visually echoes Tarzan's solo swing and Tarzan and Jane's tandem swing; those earlier swings, plus an excruciatingly slowed river battle between Tarzan and a giant python, have left us rather wearied of slow-motion effects. I understand wanting time to feast upon the perfect forms of this Adam and Eve, but do we really need to check out Cheta?

Now picture this: Tarzan lying unconscious, Jane kneeling beside him, talking to herself in the hammiest dumb blonde schoolgirl voice you've ever heard: "I've never touched a man before." Her finger runs along his leg. A small audience of chimps watches, bemused. "It's nice. It's very nice," she titters. This is Bo Derek!—the teenager for whom John left Linda Evans, and already the producer of an adult film (*Love You!*), already a two-time *Playboy* cover girl on her way to a record five, already the featured hot body in three movies including the title role in *10*, and in tens of thousands, hundreds of thousands, of young men's daydreams. Later Tarzan touches Jane for the first time, squeezing one of Bo's world-famous breasts like a twenty-year-old buying an avocado for the first time, not knowing what he's feeling for, her "oh God—oh God—oh God" an incongruous response. "It feels so strange. Like I'm reading this in a book. . . . I sure hope it has a happy ending. . . . The chapter always ended before this part." The scene ends.

The film ends with the couple's over-the-top clichéd lovemaking-at-sunset-on-the-beach. If we have taken these scenes seriously, if we have bought the film's billing as "the most erotic adventure of all time," the joke is on us. The Dereks have toyed with and exploited our voyeuristic expectations. They weren't chasing a serious story; they thought their *Tarzan, the Ape Man* would be, according to Bo, "funny."[25] When a Tarzan yodel interrupts a camp scene—the original Weissmuller yodel, heard by moviegoers for what feels like the millionth time—James Parker, played gallantly fatigued if indefatigable by Richard Harris, retorts: "Oh shut up, you boring son of a bitch!"

~~~~~

Our well-balanced, good-humored selves know better than to take Tarzan too seriously; his century-long, global popularity demands otherwise. What are we to do? His countless adventures wobble between the earnest and the playful. At his best he achieves both. *On Tarzan* embodies its impossible subject's wobbling and aspires to a hybridity worthy of the ape-man himself.

The chapters that follow proceed by subject, yet by subjects that do not stay put, and with other subjects flitting in and out. Evidence presented in one chapter might appear in another, interpreted anew. Through it all, and despite the occasional succumbing to the rhetoric of our hero's timeless appeal, runs a single historical argument: Created from the momentum of nineteenth-century American cultural life, Tarzan has lost his energy over the course of the twentieth century. As a real force and presence in the world, to rephrase Joseph Conrad, "Mistah Tarzan—he dead."

Burroughs's future son-in-law James Pierce as Tarzan in a publicity photo.
Tarzan and the Golden Lion (1927).

It seemed a foolish thing for a grown man to be doing—much on a par with
dressing myself in a boy scout suit and running away from home to fight Indians.
EDGAR RICE BURROUGHS, "HOW I BECAME AN AUTHOR" (1918)

TWO

TARZAN THE APE-BOY

Tarzan debuted in comic strip form on the same day as Buck Rogers, January 7, 1929, the first two serious adventure comic strips in history. With newspapers continuing to republish the strip even today, comic book series appearing several times through the 1990s and "crossover" books into the new millennium, and faux Tarzans swinging rampant in the comic industry, Tarzan of the comics has arguably been the most persistent of all the Tarzans.[1] The comics as a form—and graphic narratives more generally—we associate with childhood and adolescence, with boyhood.

The graphic form is the natural medium for one-dimensional action heroes. Tarzan's interior moments require no more than a single thought-bubble or caption to convey. We can see the blood and sweat, the pecs and breasts—we don't have to slog through all that (bad) prose—we never risk taking Tarzan too seriously, in obedience to Burroughs's injunction. Burroughs was himself something of a graphic artist, doodling in his spare time, illustrating stories he wrote for children, drawing his own Christmas cards, sketching pictures to accompany his signature in copies of books given to friends and family, and even daring a few political cartoons. More than a decade before writing *Tarzan of the Apes*, he sketched an ape-monkey critter in his copy of Darwin's *Descent of Man*, labeling it "Grandpa."

Children have always loved Tarzan, a truism that inspired Filmation's 1976 animated television series and Disney's 1999 animated film—the latter was the ape lord's first big-screen appearance since *Greystoke: The Legend of Tarzan* fifteen years earlier. Boys have always played Tarzan, to the profit of emergency rooms everywhere. A 1963 *Life* magazine article reported that "one day during the time of Tarzan's greatest success"—presumably sometime between the world wars—"there were 15 children in Kansas City hospitals who had hurt themselves falling out of trees while playing Ape Man."[2] Writers like Leslie Fiedler and S. J. Perelman can't write about Tarzan without reminiscing.[3] Perelman discovered Burroughs's "electrifying fable" in 1918:

> Insofar as the topography of Rhode Island and my physique permitted, I modelled myself so closely on Tarzan that I drove the community to the brink of collapse. I flung spears at the neighbors' laundry, exacerbated their watchdogs, swung around their piazzas gibbering and thumping my chest, made reply only in half-human grunts interspersed with unearthly howls, and took great pains generally to qualify as a stench in the civic nostril.[4]

Young fans growing up during the time of Tarzan's greatest success would have had available to them Tarzan knives, bows, lariats, spears, and blowguns; Tarzan ice cream, pudding, bread, cereal, chocolate, whipping cream, and bubble gum; Tarzan Big Little Books, yoyos, costumes, and vinyl pools; Tarzan bathing suits, belts, and jungle helmets. Some of them would have insisted their parents buy Signal Oil and Gas Company's Tarzan gasoline, and some teenagers' hoodlum posturing might have included Tarzan cigarettes. Burroughs, in creating his merchandizing empire, certainly took advantage of his hero's appeal to children. The Tarzan radio show of 1932–1934 considered children its primary audience; Signal Oil and Gas, the show's producer, directed an aggressive merchandizing plan at children.[5]

We tend to think of Tarzan as children's fare. Yet Burroughs wrote with an adult audience in mind, and through his lifetime and beyond—he died in

1950—Tarzan enjoyed a very large adult audience.[6] Indeed Burroughs wrote only two Tarzan books for children, *The Tarzan Twins* (1927) and *Tarzan and the Tarzan Twins with Jad-bal-ja the Golden Lion* (1936), neither of which are considered part of the Tarzan canon, and both of which he realized were awful.[7] In the late 1960s, the Minneapolis chapter of the Burroughs Bibliophiles wanted to remove the Tarzan novels from the public library's juvenile shelves: "Tarzan isn't rinky-dinky kid stuff."[8]

Burroughs got lucky by writing a book for adults that won over adults and youngsters. As the century progressed, as children stayed in school and delayed adulthood longer and longer, Tarzan the perpetual adolescent fit the national experience. At the same time, however, Tarzania would eventually lose its general adult audience. The movies especially had trouble holding their grip on older viewers, a problem foreshadowed by a ten-minute Tarzan spoof starring child star Shirley Temple, *Kid in Africa*, in 1933, the year after Johnny Weissmuller and Maureen O'Sullivan's debut as Tarzan and Jane.

Twenty years earlier, it hadn't taken long for Burroughs to recognize and benefit from Tarzan's appeal to the young as well as the young at heart. His 1915 *The Son of Tarzan* is a growing-up tale typical of much juvenile fiction, returning us to the spirit of the original novel as Burroughs had likely realized that the adult Tarzan had become a bore. The novel also contains one of Burroughs's many amusingly self-conscious moments in its first description of the ten-year-old boy. As the frustrated tutor complains to Jack's mother Jane, "His sole interests seem to be feats of physical prowess and the reading of everything that he can get hold of relative to savage beasts and the lives and customs of uncivilized peoples; but particularly do stories of animals appeal to him. He will sit for hours together poring over the work of some African explorer." When Jane frets that Jack might have inherited her husband's savagery, Tarzan assures her otherwise: "His love for animals—his desire, for example, to see this trained ape—is only natural in a healthy, normal boy of his age."[9] Efforts to quell that curiosity, he argues, could very well backfire, which they shortly do. Jack ends up in Africa, where he metamorphoses into Korak the ape-man. Or, better, Korak the ape-teen. It's a child's rendition of the Freudian return of the repressed, and a cautionary tale against too much repression.

Whether from instinct or reading, Tarzan knows what he's talking about. His plan to tell Jack about his own upbringing among the apes, and to let Jack explore his jungle fever secondhand, through books and exhibits in London (and under supervision), follows the advice of G. Stanley Hall, whose ideas about adolescence dominated the twentieth century's first decades:

> These nativistic and more or less feral instincts can and should be fed and formed. The deep and strong cravings in the individual to revive the ancestral experiences and occupations of the race can and must be met, at least in a secondary and vicarious way, by tales of the heroic virtues the child can appreciate, and these proxy experiences should make up by variety and extent what they lack in intensity. The teacher should so vivify all that the resources of literature, tradition, history, can supply which represents the crude, rank virtues of the world's childhood that, with his almost visual imagination, . . . the child can enter upon his full heritage, live out each stage of his life to the fullest, and realize in himself all its manifold tendencies. Echoes only of the vaster, richer life of the remote past of the race they must remain, but just these are the murmurings of the only muse that can save from the omnipresent dangers of precocity.[10]

Of growing up too quickly in the fast-paced, citified modern world. Children must have time to be children. For Hall, that meant being primitive. His two-volume *Adolescence: Its Psychology and Its Relations to Physiology, Anthropology, Sociology, Sex, Crime, Religion, and Education* appeared in 1904, eight years before "Tarzan of the Apes" and around the time Jack would have been a lad. With it, for all practical purposes, Hall invented the very idea of adolescence.

Hall's Darwinian model sees the "child-soul" as "animal" and "savage," full of "tribal, predatory, hunting, fishing, fighting, roving, idle, playing proclivities."[11] The adolescent finds himself at a "neo-atavistic" stage corresponding to the age of maturation "in some remote, perhaps pigmoid, stage of human evolution, when in a warm climate the young of our species once shifted for themselves independently of further parental aid."[12] Hall sees adult savages as "only children and adolescents of mature years, if unspoiled by civilization, with far more vigorous bodies and often purer lives than ours." Perhaps Burroughs had this vision in mind when in *Tarzan and the Foreign Legion* he has Tarzan encounter a group of naked pigmy savages "whom civilization had never touched. Fortunate people, thought Tarzan." And when they wave him away, demanding to be left alone, Tarzan obliges: "The Lord of the Jungle was in full sympathy with them and admired their good judgment. Were they always successful in keeping white men at a distance they would continue to enjoy the peace and security of their idyllic existence."[13] (It's a rare moment in Burroughs when Rousseau usurps Hobbes for the savage soul, a moment explained by the book's World War II publication and setting.)

Gail Bederman notes that as far as anyone knows Burroughs never read Hall, and the similarity indicates their participation in a larger conversation.[14] In the 1880s and into the early twentieth century, many if not most anthropologists, and other writers and thinkers, associated children with the lower races in a post-Darwin correspondence between ontogeny and phylogeny— between development of the individual and that of the species. Burroughs's description of Tarzan's discovery of the books in his parents' cabin portrays as much: "Squatting upon his haunches on the table-top . . . Tarzan of the apes, little primitive man, presented a picture filled at once with pathos and with promise—an allegorical figure of the primordial groping through the black night of ignorance toward the light of learning."[15]

The "primitivism" that inspired so much of modernist visual art—by veritably every major artist of the first half of the twentieth century (for example, Gauguin, Picasso, Matisse, Kandinky, Klee, Ray, Moore, Brancusi, Miro)— involved children's art as much as it did "native" art and, for that matter, art produced by the mentally ill. Such work became the focus of exhibits and artists' personal collections and was sometimes displayed alongside the artists' own work.[16] Being less developed into their civilized selves, being less corrupted by adult consciousness and more instinctive and irrational, these souls were thought to have access to the true nature of things, including humanity's primal self. The artists aspired to the condition of children.

One long passage from Hall provides a veritable blueprint for Burroughs's *Tarzan of the Apes.* A child in his middle years, from nine to twelve, has achieved a harmonious state among body, mind, and environment corresponding to "an old and relatively perfected stage of race-maturity" that characterizes some races even in Hall's day—a "terminal stage of human development at some post-simian point." Then adolescence strikes. The child unified with itself and with nature ceases to be. Disarray reigns. The teen now "must conquer a higher kingdom of man for himself, break out a new sphere, and evolve a more modern story to his psycho-physical nature." This evolution to adulthood is fraught: "New dangers threaten on all sides. It is the most critical stage of life, because failure to mount almost always means retrogression, degeneracy, or fall. One may be in all respects better or worse, but can never be the same."[17] Tarzan evolves from his childish animal stage, outgrowing his ape companions, through the savage stage represented by his first encounters with the natives, to achieve finally his civilized self, along the way battling his own urgings to cannibalism, rape, and murder that would, if he yielded to them, result in retrogression, degeneracy, or fall. Artistic primitivism's romanticizing of irrationality is reflected here in its darker aspect.

The stories of Tarzan and Jack-Korak mirror the prominent psychological theory of the day. They satisfy the natural youthful desire to read about animals and savages, and they conform to the audience's understanding of adolescence. Adults have their understanding confirmed; the youths get to live their own experiences in a purer and yet safer way. Burroughs's *The Son of Tarzan* becomes an advertisement for the entire series: buy these books for your young sons, lest they board a steamer for Africa.

Tarzan of the Apes is first and foremost a coming-of-age story, a bildungsroman, that ends in America, the endpoint of civilization's progressive westward march. Tarzan has learned English and French, has learned manners and the ways of the Western world. As he comes into his own as a human among other humans, he relinquishes the rule of his impulses (in particular his tendency to kill other people whenever it suits him). But his greatest sacrifice is of his beloved Jane. At the end of the novel, for Tarzan to reveal his identity as Lord Greystoke could only affect Jane adversely: either she would dishonor herself by breaking her engagement to his cousin and the current Lord Greystoke, William Cecil Clayton; or her honor would force her to marry Cecil and live without the Greystoke wealth and title (which would return to the rightful heir). Tarzan has evolved into his full humanity by becoming the supreme moral animal. His self-sacrifice for her sake reminds us of Sydney Carton's at the end of Dickens's *A Tale of Two Cities*, a sacrifice that also allows the beloved woman to be with another man.

The moral example of Tarzan's sacrifice perfectly fits the spirit of the times, the ideology that sent so many men to the trenches of World War I, and the Victorian and Edwardian ideology of repression. "Self-renunciation" is Burroughs's own word.[18] Many scholars of the bildungsroman consider the genre as consisting of novels "about adolescence intended for adult readers," an "inherently Romantic genre, with its optimistic ending that affirms the protagonist's entry into adulthood."[19] For adults, *Tarzan of the Apes* works as nostalgia for their lost innocence and for their coming-of-age. They celebrate their internalizing of social mores even as they long for childhood's abandon. The genius of the ending of *Tarzan of the Apes* is that it allows Tarzan to demonstrate his achieved adulthood by his noble act while also presumably sending him back to his jungle playground. We readers can't go back again, but Tarzan can, and does, in books and movies again and again and again. He gives us a simple fantasy of manhood, of leaving boyhood behind and never having to leave it behind. Indeed, the other books and the films appeal by virtue of the hero's lack of growth, development, and conflict. Tarzan is simply Tarzan; Tarzan simply is, like an animal or very small child in his lack of self-consciousness.

On the big screen, Tarzan's lack of body hair (excepting Mike Henry's chest) renders him a big kid. A close-up in *Tarzan's Greatest Adventure* (1959) shows a tarantula crawling up a leg as smooth as an ivory tusk. Screen Tarzans have used their trim athletic physiques and their hairlessness to suggest the eternal teen (perhaps preteen) even while their obvious maturity—these men were in their late twenties at the youngest—bespoke their adulthood. The downright tubby Elmo Lincoln, who at twenty-eight looked fifty, "was so hairy," recalled Gordon Griffith, the actor who played Tarzan as a lad in that 1918 film, "they had to shave him twice a day so that the audience could tell him from the apes" played by "a bunch of husky young fellows from the New Orleans Athletic Club who put on ape skins and swung through the trees."[20] (The balding Lincoln also had to wear a wig held in place with a headband, an uncooperative solution that forced a number of reshoots). In the novels, we learn in *Tarzan and the Foreign Legion* (1947) that as a youth Tarzan had obtained the secret of perpetual youth from a witch doctor, and in *Tarzan's Quest* (1935–1936) he and Jane obtain a supply of youth elixir pills.

In a movie theater, don't we adults regress to our childhood moviegoing days? Don't we escape the march of time in that dark, womb-like space, awash in sensory experience, un-individuated among the identical spectating others, and sustained through umbilical straws? At home, we curl fetally on the couch.[21] Watching a Tarzan film is quadruply regressive: in the venue, in Tarzan's youthfulness, in the return to mother Africa, and in memories of our backyard Tarzan play. Even quintuply: as we aspire to the bumbling artlessness of childhood, what could be more artless than a Tarzan movie? Weissmuller's Tarzan is especially childish, with Jane's constant mothering, his love of silly play, and most especially his infantile speech. Every sentence that isn't animal-babble is either a question or a command delivered beneath furrowed brow, looking the spitting image of my two-year-old—whose mastery of pronouns and verb conjugation puts his to shame.

For adults in the era of G. Stanley Hall, *Tarzan of the Apes* also appealed to them as parents and teachers. Tarzan served their children as a wild escapist fantasy but also as inculcation into proper, dutiful social roles—roles figured as natural, even heroic. Hall prescribed the reading of savage tales by adolescents in order to tame their youthful savagery; his psychology actually provided a strong rationale for the fledgling institutions of American public education, especially for the emergence of high school as a normal and necessary part of American life. With increased urbanization, and with real competition for jobs among their parents' generation, American youth, once indispensable contributors to the household's economy, needed someplace to be that wasn't the office or factory, the pool hall or the streets. Hall's work provided theoretical justification for keeping kids in school and indeed for prolonging that hazy period between childhood and adulthood where Tarzan thrives:

> We should transplant the human sapling, I concede reluctantly, as early as eight, but not before, to the schoolhouse with its imperfect lighting, ventilation, temperature. We must shut out nature and open books. The child must sit on unhygienic benches and work the tiny muscles that wag the tongue and pen. . . . Even if it be prematurely, he must be subjected to special disciplines and be apprenticed to the higher qualities of adulthood, for he is not only a product of nature, but a candidate for a highly developed humanity. . . . Never again will there be such susceptibility to drill and discipline, such plasticity to habituation, or such ready adjustment to new conditions. . . . This is not teaching in its true sense so much as it is drill, inculcation, and regimentation. The method should be mechanical, repetitive, authoritative, dogmatic. The automatic powers are now at their very apex, and they can do more and bear more than our degenerate pedagogy knows or dreams of.[22]

Read Tarzan, play Tarzan during recess, but otherwise transform yourself into an indoor automaton, a productive factory cog or office stool, working for someone trained on Frederick Winslow Taylor's efficiency principles. "In the past, the man has been first," wrote Taylor in his 1911 *The Principles of Scientific Management*; "in the future the system must be first."

Tarzan's education similarly pretends one thing to kids but teaches another. On the surface Tarzan doesn't need anyone, and he certainly doesn't need school, to learn all he needs to know. He learns from the school of hard knocks, even teaching himself to read. But the novel also quite clearly argues for education, for book learning. Tarzan learns a lot from books. He learns that he is a man—a white man. He learns how to be a man, and how to treat women, and as a result he gets the girl. And he can teach himself to read only because of his aristocratic genetic inheritance, something lacking in American schoolchildren, the mutt children of a mutt nation. American kids need teachers. Eventually even Tarzan needs a teacher, the estimable Frenchman, Paul D'Arnot.

In 1912, more American youth could read than ever before; more American youth had time to read than ever before. Large numbers had left the farm and its endless chores and found themselves in cities and towns, and in school. The world of American childhood was changing, and Tarzan managed to speak to the world we had left behind and the strange new one in which we found ourselves.

～～～～

Tarzan of the Apes appeared at the apex of the greatest immigrant influx in American history. With over thirteen million immigrants, the first fifteen years of the new century more than doubled the number from the prior fifteen years, a period that itself had been a record high. No single year had brought in over a million immigrants until 1905, and then again in 1906, 1907, 1913, and 1914[23]—this great wave brought to America Johnny Weissmuller from Hungary and Maureen O'Sullivan from Ireland. Many of those reading about Tarzan learning to read a new language had themselves only recently learned to read a new language. Like Tarzan, they came of age in a polyglot world, their mother tongue different from and "inferior" to the language they were now supposed to know. Like Tarzan, they had to reconcile their old native identity with their new modern one. Their polyglot world was a polyself world.

Tarzan the immigrant: first as a human in the jungle, an Old Europe child alone in a dangerous new world, but more pointedly as an "ape" going human—torn between his ties to his familial and cultural roots and his compulsion to reinvent himself, a compulsion that drives him to the United States. Tarzan never knows home; he is the ultimate diaspora figure. Among the apes he misses his own kind; among humans he misses his own kind. Immigrant youth at the turn of the last century had no help from their parents in learning their new selves, the parents who were themselves basically young adults learning the ways of the world. Like Tarzan, they all had to teach themselves. To reinvent themselves. Tarzan's triumph would have been the shining exemplar of American promise, of a meritocracy of ability, adaptability, and character. He even looked like a lot of immigrants: black hair, gray eyes, and dusky, in a land that valued blond hair, blue eyes, and the fair. An ugly duckling despite his obvious beauty.

These immigrant youth, without any parental guidance in or real inherited connection to their new world, would feel a lot like orphans. The orphan too is a diaspora figure, belonging and not belonging. *Tarzan of the Apes* is, after all, a Horatio Alger tale transplanted from New York City's streets to the Dark Continent's jungles. Burroughs's Tarzan is doubly orphaned, losing first his English parents and then his ape foster mother. The fact of his orphanhood, though instrumental only to the first book's plot, informs all the rest.

From the 1930s onward, however, the movies of Tarzan's golden age on the screen ignored everything about Tarzan's background and presented him as a fully formed adult. The production companies eventually discovered that they needed a character with whom the children of their primary market could identify. They needed an orphan. Starting with 1939's *Tarzan Finds a Son!* and running through all but the last Weissmuller Tarzan film (*Tarzan and the Mermaids* in 1948), we have Boy, played by Johnny Sheffield. In *Tarzan's Savage Fury* (1952), Tarzan and Jane's son is not an adopted baby they name Boy but an adopted child, Joey. In the Jane-less *Tarzan Goes to India* (1962), the young orphan sidekick role falls to Jai the elephant boy. Jai returns to cavort with Tarzan for the 1966–1968 television series, which also never bothered with a Jane character. The child actor who played Jai in the TV series, Manuel Padilla Jr., played different orphan characters in two Tarzan films during the years the TV series aired, *Tarzan and the Valley of Gold* (1966) and *Tarzan and the Great River* (1967).

Americans have historically loved orphan literature because America is an orphan nation, a nation born from a crew of preteens running away from home, and a fictional orphan has, narratively speaking, done away with his parents. In the late nineteenth and early twentieth centuries, long before birth control and modern obstetrics, America also had a lot of orphans in its city streets. The country had so many orphans that between 1853 and 1929, some 200,000 orphans were loaded onto trains and shipped from the East Coast to join families needing hands to help tame the West.[24] Moreover, with the Industrial Revolution and the rise of office labor taking parents away from the home more and more, and with children either working in a factory or relegated permanently to the school system, an entire generation experienced an odd sort of orphanhood. As America approached and entered the twentieth century at the forefront of the new modern world, a post-God, post–Great War world, the collective experience must have felt a lot like an orphan's coming-of-age self-creation. This was, not coincidentally, the golden age of children's literature in the United States.[25] One might easily enough argue that feelings of homelessness and displacement marked the modernist generation and its literature, the generation Gertrude Stein famously labeled "lost."

Neither Tarzan nor orphan literature appealed strictly to Americans, of course. The plight of orphans and the mystery of their parentage had long been a staple plot device of English literature, from Henry Fielding's *Tom Jones* (1749) to nearly every Charles Dickens novel. Indeed, we might credit Tarzan's popularity to the return to a time-proven tale, satisfying if sentimental, abandoned—orphaned, as it were—by the new "serious" literature. *Tarzan of the Apes* appeared after the new divide between high culture and popular culture had opened,[26] and during that divide's culminating era of high modernism dominated by such reader-unfriendly authors as James Joyce, William Faulkner, Virginia Woolf, T. S. Eliot, and Gertrude Stein.

Orphan literature also appeals to many readers on a more fundamental and personal level. As Daniel Karlin notes, Kipling's Mowgli finds himself "separated from his real parents as every child both dreads and longs to be."[27] This overgeneralization nevertheless resonates. Tarzan has it both ways, an orphan with a parent, Kala, who as an ape doesn't actually count as his parent. Orphan fiction is thus a narcissistic fantasy genre of complete self-determination disguised in superficial if genuine moral tales. Yet the orphan story as a fantasy of life without parents is too easy a conclusion. Parents are a necessity, after all, and only-children hardly need to fantasize about being the center of the universe. Orphan fiction is also the fantasy of life without siblings, more specifically life without older siblings, and probably most purely life without older brothers. Burroughs hides the fraternal rivalry in Tarzan's relationship with William Cecil, his cousin, Jane's suitor and first fiancé, and the current natural inheritor—like an older brother—of the Greystoke name. The movies play out this fantasy through Boy in his various guises.

It takes one to know one: Edgar Rice Burroughs was the youngest of four sons; I'm the youngest of three. Ed's two oldest brothers went to Yale; Ed failed to gain admission to West Point and never tried to go to college again. Twice he worked for George Jr. and Harry and their Yale classmate in Idaho, working a ranch named the Bar Y after their alma matter and then dredging for gold on the Snake River, along with the third brother, Frank. One of the dredge boats they named Yale, and a large Yale banner decorated the main cabin of the houseboat where the four Burroughs bothers and their families lived. The dredging company had two names: the Sweester-Burroughs Mining Company and the Yale Dredging Company. Desperate for money a few years later, Ed took a job at Frank's stationery store though his older brother could hardly afford it. He quit as soon as his writing career promised fiscal relief.[28]

The fantasy of having no siblings reflects the catch-22 of a youngest son's desire to compete for his mother's affection while also wanting desperately to grow away from her in order to best his brothers by—paradoxically—growing up like them. It's the catch-22 of always being her baby in her eyes and having to play up that role to secure her attention, even while rebelling against it, even while nesting in it. Being the baby after all distinguishes him from his older siblings. With Tarzan, Burroughs solves his birth order's dilemma. With Tarzan, Burroughs also solves the struggle every child undergoes: the desire to separate and individuate from the mother versus the desire to curl up in that lap forever. The death of Tarzan's mother Alice Clayton and his adoption by Kala, who adored him as much as Alice would have, allows him to have it both ways: he can individuate but still gets to clutch her teat. And for an adult Burroughs and his adult readers, Tarzan the singleton satisfies their longing for the narcissism of childhood, when they were the center of the world. With his two adoring mothers he is, as a child, doubly the center of the world and, as a man, doubly individuated. Even with Alice and Kala both dead, Tarzan's African home serves as both womb, the bushy dark place of his origins, and the very proving grounds of his singularity.

Did Ed Burroughs's decision to become a writer stem from a youngest son's desire to have a voice and be heard? "We like to speak casually about 'sibling rivalry,'" wrote Ernest Becker in his Pulitzer Prize–winning *The Denial of Death* (1973). But "Sibling rivalry is a critical problem that reflects the basic human condition: it is not that children are vicious, selfish, or domineering. It is that they so openly express man's tragic destiny: he must desperately justify himself as an object of primary value in the universe." Children want to count more than their siblings; adults want to count more than their peers; civilization exists to "*make man count* for more than any other animal."[29] In childhood one first feels the terrifying and impossible challenge of creatureliness. In adolescence in particular, we grow into our most abstractly capable and our most biologically purposed selves. Young Adam and Eve achieve abstraction—the knowledge of good and evil, and of mortality—and simultaneously become sexual beings; thus Tarzan the teen learns to read and conceptualize during his own sexual maturation.

To the degree that the child's plight bespeaks everyone's—that the child is the parent of the person—Tarzan symbolizes the desperate human hope that we are, in a post-Darwin, post-God world, more than the animals around us. Tarzan's victory over his older foster ape-creature brother Terkoz, by which he wins Jane, expresses this hope. Through Tarzan, we vicariously kill animals to kill the animal within. A kind of zoophobic violence. We get to kill representatives of that messy adult civilized world, too. Adults losing themselves in a good Tarzan yarn travel back to the time when they didn't understand what was happening to them or what was at stake in the battle, to the time before what Becker calls the Pyrrhic victory of adulthood:

> The child emerges with a name, a family, a playworld in a neighborhood,
> all clearly cut out for him. But his insides are full of nightmarish memories
> of impossible battles, terrifying anxieties of blood, pain, aloneness, darkness;
> mixed with limitless desires, sensations of unspeakable beauty, majesty, awe,
> mystery; and fantasies and hallucinations of mixtures between the two,
> the impossible attempt to compromise between bodies and symbols. . . .
> To grow up at all is to conceal the mass of internal scar tissue that throbs
> in our dreams.[30]

By returning to that time in their lives through Tarzan, adult readers master the experience by transforming it from bodily and emotional reality to mental abstraction. Like the visual artist so taken with primitivism, they re-immerse themselves in those swirling days only through strict control. Tarzan is the fantasy of conquering the teeming chaos of one's own nature (though we should not forget that children aspire to the wholeness and surety of adults, that Adam and Eve wanted to grow up and get their own place).

Yet Tarzan has one distinct advantage over the rest of us. As a child he never knew his parents, he discovered his humanity without any adult humans around, and he never connected the former occupants of his parents' cabin to himself. As far as he knew, his existence lacked natural origin, lacked any bodily source. He would have experienced himself as an abstraction, beyond biology and apart from animal existence even as he had suckled at his ape-mother's breast. Talk about having it both ways.

~~~~~

None of which Burroughs intended: "I recall that when I wrote the first Tarzan story twenty years ago I was mainly interested in playing with the idea of a contest between heredity and environment."[31] Yet he wanted a victory by human nature, not a victory over human nature. *Tarzan of the Apes* was no experimental naturalism à la Zola, who dropped his characters into situations as experiments, to "observe" the "natural" outcome. If honestly observed, Burroughs full well knew, baby Tarzan would not have survived, and if he had, he would have been "cowardly" and "under-developed" and would have possessed "a most abominable disposition." So he gave "heredity some breaks."[32] Thus Tarzan overcomes creatureliness by becoming lord of the jungle even as the heroic ape-man, suckled by an ape-mother, thrives by means of creatureliness.

The basic question Tarzan and his readers face—Are we products of nature, nurture, or self-determination?—is the question that initially confronts all of us in adolescence and that pesters us the rest of our lives. It's no wonder that Burroughs's Tarzan plays a god to the superstitious natives time and time again, godliness of course being the fantasy of ultimate authority over one's self and one's world. The common conclusion that Tarzan represents nature's unqualified triumph over nurture, of heredity over environment, even as mere fantasy, does not hold. Burroughs intuited the speciousness of the nature-nurture dilemma—it took the Greystoke noble blood *and* the Kerchak ape clan to make the Lord of the Jungle. Tarzan's father John Clayton, with the same genetic inheritance and the advantage of a lifetime of civilized and martial training, does not survive. Tarzan's surrogate twin, his cousin and Jane's fiancé William Cecil Clayton, would not have survived and in fact does not survive the second book, *The Return of Tarzan*, letting Tarzan get the girl after all.

Tarzan also succeeds through more material handicaps from his environments: his father's knife, the knowledge imparted by the books his parents left behind, and the weapons, clothing, and knowledge gained from the nearby cannibal African tribe. After all, it's from his parents' books, not their noble blood, that he learns he is not an ape, that he should wear clothes and shave, that he is not an ugly duckling in comparison to his "handsome" ape-creature brethren.[33] From books, not noble blood, he learns to treat Jane gently rather than rip off her clothes and slake away.[34] The Tarzan tales' argument for inherent and essential gender and racial roles and traits self-deconstructs. Cultural relativism rears.

Tarzan finally succeeds because he's the luckiest person, real or fictional, in the history of the race. Burroughs usually cites Providence, but he means luck (and here again Burroughs gives his hero a break by rigging literary naturalism's use of the role of "chance" in human affairs). Anyone who has read even one Tarzan novel knows the burden of suspending disbelief required by all those coincidences, like Jane and her entourage's landing at the exact spot where Tarzan's parents landed twenty years earlier. The importance of Tarzan's luck can't be overlooked, because it indicates another reason for his appeal—to those readers who, despite their fine character and intelligence and physical aptitude, have not been so fortunate. People like Ed Burroughs, who despite his talents scraped through roughly twenty occupations and ventures before Tarzan saved him, in his late thirties, from a less secure financial life and perhaps from a less secure sense of manly selfhood. Burroughs spoke frequently about the role of luck in human affairs; Tarzan's extraordinary popularity and Burroughs's resultant success surprised him his entire life.

In the context of the novel's reconciliation of nature and nurture, the last lines of *Tarzan of the Apes*, when Tarzan relinquishes his claim on Jane by denying his true identity as Lord Greystoke, are positively brilliant. "How the deuce did you ever get into that bally jungle," cousin Cecil has asked him. "'I don't know,' said Tarzan quietly. 'I was born there. My mother was an ape, and, of course, she couldn't tell me anything about it. I never knew who my father was.'"[35] Tarzan's reply points to his nurturing by apes; it signifies humankind's animal nature and ancestry; and, in its self-renunciation—more of a noble half-truth than a noble lie—it reveals his fine breeding, the paragon of civilized humanity. Even his aristocratic breeding, a kind of genetic nurturing, challenges the nature versus nurture dilemma. What do we do with Tarzan, who sometimes revels in his creatureliness, who other times transcends it—"nature"—by way of his genetic nature, his creatureliness?

Tarzan's contradictory nature enables contradictory sympathies. For the immigrants, orphans, and poor, fighting the elements in their rudimentary homes on the Great Plains or fighting the savage urban jungles of America, the swarthy Tarzan is their godsend, their fantasy, their hope. For the others, those running scared from the immigrant invasion and insecure in their own national and racial identity, those "native" Americans—many of whose parents were poor, uneducated, non-English immigrants—clamoring for the preservation of the purity of their Anglo-Saxon roots and promulgating the "Americanization" of the newcomers to erase all vestiges of their backward foreign selves, the blue-blooded Tarzan is their godsend, their fantasy, their hope (racism was hardly a simple black-white affair). For Europeans, he can be old blood, old money, or representative of the new breed. All of these identities and none of them, like America itself: "Tarzan of the Apes" ends in America, looking back simultaneously and confusedly to its origins in the great halls of Europe and in the wilds of nature.

Tarzan also fits perfectly his genre, the novel, with its roots in middle-class popular culture. The novel, like the middle class, is anxiously both and neither the working class and the aristocracy. During the Depression of the 1930s, struggling Americans would have appreciated the screen Tarzan and Jane's rejection of materialism and celebrated their Yankee ingenuity in the outfitting of their tree house with animal-powered faucet, stove, refrigerator, and elevator—even if Steinbeck's Joads didn't have a chimp and an elephant handy, and even as those jerry-rigged luxuries reinforced the materialistic bourgeois lifestyle ideal. Tarzan is the prime early example of how mass culture can serve superficially to unite antagonistic classes, to defuse through distraction the potential for material conflict, and thus maintain the status quo. The century's precipitous transition to a workforce of professional specialization, and the consequent loss of common knowledge and experience, only increased the desperation for the unifying force of popular culture. People need to have something to talk about.[36]

Tarzan isn't a Rousseauian noble savage; he is a noble and a savage. He is and isn't an immigrant. He is and isn't an orphan. He is and isn't working class. He is and isn't educated. He is and isn't well bred. He is and isn't a youth, is and isn't a mature adult. He is and isn't whatever you or I want him to be. His white hairless body is our blank slate.

This fundamental ambiguity of Tarzan's character boils down to the fundamental question of Burroughs's immediate post-Darwin era: Are we men or beasts? Orphaned by God's sudden absence, we were on our own. The self-determination of existentialism would slither and crawl out of this morass to breathe on its own. (Terry Eagleton has remarked that existentialist self-determination is "a rather adolescent kind of ethics" because of its self-centeredness, because "it is this proprietorship that matters, not the nature of the values themselves.")[37] Not coincidentally, *Tarzan of the Apes* plays with the detective fiction genre, as Tarzan and his French mentor Paul D'Arnot seek evidence of his identity, the cause of his situation, and they find it with the new forensic tool of fingerprinting. Not coincidentally because detective fiction came into its own after Darwin, the genre's premise being this very analytical quest, backward in time, for cause, origin, identification.[38] The endless controversy over the origin of Burroughs's idea for Tarzan recapitulates this very issue: Who are we? Where did we come from?[39]

Tarzan's identity confusion resonates perfectly with that of his adolescent reader. Amnesia afflicts Tarzan more than once. A Tarzan imposter in Burroughs's *Tarzan and the Golden Lion* (1922–1923) comes to believe he is Tarzan; in a later novel, *Tarzan and the Lion Man* (1933–1934), Tarzan and a man playing a Tarzan-like character for a jungle film are frequently mistaken for one another—this is the novel in which Tarzan fails to land a movie role playing himself. The mad man of *Tarzan and the Mad Man* (1964) idolized Tarzan, and when he develops amnesia in the jungle he too believes he is Tarzan. Written in 1940, no publisher wanted this story because, as one said, "Tarzan doesn't seem to be Tarzan any more."[40] Did we ever, did he ever, really know who he was?

"Wanna see me be a leopard?" the boy Tarzan asks his ape-mother in the animated Disney film. "Why don't you just come up with your own self?" Kala rejoins. Disney's 2005 straight-to-DVD *Tarzan II* focuses even more squarely on the issue, with its theme song "Who am I?" and Tarzan's surrogate father Zugor's final pronouncement: "You're a Tarzan!" The DVD's accompanying music video of "Who Am I?" is set in a classroom, with the song sung by a preteen, her classmates dancing behind her. The fact that an apparently middle-class African American girl performs this number attempts to universalize Tarzan's appeal and ripeness for identification, effectively nullifying the historical context of immigrants and orphans and asserting a common denominator of normative adolescence that trumps all differences. The music video speciously portrays an achieved equality of self-determination for all, regardless of skin, class, or gender; or, more generously, it portrays an ideal to advance its realization. Then again, are we to read this young woman's singing "Who am I, tell me?" "Where do I come from?" and "Where do I belong?" while visually transported to a jungle as black prideful heritage-homecoming or as white racist expulsion? Cuts between her jungle dancing and Tarzan's jungle swinging, though ideally identifying her with him beyond race and gender, potentially subvert his race and gender: Tarzan as adolescent and as savage, per Hall? and as a girl?[41]

Yet I, too, as you've observed in my own reaction to Tarzan, vacillate between the historicizing and the universalizing impulse, and wind up generating more questions than answers. I want to read him in the context of Hall's notion of adolescence, but also as the eternal adolescent, caught and screaming in a net of determining and often unknown forces: his familial history, his cultural legacy, his immediate surroundings, his own body. As the eternal adolescent for whom Tarzan embodies the fantasy of self-possessed adulthood. And I want to read him as the adolescent loitering inside all adults, indeed as the eternal adult, nostalgic for the days of virility and the potential, however illusory, for future self-determination. As the adult for whom Tarzan embodies the fantasy of childhood's simplicity, grace, and, yes, self-possession.

And sometimes I want to throw my hands up and say: None of the above. He's just an escapist action hero. Readers and viewers lose themselves in Tarzania, and wallow in their lostness.

~~~~~

T. S. Eliot's poem "The Love Song of J. Alfred Prufrock" appeared in 1915, only a year after the book version of *Tarzan of the Apes*, and in a magazine, *Poetry*, based in Burroughs's hometown of Chicago. Roberta Seelinger Trites's book *Disturbing the Universe* explains that the poem, written by Eliot in his early twenties, "asks a question as germane to adolescents as it is to the middle-aged: 'Do I dare disturb the universe?'"[42] The middle-aged Prufrock's dilemma involves the women at a tea toward which he is heading. Should he speak with them? What would he, could he, should he, say? The poem details his agony, which feels a bit like that of a shy boy on his way to a junior high school dance: Dare he talk? Will they laugh? Dare he disturb the universe? Dare he even eat a peach?

Driving Prufrock's trivial anxieties is the greatest anxiety of all, per Becker: "The irony of man's condition is that the deepest need is to be free of the anxiety of death and annihilation; but it is life itself which awakens it, and so we must shrink from being fully alive."[43] Raised a jungle animal who witnessed death daily, Tarzan does not fear it—as Burroughs reminds incessantly—so he does not fear life. He became our answer to Prufrock.

The fantasy of fearlessness and power certainly appealed to Burroughs's male peers, who found themselves increasingly working for bosses in offices and factories. Tarzan has no boss, he works in the jungle, and he has an uneasy relationship with money, for us the supreme boss, for him an unnatural constraint and an inducement to compromise. The jungle setting allows for the escapism and allows the power fantasy to work by masking it through displacement. Children's natural feeling of disempowerment would have been exacerbated by the turn-of-the-century's lengthening of adolescent limbo, while disempowered adult men would have felt treated like children themselves—Tarzan's Africa as manly fantasy and maternal embrace.

Orphans and youngest sons epitomize adolescents in their need, as Trites describes it, to "learn their place in the power structure." Trites finds this issue central to adolescent literature: "Although the primary purpose of the adolescent novel may appear to be a depiction of growth, growth in this genre is inevitably represented as being linked to what the adolescent has learned about power. Without experiencing gradations between power and powerlessness, the adolescent cannot grow."[44] It's the stuff of Harry Potter. Both Tarzan and Harry, after losing their parents as infants, are raised by an apish foster family living outside the child's proper environment. A scar on the forehead, from an early life-or-death encounter, throbs scarlet whenever real danger presses. Every Harry Potter novel is a detective story involving an inquiry into the past for the self-understanding necessary for managing the present.

It's also turn-of-the-twentieth-century America. Discovering the relationship between power and identity, learning one's position in the world—the United States circa 1912 was a nation struggling with exactly these issues. It was an adolescent nation, an immigrant and a self-orphaned nation frantic about self-determination, anxious to maintain the integrity of a still-vague self-conception, a youngest child longing to be treated alongside those much older countries, finally, as an adult.

Cpl. Vernon Davis (left) coaches and S/Sgt. Edmund V. Feliz (right) drapes a lei of machine gun bullets around him as Edgar Rice Burroughs, author of the Tarzan novels, shoots a few machine gun rounds at a target at the Jungle Training Camp somewhere in the Central Pacific. AP / Wide World Photos, 1944.

From the records of the Colonial Office and from the dead man's diary we learn that a certain young English nobleman, whom we shall call John Clayton, Lord Greystoke, was commissioned to undertake a peculiarly delicate investigation of conditions in a British West Coast African colony from whose natives another European power was known to be recruiting soldiers for its army, which latter [sic] it used solely for the forcible collection of rubber and ivory from the savage tribes along the Congo and the Aruwimi.

NARRATOR, "TARZAN OF THE APES" (1912)

THREE

THE HOLLER HEARD 'ROUND THE WORLD

The Boy Scouts of America incorporated in 1910, two years before Burroughs published Tarzan. Like Tarzan, the Boy Scouts have always blurred the line between childhood and adulthood, the scouts playing little men while their leaders play little boys. In a publicity photo from 1927, Tarzan actor James Pierce poses in his over-the-shoulder leopard-skin costume and shakes hands with the oldest of five scouts of varying ages, from casual youngsters to upstanding young adult. A group of dark-skinned shaggy-haired spear-clutching "natives" gathers behind them. The allegory taunts: Is Tarzan the transitional link on the way from savage blackness to civilized whiteness, or is he the white male ideal to which civilized boys aspire? Either way, the Africans literally constitute the background to the making of white manhood. Like the Boy Scouts, the original Tarzan curiously blended the American frontier spirit and the British imperial one, and at the exact moment when the United States began fancying itself as the world's next great empire.

On the home front, on March 23, 1922, Tarzan's creator became the first writer known to have incorporated himself: Edgar Rice Burroughs, Inc.; the first official Tarzan merchandise, a line of toy primates, appeared later that year,[1] the year that also brought out those highbrow monuments *Ulysses* and *The Waste Land*. Burroughs was the first to take full advantage of the secondary product market, truly the pioneer of the practice that has come to dominate America's entertainment industry. For his time he achieved an unprecedented synergy with the books, the comics, the illustrated books, the radio shows, the movies and television shows (live and animated), and the products. Were I writing this book in the late 1920s, I would surely be typing it on Tarzan bond paper (and in the 1970s, perhaps in my "Me Tarzan" bikini underwear). And all the rest: ladders, coloring books, art-by-the-numbers, Picturama Rub-ons, jigsaw puzzles, adult jigsaw puzzles, sweat shirts, 3-D Viewmaster pictures, suspenders and garters, notebooks, wallets, several games, stickers, playing cards, stamp albums, handkerchiefs, gloves, rice bowls, knapsacks, beach balls, and thongs. Perhaps my brothers and I would have started our own Tribe of Tarzan or Tarzan Clan of America chapter— except that these efforts failed to thrive, largely because of Tarzan's deep kinship with the already-established Boy Scouts.

Tarzan's empire reached far and wide. The trailer for the infamously racy 1934 *Tarzan and His Mate* introduced our hero as "the best known . . . the most loved character . . . ever conceived in the mind of man." That's a bit precious. Yet the American century *was* Tarzan's century, at home and abroad. According to Sol Lesser, "about 75 percent of the film grosses came from foreign countries during the period when I was producing the films," from 1933 to 1958.[2] In an article for the *San Francisco Examiner*, Lesser wrote that at the time—1949—"Nearly half a hundred Tarzan movies have been made" of which "almost one-half are still in constant circulation." He continued by focusing on foreign markets:

> Some motion picture theaters run each Tarzan picture as often as eight and ten times. Some European and South American audiences accept new Tarzan films grudgingly—they prefer to see the old ones over and over again.
>
> One theater in Ecuador obtained prints of eight Tarzan pictures. These were strung together and run off without pause for an audience which

brought its lunches and dinners, then had to be shooed from the theater at the conclusion of the thirteen-hour show![3]

According to Johnny Weismuller's fourth wife Allene Gates, "In Shanghai, Bombay, and Egypt, Tarzan broke the record of all the movies released by RKO in its history. Quite a feat, considering RKO also had the Astaire-Rogers films and those of Walt Disney." She also recounts the mobs that her husband inspired in foreign cities.[4]

In the early 1950s, when UNICEF had trouble getting Indonesian children to submit to tuberculosis immunizations, "a farsighted theater operator booked an old Tarzan picture and fixed the children's admission price at submission to immunization. The film played to standing room only for days, and a number of grownups tried to get in on the same terms."[5] Once during the 1948 Arab-Israeli War, three Israeli soldiers stopped a car with an American attorney and several UN officials. They wanted a ride to Tel Aviv, twenty-five miles away, to see the opening of a Tarzan picture. "The crowds that swarmed to the opening were so large and unruly that a police riot squad was called out. More men were needed to maintain order than were assigned to guard the Mandelbaum Gate in Jerusalem, which separated the warring Arab and Jewish quarters of the city."[6]

Overseas Tarzan came to symbolize American culture as a phenomenon audiences both loved and loved to hate. In 1924, a Moscow newspaper complained, "We publish books and pamphlets about Marxism and our great revolution. We encourage young authors to interpret its spirit and inspire the masses. We even issue cheap editions of the Russian classics. But the public reads—what?—'Tarzan.'" One member of the Soviet literati harrumphed: "In my opinion this alone proves the necessity for some dictatorship over the proletariat." Twenty years later, Hollywood triumphed in British territories in Asia because it produced "simple, inartistic action pictures, comedies and musicals, which even the coolies underst[ood] sufficiently to enjoy," and "let the British have 'art.'"[7]

Unauthorized Tarzan rip-offs and faux-Tarzans popped up around the globe in print and on screen—the Spanish film *Tarzan and the Grotto of Gold* was in some markets distributed as *King of the Jungle* with the hero named "Zan" as the first syllable was dubbed out. *Tarzan Roi de la Force Brutal* similarly became, in English, "Taur the Mighty." One Italian film, *Jungle*

Master (1972), starred "Johnny Kissmueller" as Kazan. In Israel, by the early 1960s "there were 10 competing Tarzan series on the stands, all originals & all without the knowledge of the American publisher. . . . In all, some 900 such issues were published by some ten competing publishers . . . [resulting in] many lawsuits . . . between the various unauthorized publishers. . . . At the same time, Syria and Lebanon were issuing similar unauthorized series about Tarzan in which he was presented as fighting the evil Jews and their attempt to achieve world domination."[8]

Though Tarzan's popularity in Israel dates back to the 1930s, it peaked in the decade between 1954 and 1964, no doubt a direct result of the U.S. government's intervention. In 1953, the United States Information Services, battling the Soviet Union to win the hearts and minds of Israelis, subsidized Hebrew translations of $3 million worth of American books, including twelve Tarzan volumes, making Burroughs the top-translated writer of this project.[9] Paranoia over Tarzan among foreign governments was therefore not entirely unjustified. Hungary banned ten thousand "bourgeois" books, including several Tarzan titles, in 1951.[10] The Tarzan films were banned in Egypt from the mid-1960s until 1968 because the Ministry of Culture deemed they "reflected a colonialist outlook, . . . embodied imperialist ideals in achieving fictional mastery over the jungle, . . . [and] presented Africa and Africans in an unsympathetic or patronizing light"—an anxiety perhaps fed by the fact that 80 percent of Egypt's foreign films came from the United States.[11] Another reporter wrote, more bluntly, that Cairo banned Tarzan "on the grounds that he was a CIA and, what's worse, white agent of the imperialists."[12]

For some time the Tarzan films were banned in the Soviet Union, but Russian soldiers made off with German-dubbed versions when they pillaged Berlin in 1945.[13] The films hit the movie houses, "thrilling Moscow audiences" in February 1952—though at the front-end of that first film, the 1932 Weissmuller-O'Sullivan *Tarzan the Ape Man*, an official preface noted that Tarzan, "raised in native innocence by monkeys," never "encountered the influence of bourgeois culture until he met the American explorer's party."[14] By December 1953, the old Weissmuller Tarzan films had become "the most popular movies in the Soviet Union," causing much consternation to the Soviet Communist Party. Among other complaints, the party charged that in villages throughout Russia, Tarzan's holler, African drums, and the cries of wild beasts sent chickens and pigs into a frenzy.[15] Postcards of Weissmuller as Tarzan became a hot under-the-counter item in a Russian market, and when four American college students visited the Soviet Union in 1954, the Soviet youth they met peppered them with questions about whether "new Tarzan pictures were being made." When Johnny Weissmuller died in 1984, "the Russians played his Tarzan yell in Red Square for twenty-four hours straight."[16]

The significance of Tarzan's international dominance cannot be understated. The isolation of the United States after World War I applied to the armed forces only. The federal government might not have officially entered the game until 1938 with the creation of the State Department's Division of Cultural Affairs, but between the wars it supported and cheered the private sector's overseas economic expansion, an expansion that took full advantage of Europe's devastated economy and industry. In 1923, the *London Morning Post* had already sent up a warning cry: "The film is to America what the flag was once to Britain. By its means Uncle Sam may hope some day, if he be not checked in time, to Americanize the world."[17]

If Hollywood led the charge, Tarzan was its point man. In the 1930s and through 1941 in *Tarzan's Secret Treasure*, Johnny Weissmuller's Tarzan was only nominally a hero of isolationism. All five of these MGM films begin with unwelcome white intruders invading Tarzan's space, the Mutia escarpment where he, then he and Jane, then he and Jane and Boy, live peacefully in this land of plenty. The white intruders scheme to involve Tarzan and his family in their greedy plotting. Tarzan will have none of it; but Jane or Boy is suckered, inevitably bringing on a small war in the jungle from which Tarzan must save them. The brilliance of these films lies in the ruse of the isolationist message in an imperialist context. Not only do we have a white man ruling the jungle, animals and natives alike—a British nobleman, if we know the full story—but the films themselves participate in U.S. cultural colonization of the rest of the globe as the nation exerted its worldwide influence as never before.

Tarzan's New York Adventure of 1942 provided comic relief from the other Tarzan stories as well as from the war, even while Jane editorializes to Boy about how people outside their jungle paradise "do terrible things. They even destroy each other." RKO and Sol Lesser took over from MGM beginning with another 1942 film, *Tarzan's Triumph*. After the Nazis invade the jungle despite Tarzan's saving a Nazi soldier downed in a plane crash, Tarzan leads an army of Palandrians, a hidden, peace-loving African society, to victory.

Tarzan had resisted involvement until the Nazis kidnap Boy: "Took away? Boy? . . . Now Tarzan make war!" Some audiences apparently gave the line a standing ovation. The federal government directly controlled this film's message, its movement from isolationism to war, as its producer Sol Lesser told an early Burroughs biographer:

> It was during the early part of World War II and the State Department was *most* anxious to see that there was no material in a Tarzan film that was in-imicable to the best interests of democracy. The department made it clear to me that there was no greater potential that could reach the minds of people with a message than that contained in a Tarzan picture. . . . Tarzan was the epitome of what the American mind was at that time.[18]

Tarzan's Triumph would be the greatest moneymaker of all seventeen of Sol Lesser's Tarzan films. His *Tarzan's Desert Mystery* appeared in 1943, and its chief villain was an undercover Nazi ruling an Arab tribe. Jane in Burma tending to sick British soldiers has written to her husband asking him to fetch medicine from certain vines in a jungle across a vast desert, where most of the action takes place. Weissmuller's Tarzan had left the jungle for the first time.

After World War II, America once again took advantage of the rest of the world's decimation. The Cold War was as much a culture war as a nuclear arms race—even as the U.S. 1950s "Program of Truth" sounded eerily Or-wellian. Investigations of the film industry by the House Committee on Un-American Activities suggest how deeply many felt this motivation. A 1954 *Study of USIA [United States Information Agency] Operating Assumptions* summarizes the deliberate use of film as a weapon:

> The film program abroad helps not only American foreign policy or propaganda objectives, but also the American economy. This occurs in two ways: through direct cooperation between USIA and private American companies, and through stimulation of consumer interests by films which document the American style of life. . . . Films effectively convey information. . . . They are an excellent medium to use to expound foreign policy without the audience being aware of it. . . . Films are the best substitute for word of mouth persuasion. The purpose of USIA films is attitude formation, not information.[19]

Or, as a Department of State Inquiry phrased it more pointedly, "the rifle the film industry had shouldered in World War II could not be put down; it had to keep marching to the drums of another martial conflict—the Cold War with international and domestic communism."[20] Hollywood's postwar control of the international film industry would lead one British filmmaker to remark, "to be an Englishman in the film industry is to know what it's like to be colonized."[21]

From 1947 to 1956, the U.S. government increased the budget for its Foreign Cultural programs from $19 to $110 million, and the staffing from 3,008 to 10,038.[22] In 1947, "earnings of Hollywood productions are surpassing pre-war boxoffice records throughout the Far East" as American films "encounter 'no competition' from British films, even in British territory, where restrictions and discriminations operate against American entertainment enterprises." In Bangkok that year, a Tarzan film "with a Siamese-language sound track, broke all records";[23] in Korea three years later, a nine-year-old orphan "adopted" by a U.S. Marine talked frequently about "Tarzan and Jungle Boy" from having seen the films.[24]

The next RKO-Weissmuller films continued the globalization of Tarzan's adventures in subtle ways. Starting with *Tarzan and the Amazons* (1945), Lesser's production team, apparently bored by the clichéd African natives of the previous films and unable to reinvent them satisfactorily, peopled its four Tarzan films of the late 1940s through the late 1950s with actors who looked like they came, and frequently did come, from south of the U.S. border—just as Amazons should, even though they portrayed indigenous Africans. Some of these films employed no black actors, and some a sprinkling for effect yet without acknowledging any difference. The use of extras from Latin America or of Latin American descent, both European and indigenous, helped draw Latin American audiences to the U.S. Tarzan films.

Tarzan's Latin American turn matched exactly the new focus of the U.S. government's cultural imperialism. Before, during, and after the war, the political trustworthiness and economic stability of these nations in America's own hemisphere was a serious concern.[25] In 1934, three Hispanic Hollywood performers were investigated for "alleged support of communistic activities": Dolores Del Rio, Ramon Navarro, and the legendarily hot-blooded Mexican starlet Lupe Velez, who at the time happened to be Johnny Weissmuller's wife (and who was so beautiful that when she filed for divorce and claimed her husband "did not want her to go places, even to a beauty parlor," the judge couldn't help but reply, "'He probably thought you didn't need beauty treatments'").²⁶ The Office of Inter-American Affairs was established in 1938, the same year as the Division of Cultural Affairs. By 1943, Hollywood had recovered from the war's initial adverse impact on the overseas market by targeting Latin America. "Through the significant political and financial support of the Department of State, the U.S. film industry was able to expand its position massively in Central and South America to such a degree that the U.S. share of the market was just under 100 percent in many countries."²⁷ After the war, the U.S. film industry did not relent in its efforts in the region, seeing instead a real economic, cultural, and ideological opportunity.

The industry worked especially hard to undermine Mexican film production, the region's only threat to the U.S. industry.²⁸ RKO specialized in "mid-to-big-budget musical comedies set in either Latin America or in the USA but featuring, in addition to recognizable US stars, fairly well-known Latin American actors and entertainers."²⁹ RKO also co-owned Mexico City's Churubusco Studios, which it used for *Tarzan and the Mermaids*,³⁰ the first feature since *The New Adventures of Tarzan* (1935) to be shot outside the United States. Much of the filming occurred in Acapulco, complete with scenic Aztec ruins despite the story's African setting.

While most of the Tarzan pictures of this Latin period downplayed this cultural colonialism in the stories themselves, *Tarzan and the Leopard Woman* tackled aggressive anti-colonial nationalist movements head-on. The bad guys are a native group, the leopard clan, bent on keeping the whites out of their jungle. The clan members' behavior suggests a communist kind of totalitarianism—they address one another as "brother," they have no identity beyond group membership, and they swear fealty to their power-mad leader whom they call "brother," too. This man, Dr. Lazar, is a native (or mixed-race) doctor presumably trained in Europe who works for the British colonial authority. His training and his class status thus portray a man like other nationalist-communist leaders of the era, the Western-educated men leading the proletariat against the colonial powers, men like Ho Chi Minh, who was leading the Viet Minh rebellion against the French at the time of this movie's release. These leopard men are clearly godless savages, perhaps even cannibals. Tarzan's victory over the leopard clan assumes biblical dimension when, Sampson-like, he pulls down the pillars holding up the roof of the clan's cave, reminding viewers of the divine backing of America's Manifest Destiny.

Everyday Americans might not have known of America's cultural warfare south of the border, but the rest of the world knew. *Reconstruction*, an anti-U.S. opera, premiered in Amsterdam in 1969, with American economic imperialism in South America as its subject and, as one of its villains, an American businessman who turns out to be Tarzan. His company, the Total America Company, "controls and exploits all of Latin America" with CIA backing.[31] The show's allegorical plot focuses on an American Don Juan figure who seduces women "on a bed shaped like a map of South America," in a clever revision of the metaphorical and actual sexual exploitation by European colonialism. In one scene "a young woman called Cuba takes off her wedding gown and stands tastefully au naturel for a few seconds, and then puts on a shirt and breeches, presumably symbolizing her new status as a Castro convertible."[32] In fact, the titles of all four Tarzan films of this Latin American turn pit Tarzan against women: *Tarzan and the Amazons* (1945), *Tarzan and the Leopard Woman* (1946), *Tarzan and the Huntress* (1947), *Tarzan and the Mermaids* (1948). In *Leopard Woman*, Dr. Lazar may have served as the leopard clan's brain, but its heart, its soul, resided in the leopard woman, played by the exotic beauty Acquanetta, known as "The Venezuelan Volcano" despite her claims of mixed Native American and European ancestry, due to a suspicion of her South American roots.

~~~~

In the early 1960s, our newly global celluloid Tarzan found himself in South and Southeast Asia, in *Tarzan Goes to India* (1962) and *Tarzan's Three Challenges* (1963), two of only a handful of Tarzan films shot entirely on the actual location of the general fictional setting and employing local talent. *Three Challenges* opens with Tarzan parachuting into Thailand, cutting the familiar figure of a paratrooper with a round drab chute above him and a reserve tucked into his belly. He then makes his way upriver, up a palm-lined river, to the interior, his small thatch-roofed boat ambushed along the way, to help the good guys win rule of the land. Significantly, this turn to Asia occurred just when U.S. neocolonialism was on the verge of its most nefarious—and its final—phase: the American war in Vietnam. (Born in 1967 at the height of both the Cold War and the war in Vietnam, I inevitably find myself drawn back to these seminal facts of the world that brought me into being.)

Neil Sheehan's dazzling hybrid history-biography-memoir *A Bright Shining Lie: John Paul Vann and America in Vietnam* describes America's Cold War neocolonial project:

> Having overt colonies was not acceptable to the American political conscience. Americans were convinced that their imperial system did not victimize foreign peoples. . . . Americans perceived their order as a new and benevolent form of international guidance. It was thought to be neither exploitative, like the nineteenth-century-style colonialism of the European empires, nor destructive of personal freedom and other worthy human values, like the totalitarianism of the Soviet Union and China and their Communist allies. Instead of formal colonies, the United States sought local governments amenable to American wishes and, where possible, subject to indirect control from behind the scenes.[33]

Sheehan characterizes the American spirit behind the intervention in Vietnam as one of absolute confidence in the rightness of America, and of absolute faith in eventual success based upon that rightness. That spirit found itself embodied in men of ingenuity, perseverance, and might, men of action who never entertained a moment of self-doubt—Graham Greene captured this ideological enthusiasm in the fictional Alden Pyle from his 1956 novel *The Quiet American.*

Sound familiar? The men who dragged us into the war in Vietnam were a troop of Tarzans.[34] A man of supreme surety, Tarzan on page and screen is never wrong, he knows he's never wrong, and we forgive and forget his arrogance because he always proves himself—and because, if we're Americans, he's one of us. It's the new natural order. That in 1944 the U.S. film industry "controlled 80 percent of the world's screentime" was only "the natural order of things," according to the Motion Picture Producers and Distributors of America.[35] Tarzan too, whether in the novels or on the screen, rules the locals without ruling. Benevolently and wisely. His presence behind the scenes of native affairs provides order and a civilized touch without overt interference. When he does interfere, he has no choice: moral circumstance demands it, and it is always welcome. Right makes might makes right. How fitting, then, that the Tarzan novels saw their great revival in the early 1960s, from verging on oblivion to "accounting for ten percent of all paperback sales." New editions appeared, "Barton Werper" brought out his five unauthorized Tarzan novels, and Tarzan of the comics was also rejuvenated after languishing through most of the 1950s. As Tarzan.com comments un-ironically, "By the early 1960s the Cold War was in full swing, major social and cultural changes were in the air, and America was getting itself mired in Vietnam. The perfect time for the return of a legendary hero!"[36]

Responding to Tarzan's resurgence alongside the increased U.S. presence in Vietnam, a *New Yorker* cartoon from 1964 depicts Tarzan and Jane crashing a herd of elephants through a fence and sending the town's inhabitants fleeing for their lives, one of them saying to another, "You can just bet the C.I.A. is behind this!" Tropical palm trees, a mountain in the background, and a building named "REPUBLIQUE DE . . ." are all the identifying information we need.[37] (It's tempting to read a disdain informed by anxiety from this highbrow and left-leaning magazine toward both Tarzan and U.S. foreign policy). In December 1965, Gold Key revived its comic book Tarzan by basing its stories on Burroughs's originals, and conveniently enough this meant, in early 1967, having Tarzan do battle with Germans and their jungle allies during World War I—a choice updating of Burroughs's 1919 tale *Tarzan the Untamed.* The cover of the first of these two issues shows a bare-chested Tarzan firing a machine gun too big to be held, Rambo-style (Rambo, Vietnam vet and self-righteous savage, is very much a child of Tarzan). In the next issue, Tarzan fights the Xuja, a light-skinned race with Fu Manchu moustaches, pointy beards and eyebrows (and ears), and yellow tunics. Then Gold Key in 1969 matches Tarzan against a Russian communist in a storyline adapted from Burroughs's early 1930s titles *Tarzan the Invincible* and *Tarzan Triumphant.*[38] Tarzan's own comics house, Dell, produced an eleven-issue series from July 1962 to April 1965 called *Jungle War Stories.* The first issue's cover transitions its readers from typical jungle adventure to the war simmering in Vietnam: "THE JUNGLES OF ASIA AND AFRICA HAVE BECOME FLAMING BATTLEGROUNDS." The last issue's cover portends ominously with an American soldier falling from a helicopter in flames: "HELICOPTERS AREN'T ALWAYS THE ANSWER AGAINST THE STINGING FIRE OF THE VIET-CONG GUERILLAS. A DESPERATE PLAN IS NEEDED . . . BRING IN THE ALLIGATORS!"

Covers from men's adventure magazines associated jungle cannibalism and rapacity with communist Vietnam. The March 1962 *Man's Action* entices us with "Nude Queen of the Communist Cannibals" and "The Vicious Virgins of Vietnam," while the January 1960 *Man's Adventure* shows Asian (communist) soldiers guiding a group of white prisoners through a jungle as it blurbs: "They Made Me Eat My Mate!" (that the blurb fits a different story does not lessen the instant association). "Marine Dog, We Drink Your Blood" shouts the *Men Today's* May 1966 cover, as two bare-chested Viet Cong men threaten two white women in torn Red Cross uniforms in a rice paddy. Other covers recast familiar scenes of ritual and implicitly cannibalistic sacrifice with Asian villains, both soldiers with red-star caps and other communist agents, instead of savage African natives.[39]

Above my office desk hangs a William Weege political art poster from 1967, from before President Johnson dropped out of the 1968 election. In one corner we see a still image of Weismuller's Tarzan and O'Sullivan's Jane from *Tarzan and His Mate*; Tarzan's arm reaches up and out of frame, turning into a drawing from *Gray's Anatomy* suggesting both a corpse and a Nazi salute. Down the arm run the words, "ALL THE WAY WITH L.B.J." Above the still image is a Christmas verse: "And lo a voice / from Heaven / saying this is / My beloved Son / in whom I am / well pleased." The campaign slogan and the Christ reference are used ironically—Tarzan will be nobody's savior in Vietnam. On the other side of the poster, an upside-down chicken hawk cries "Help!" as arrows push it down, expressing Weege's hope for the end of the Johnson administration, the end of the war, the end of American neocolonial self-righteousness.[40]

Then this random piece of evidence: in 2005 Pat Sajak, host of the classic American television game show *Wheel of Fortune*, said on the show that "due to his own service in Vietnam . . . he was a big Tarzan fan."[41]

In 1912, Edgar Rice Burroughs set "Tarzan of the Apes" in a colonial context, as Britain has sent Tarzan's father and his pregnant mother to Africa to investigate a European squabble over proprietary rights and resource utilization, the property and resource being, of course, people. Africans. The driving conflict in nearly every film and novel occurs between whites. The blacks become part of the battlefield terrain—the resources, the hindrances, the local terms of the global conflict. Once again, American Cold War neocolonialism resounds. Tarzan the eco-warrior ironically paves the way for civilization; sometimes wittingly and sometimes not, Tarzan enables other whites to find the ivory and the gold. His custodial attitude is paternal and superior; he protects his environment by conquering it, and only insofar as it provides for him and his. In the third and fourth Burroughs novels, we learn that Lord Greystoke and his family split their time between two homes: one in London and a "vast estate" getaway in Africa.[42]

To rephrase Kyle Chrichton's 1948 review of the western *Red River*, nobody can yell "propaganda" at a movie full of chimps, hippos, jungle play, a near-naked woman, and an even more naked man.[43] The strategy of using films as subtle propaganda worked domestically as well. An American audience watching a Tarzan movie in the 1950s would hardly have stopped to consider the geopolitical implications. If Americans thought in terms of empire at all, it would have been about the going-going-gone European brand. When in *Tarzan's Peril* (1951) Queen Melmendi (Dorothy Dandridge) tells her British colonial commissioner, "You are our father, and our mother," American audiences might have tittered bemusedly over the dead paternalism of the old European colonial system. How silly it all was! And exploitive! And how above it we are! Or they might have felt a little virtual nostalgia for a system that was part of their Anglo-European cultural DNA but that never found expression in their history—a system Americans never had the chance to enjoy. A nostalgia that perhaps motivated the country's quiet neocolonialism. Either way, this American audience would hardly think about its own colonial system.

But the rest of the world understood. At the Galeria Havana in Cuba, images from the American war in Vietnam and from Tarzan movies anchored an anti-U.S. exhibit dedicated to the third world and on display during a meeting of the International Cultural Congress. "The final part of the exhibition is a United States combat film showing a soldier of the Green Berets, or Special Forces, wildly firing a machine-gun and throwing hand grenades into a peasant's shack." A few moments later, we see "a picture of a Vietcong brandishing a rifle and a sign that says: 'Vietnam—many, many, many.'" The Tarzan film sequences were used to "satirize the 'white supremacy' of Johnny Weissmuller in relation to African tribesmen," a racism implicitly connected to America's military misadventure in Southeast Asia.[44]

Had the Cubans gotten their hands on a more recent Tarzan film, they might have seen closer approximations of the war in Vietnam. Played by local Mexicans and Brazilians, the natives of *Tarzan and the Valley of Gold* (1966) and *Tarzan and the Great River* (1967), respectively, look more Vietnamese than Tarzan's usual African extras. In both films Mike Henry as Tarzan arrives by jet plane and must shed his fitted suit before plunging into the jungle; his accent is unmistakably and dully American. Every advertisement and poster I've seen for *Valley of Gold*—its working title was *Tarzan '65*—promises a fight against "THE WORLD'S MOST MODERN WEAPONS," and the film gives us automatic rifles, large-caliber machine guns, hand grenades, a half-track, a tank, and a fighting helicopter. In an early scene native soldiers in mufti produce automatic weapons and a machine gun, shoot up the adults, kidnap a boy, and torch the thatch-roofed house. The Viet Cong allusion is furthered by the posters that tempt us to "SEE A BEAUTIFUL WOMAN BECOME A HUMAN BOMB," though the film hardly delivers on this score (she's white, blonde, unwilling to explode, and Tarzan saves her). There are tunnel fights and indigenous soldiers invading the land of their peaceful prosperous brethren, and leave it to Tarzan, who has come all the way across the ocean to rescue the latter, to prove that "Sometimes one has to use violence." The animals of Tarzan's army bear telling names: Major the militant lion, Bianco the white leopard, and Dinky the comical and fearful dink—chimp, that is.

This film also gives us the most astonishing convergence of American capitalism, cultural imperialism, and violence I know, with Tarzan as the focal point, when in the Plaza de Toros, a cultural landmark, he crushes a Mexican foe with a giant Coca-Cola bottle.

The villains of *Great River* are also indigenous "rebels" who emerge from the jungle to raid and destroy the villages of other indigenous groups, killing, recruiting, or enslaving the villagers. As David Fury rightly concludes in his history of Tarzan in cinema and television: "In fact, this Tarzan was the most cold-blooded ever portrayed on the screen. In one scene a dozen or so of Barcuna's men were torched with a gasoline bomb before they even lifted a finger to attack."[45] The movie was released in 1967, the same year as the My Lai massacre. I don't think it requires too great an imaginative leap to see Barcuna's men as a neocolonial grotesque version of the Viet Cong, and to see Tarzan's ambush and gasoline torching of probable combatants as just that.[46] The following year, Mike Henry starred in his last Tarzan film, as well as in John Wayne's pro-war propagandistic *The Green Berets* as Sergeant Kowalski, dubbed "the killer" by the trailers.

Kowalski's death in the jungle during a Tarzan-like hand-to-hand combat scene with four or five darker-skinned foes was for John Wayne a patriotic self-sacrifice; for me, it suggests something else. When we lost the war in Vietnam, Tarzan took a leave of absence. In the fifty-two years from 1918 to 1970, the United States produced forty-three Tarzan feature films at an average rate of one every fourteen and a half months, a conservative calculation that treats serially released films as single titles and does not account for unofficial productions or faux Tarzan rip-offs (the faux Tarzan films, books, and comics are far too numerous to list, even in a note). Then not a single Tarzan feature film for the next eleven years. For one thing, Tarzan's theatrics couldn't compete with new images of actual jungle combat. In 1964—the same year *Jungle War Stories* ended its run—CBS scrapped plans for a weekly one-hour Tarzan television series largely because of the challenge of "injecting realism into modernized Tarzan stories."[47] Soon enough Hollywood used Vietnam to bring such graphic realism to the screen with films such as *The Deer Hunter* (1978) and *Apocalypse Now* (1979). But I wonder if the reason for Tarzan's demise runs deeper. Perhaps the lost war in Vietnam destroyed the American character that Hollywood's Tarzan stood for, the character behind the war.

One Tarzan television series, Tarzan's first, did make it to the air. It ran from 1966 to 1968, ending at the turning point of the war and coevally with Kowalski's death. The two Tarzan feature films of 1970, in fact, were compiled from episodes of this series that originally aired in 1966 and 1967. The series was deliberately ambiguous, never specifying its geographic setting.

On the heels of the television series came ABC's Saturday morning cartoon parody, *George of the Jungle*, which ran until 1970. The Tarzan comic book industry also began slowing down in the early 1970s, and it's at this time that Philip José Farmer, a prodigious science fiction writer and a fan of Tarzan from childhood, began writing his several Tarzan parodies. The most outrageous of these, *A Feast Unknown* (1969), exploded the masculine confusion of violence and sexuality that has now become a cliché of war literature and film, especially Vietnam stories. Marvel Comic's *Spoof* issue #2 in November 1972 and *Mad Magazine*'s September 1973 issue both had their fun with the loincloth hero. The *Spoof* spoof opens:

The Lord of the Jungle! For more than half a century, adventure fans the world over have thrilled to the daring exploits of the greatest Apeman of them all! The tale of how he was raised by a savage she-ape has enthralled millions! His name is a household word—his thundering bull-ape cry is known to one and all! So okay—we figure you are probably sick to death of him by now.

Tarz, duped by Jane out of his inheritance of the "Greatstroke" estate, returns to Africa only to find a modern urban Nairobi that no longer needs him. The adult leader for a black scouting troop points Tarz out to his charges as "a perfectly preserved example of primitive man," a "savage . . . obviously in the throes of hysteria, due to lack of social acceptance." In the end, a black man offers Tarz a job as a safari gun-bearer—along with nine unemployed Tarzan actors.[48] Our big-screen hero was reduced to Filmation's animated television show (1976) and such silly films as *Carry On up the Jungle* (1970), *The World's Greatest Athlete* (1973), *Tarzoon: Shame of the Jungle* (1975), *Trader Hornee* (1970), *Tarz and Jane and Boy and Chimp* (1976), and several bad, R-rated femme-Tarzan flicks. Almost weekly from 1967 to 1978 the comedian Carol Burnett entertained her television show audience with her mock Tarzan holler.

It's only fitting that the American president in office during the death-spasm years of the failed policy in Vietnam, Gerald Ford, once went by the secret service code name Tarzan. His wife Betty was Jane, and his chief of staff, Richard Cheney, was Chimpanzee.[49]

~~~~~

When Tarzan reappeared on screen in the 1980s, he dodged the issues that had driven him into exile. Whereas the films up until 1970 had contemporary settings, both *Tarzan, the Ape Man* (1981) and *Greystoke: The Legend of Tarzan* (1984) were deliberately historical retellings of the romance, set like Burroughs's first novel around 1910. The only other Tarzan appearance in the 1980s was a television movie whose title says it all: *Tarzan in Manhattan* (1989). This film piloted a new series that never got off the ground; if its creators had seen 1987's urban faux-Tarzan parody *Wild Child*, they probably would have wisely canned their idea. All three of these Tarzan movies reflect a post-Vietnam American isolationism: In *Tarzan, the Ape Man*, we last see

Tarzan and Jane skipping away into their private jungle; in *Greystoke*, Tarzan even leaves Jane behind when he returns to the jungle; and in *Tarzan in Manhattan*, we might read a certain U.S.-centric narcissism.

The end of the decade brought with it the end of the Cold War, the triumph of the United States as the world's sole superpower, and a return of Tarzan. After the Persian Gulf War of 1990–1991, Tarzan hit television for the 1991–1992 season, and again in a separate production for the 1996–1997 season. Dark Horse comics began running its Tarzan titles in 1995, and the decade—the century—closed with the 1999 release of Disney's *Tarzan* animated feature. "Oh, great!" says one chimp to another as Tarzan swings into view in a 1999 *New Yorker* cartoon: "Here comes the policeman of the world again." On the opposite page, another cartoon connected the present with the past when a father explains to his child, "Son, everyone went to college in the sixties—there was a war going on."⁵⁰

Disney's follow-up animated television show *The Legend of Tarzan* first aired eight days before September 11, 2001. The day that changed the world did not stop Tarzan: Dark Horse put out a few more comic books into the new millennium; The WB (Warner Brothers Television Network) broadcast its *Tarzan* television series in 2003; *The Tarzan Collection* DVD set of all six MGM Weissmuller-O'Sullivan films and a new documentary appeared in 2004, followed by the six RKO Weissmuller films (sans O'Sullivan) in *The Tarzan Collection Volume 2* in 2006; Disney put out its *Tarzan II* DVD in 2005 and took its story to Broadway in 2006; and in 2006 Warner Bros. announced plans to bring out a new feature film.

~~~~

We should recall that the neoconservative movement that led to the 2003 U.S. invasion of Iraq had its roots in the 1990s. One might very well connect neocolonialism's rebirth as neoconservativism with the coeval Tarzan resurgence. In *Tarzan's Triumph* of 1942, the film in which Tarzan must save Boy from the Nazis, a character mocks Tarzan's initial isolationism: "Tarzan is arrogant. He doesn't need the rest of the world." Sixty years later, liberal Americans will argue that their nation's forty-third president embraced such an arrogant disregard for the rest of the world in a foreign policy that was anything but isolationist. Yet it should also be said that just as U.S. neocolonial-conservatism has failed to win over the entire U.S. population (much less the globe) and has struggled to maintain itself as a viable strategic policy, so too has Tarzan. The 1991–1992 series had another season's worth of shows never broadcast in the United States. The 1996–1997 series was more fantasy than jungle adventure, and it too was short-lived. Tarzan of the comics appeared sporadically, the animated *The Legend of Tarzan* died its second year, The WB's show did not see a second season, and Broadway's *Tarzan* has also failed to thrive. In 2005, when the full challenges of President George Bush's manly and shortsighted bumbling into war in Iraq became widely apparent, the Cartoon Network announced plans to produce a new George of the Jungle series. After a Christmas episode in December 2007, this George's misadventures officially premiered in January 2008, followed by a DVD release of the original episodes, and reprising the original's opening number: "George, George, George of the Jungle, Watch out for that tree!"

If Tarzan has so thoroughly epitomized the American mind over the century, how do we explain his appeal to the enormous foreign market? Tarzan aficionados talk about the universal appeal of his manly independence, of his harmonizing of the animal and the civilized. He's a veritable archetype. It's the same reasoning offered by the Motion Picture Producers and Distributors of America (MPPDA) in 1944 for the global dominance of Hollywood: "These [images, values, and sentiments] are the imperishable things of which pictures are made. And they are the same the world over. Geography leaves them untouched. They are the common ground of all men everywhere."[51] That the film-producing capacities of rival nations had been destroyed by the war seems not to have figured into this analysis.

When during his tour in Vietnam Lt. Clark Welch visited a Catholic school in Ben Cat and saw a group of boys reading a Tarzan comic book— "*Tar-san cac con truong*, Tarzan, leader of all the animals"[52]—what would they have said if he had asked them why they liked this American icon? Would they have praised those American values espoused as universal by the MPPDA? Or would their answers have gone in a different direction? The Vietnamese writer Ly Lan's suggestively titled story "Tet," set in the 1950s of her childhood, has children playing by trying to out-Tarzan one another.

Communist China produced the first overseas Tarzan rip-off in 1940.

By April 1947, MGM, the company behind the first wave of Weissmuller Tarzan films, had released a number of films in French Indo-China.[53] We can safely presume a Tarzan film or two in the bunch. Weissmuller's fourth wife reported that "in some Asiatic countries, the arrival of a new Tarzan film was the occasion for a white-tie-and-tails premiere, with the local populace fighting to get seats," and when Weissmuller died in 1984, "even mainland China's state-run television reported it. Their nightly news devoted nearly four minutes to Weissmuller, showing clips of harrowing scenes from his Tarzan films."[54]

Pham Xuan An, an intelligence agent feeding information to the North Vietnamese while working as the Saigon reporter for V.T.X, Reuters, and finally *Time* magazine, had grown up watching "all the films with Johnny Weissmuller swinging through the trees as Tarzan. 'It was a beautiful dream of freedom in the jungle,' An says of those movies. 'I thought under Communism I would live like Tarzan. I put this dream into the revolution. Look at Tarzan!' An exclaims. 'What does he have? Only his loincloth.'"[55] Tarzan and his family live a peaceful, communal, and comfortable existence without money. And when he fights, he inevitably does so to repel the invading and exploiting whites. He fights to defend his neck of the jungle, for himself, his family, and their native neighbors. In *Valley of Gold*, Mike Henry's Tarzan is more VC guerilla than regular army, bringing down a helicopter with an improvised hand grenade sling and stealing the bad guys' American tank. Does he then represent the America working and fighting for South Vietnam's independence in the 1960s—the neocolonial America that installed failed puppet government after failed puppet government—or does he represent the America appealed to by Ho Chi Minh in the late 1940s, for support of a unified Vietnam independent of external rule for the first time in centuries? Or even Ho the communist? Ho's cult of paternalistic personality characterizes Tarzan, too.

The attack on American materialism pervades Tarzania. On the big screen, Tarzan and Jane preach about money's lack of necessity and reject its temptations without a blink. Greed always motivates the movies' villains; greed motivates most of the novels' villains, too. In both media, money corrupts. In Burroughs's *Tarzan of the Apes*, Tarzan upon entering civilization kills a lion barehanded to win a bet, apparently forgetting his principle to kill only to feed or defend himself. Burroughs's Jane very nearly marries the petty

Robert Canler as a way of paying off her father's deep financial debt, and it's clear that Canler only values Jane as more, and mere, booty. In America, money gets the girl. This near-marriage from which Tarzan saves Jane echoes the near-rape by an ape-creature from which Tarzan had saved Jane in the jungle—Canler's consuming materialism is as base as the ape-creature's consuming lust.

Tarzan is thoroughly a lad of the working class. He labors with his body. He sweats. He struggles to survive. He depends on himself, not an infrastructure of social privilege, not on fine breeding—in most film and television versions, we never learn the backstory, we have no reason to imagine him noble, or aristocratic, or otherwise bourgeoisie. His association with apes and with blacks places him firmly in the working-class world according to the racist, classist logic of the day; his tan also groups him with the only other sun-tanned whites in the first book—the villainous, mutinying, and eventually cannibalistic working-class sailors.[56] His antagonistic relationship with language in the first novel renders him akin to the illiterate working-class sailors whose mutiny results in his parents' abandonment on the African coast, the blokes whose speech is more butchered than the speech of Burroughs's apes. In the films, Tarzan's limited speech and many denunciations of *too much talk* reflects a working-class hostility to intellectualism's sabotage of a simple, underdeveloped Forrest Gump approach to the world. "Books little value in jungle," says Gordon Scott's Tarzan in *Tarzan and the Trappers*: "What man does is more important than what man read or say."[57]

No wonder Tarzan was so popular among the Russian proletariat. No wonder Brazil, in 1937, banned Burroughs's *Tarzan the Invincible* because the police felt it taught communism.[58] Should it surprise us to learn that one Tarzan screenwriter, Gordon Kahn, was one of the "Hollywood 19" investigated by the House Committee on Un-American Activities in 1947, and as a result was blacklisted by Hollywood?[59] Kahn worked on the script for *Tarzan's New York Adventure* (1942), "by far," according to *Blacklisted: The Film Lover's Guide to the Hollywood Blacklist*, "the most political of the Tarzan feature films," and one of only twenty U.S. films approved by the Ministry of Trade in 1950, "after two years of negotiation," for distribution to Soviet theaters.[60] Perhaps the Soviet Union, even more than its proxies like North Vietnam, could delight in Tarzan. He satisfied its atheistic, anti-material ideology, and its imperial hunger and white superiority. He comported himself as a benevolent big brother. Arguably, he epitomized the twentieth-century Soviet mind far more exactly than he ever did the American.[61]

The title character of the 1966 British film *Morgan: A Suitable Case for Treatment* obsesses over primates, Tarzan, and Karl Marx. In one scene, this painter from a working-class family visits Marx's grave, snaps to attention before the giant hollow-eyed bust, and beats his chest and hollers in a true Tarzan salute. Earlier, he imagines men working on a scaffolding as apes swinging on bars in cages, and leaving the underground in another scene he salutes the man working the cage-like booth in the same manner he later salutes Marx.

Still, we can qualify Tarzan's communist appeal. Morgan has an eye only for well-heeled women. He refuses to grow up; his crazy charm is his childishness; his idealization of Tarzan and Marx a self-implosive naïveté. He ends up in a mental hospital. Marx, after all, is dead, buried, done—one wonders if the movie drew on the Cobra art scene in Europe (1948–1951), another movement inspired by the art of "primitive" peoples, of children, and of the insane, this one with Marxism's philosophy of revolution as its "profound driving force."[62] In the movies, Tarzan owns the land he defends from intruders; he actually uses the language of ownership to challenge their encroachment. His lifestyle project is that of a very American nuclear-age nuclear family complete with pets, not a communal organization. (Beginning in 1939 when Tarzan and Jane find Boy, Hollywood's Tarzan family promulgated the independent nuclear family as the normative ideal during the heady early decades of suburbanization and geographic dispersion among American families.)

And, of course, to watch a Tarzan movie or read a Tarzan novel is literally to buy into the capitalist system that produced them. If the film Tarzan's language use linked him with the working class, it also meant more cost-efficient repackaging and accessibility for the foreign market. Weissmuller's invented, all-purpose "African" word *umgawa* is *umgawa* in America, Kenya, Peru, and the Philippines. One might make the case that Tarzan's defense of property rights in the name of anti-capitalism reveals the contradiction between a communist state's nationalism and its communist ideals, and that its leadership's dismissal of its own proletariat's affection for Tarzan reveals a fundamentally aristocratic social structure.

In 1968, in the wake of the Soviet invasion of Czechoslovakia, Romanians "enjoy[ed] a warm, sunny holiday weekend" by, among other pastimes, forming long queues in Bucharest to see an old Tarzan film.[63] How perfect, how apt, in its ambiguity. Did Tarzan speak to them as anti-capitalist members of a steadfastly communist state? Or as a people asserting its independence, its right to self-determination, of national ownership, in defiance of Soviet authority and the larger global collective?

~~~~~

So what is Tarzan? Who is he?

Marianna Torgovnick's analysis of the Western world's slippery conception of *the primitive* speaks to Tarzan's ambiguous identity. According to her *Gone Primitive*, the primitive represents the opposite of and antidote to whatever one chooses to condemn about the present and modern. If we are repressed, they are uninhibited; if we are decadent, they are innocent: "The primitive does what we ask it to do."[64] For Americans, Tarzan can epitomize American self-made manhood and how that manhood operates in the world arena. He can be "yet another American rejection of European civilization" as he "rejects his inheritance as Lord Greystoke, denying his European heritage in favor of Africa, and embracing the new and the American girl."[65] For Europeans, Tarzan, restored to his English title by the second book (suitably titled *The Return of Tarzan*), clearly validates his superior breeding. He can also, especially his Hollywood self, represent negative European stereotypes of Americans: inarticulate, uneducated, self-absorbed, and self-righteous brawn.

The ambiguity of Hollywood's Tarzan's origins is exactly right. We need not necessarily separate European and American responses to Tarzan. We should heed Reinhold Wagnleitner's remonstrance, that "behind the phenomenon 'Americanization' lies the actual 'Europeanization' of the world. . . . [T]he 'American dream' is a Euro-American dream."[66] More so than its assertion of an American identity distinct and better than a European one, twentieth-century American culture asserted a white Euro-American ethnicity distinct from and better than any other—than any of the darker races of the third world. Nor should we forget that America found itself at war in Vietnam in the 1960s largely because in the 1940s and 1950s it continued to support European colonization (which it reinvented in its own neocolonialism).

Torgovnick notes that "while the Tarzan novels [from 1912 through the 1920s] could afford to condemn colonialism in Africa and brutality toward

African people," we must not "assume that because the United States had no African colonies it had no stake in colonialism and in the host of issues associated with it." She cites the U.S. treatment of Native Americans and Mexicans as matching Europe's treatment of Africans; she links European exploitation of Africans with American slavery; and she reminds us that when "Tarzan of the Apes" first appeared in 1912, the nation "had recently embarked on imperialist adventures in Cuba, Hawaii, and the Philippines" (Bederman's *Manliness and Civilization* and Eric Cheyfitz's *The Poetics of Imperialism* firmly establish the racism informing these adventures and Tarzan's[67]). Perhaps U.S. overseas adventures at the beginning of the twentieth century, both actual and fantastic, became a means to practice racism simply and clearly, to escape the racial confusion of post-emancipation America. The American rhetoric of imperialism of the day, especially as espoused by Teddy Roosevelt, defined its mission and motivation in terms of manhood, yet as Matthew Fry Jacobson has pointed out, the racial context of Roosevelt-style man-making imperialism was inherently contradictory: "If Roosevelt and others identified a renewed, 'strenuous' barbarianism as a salve to the encroachments of modernity, the 'barbarism' of national or racial 'inferiors' also provided a ready-made rationale for conquest and domination."[68] How does one go native and exterminate the brutes at the same time?

American neocolonialism also aped its European model's paternalism. I can't help but relate Jai and the several other ethnic orphan sidekicks of the 1960s films—including Mike Henry's thinly disguised Vietnam-Tarzan films—to the Vietnamese orphan adopted by U.S. soldiers in *The Green Berets*. In the last scene, Wayne's character, Colonel Kirby, takes the boy's hand for a sunset stroll along the beach. "You're what this war is all about," Kirby tells the boy. In the 1950s, Senator John F. Kennedy had argued for U.S. commitment to Vietnam by referring to it as "our offspring." From 1966 to 1967, the aptly named gum company Anglo Confectionary produced a series of sixty-six Tarzan cards telling a story about Tarzan finding and saving a boy. No Jane at all here, and the back of the cards fit together to create a six-by-eleven card poster of Tarzan and Boy walking hand in hand—at least in the poster, the dark-haired boy with prominent incisors evoked the era's classic racist illustrations of Asians.

For European moviegoers after World War II, Tarzan might have also evoked a real nostalgia for the good ol' days when they owned the globe. But back in 1912 European readers of Burroughs's novel would have experienced something other than nostalgia:

> When Dutch children in the colonial Indies were forbidden to play with the children of servants because officials thought they might become too comfortable "babbling and thinking in Javanese," when Javanese nursemaids were instructed to hold their charges away from their bodies so that the infants would not "smell of their sweat" . . . , there was more going on than peevish squabbles over cultural style. These were part of a wider set of standards framed to ensure that European children in the colonies learned the right social cues and affiliations—and did not "metamorphize" into Javanese.[69]

What else could images of baby Tarzan babbling in ape-creature-speak and breastfeeding from an ape-creature evoke but fear of racial degeneration? In the faux-Tarzan film *Forbidden Jungle* (1950), the native women adopt abandoned chimps for their own—as a paternalistic white trader explains when we see a young woman with a chimp and a child, one on each hip.

If white youth were imagined to be psychically half-savage, imagine the consternation over the half-European, half-native (métis) child. For Ann Laura Stoler, the fact that "métis children living in native homes were sometimes *sought out* by state and private organizations and placed in" orphanages run by civilized Europeans evidences deep fear of the children's darker blood.[70] Kipling's Mowgli from *The Jungle Books* would have spoken directly to the European obsession with wild orphans on the loose in the colonies in the eighteenth, nineteenth, and early twentieth centuries. Tarzan in Africa, who believed himself the issue of a "strange white ape" and his ape-mother Kala,[71] embodied colonial fears of the best of Europe gone barbarous, of European men fathering monstrous hybrids with native women. Perhaps the 1981 *Tarzan, the Ape Man*, a film explicitly set in 1910 in British Africa, has James Parker repeatedly call Tarzan *bastard* and *son-of-a-bitch* to evoke the métis orphan. Nearly every white person in Tarzania is scared by Tarzan. Tarzan survives degeneracy not because he's the best of Europe, but because and only because he's fantastical. Instead of allaying fears that the métis orphans' blue blood would triumph, this impossible hero would have reinforced the need for orphanages. For control. Given the paternalistic stance of the colonizers, the métis orphan is truly the controlling metaphor for the colonized world and its hybrid culture. The colonists feared métis offspring becoming "patricides, and anticolonial revolutionaries" (which amount to the same thing);[72] Tarzan's living up to his blood and becoming civilized is a fantasy victory over these deep anxieties, anxieties giving him an edge, a bite, now long lost to readers.

Stoler's *Carnal Knowledge and Imperial Power* records how the European colonial powers, having had long-standing policies restricting white women from going to the colonies, finally reversed that policy to counter the growing mixed race population and to counter the potential that their men, in cohabitating with the natives, would themselves go native. The white women would save them all.[73] So Burroughs's Tarzan comes of age, raised as an ape-creature and dressed in the garb of a local African tribe and trying to decide just what exactly he is, and if nothing happens soon he'll go bestial or native because he has no other choices.

Lo! There's Jane now.

Ape and Jane (Maureen O'Sullivan) posing for a publicity photo.
Tarzan the Ape Man (1932).

"Say, a broad I meets on the boat tells me some of these smokes eats people."

THE "GUNNER," *TARZAN TRIUMPHANT* (1931–1932)

FOUR

NATIVE SON

Racism abroad, and racism at home:

A movie of Teddy Roosevelt's widely publicized 1909 African safari came to the Chicago area in 1910. In October 1912, the very month "Tarzan of the Apes" appeared in *All-Story Magazine*, a stampede of lectures on African topics overran Oak Park, Illinois, a community just outside Chicago. According to the local paper, the lectures "have awakened great interest and especially in view of the fact that Africa is the subject that Oak Park people will study in preparation for their part to be performed in the World in Chicago exposition." By March 1913, the paper reported "nearly 400 in classes in the churches studying Africa and reading about it" as they prepared "to serve as stewards, or explainers, in the Africa section of the exposition . . . wear[ing] the native costumes." In March 1913, Oak Park's Third Congregational Church's choir performed in celebration of the David Livingstone centennial; in May, another performance featured the choir's "chorus scenes in Africa" along with the Young Ladies quartet singing ":in the Congo dialect," the same month *New Story* magazine published "The Return of Tarzan"; in June, a native Zulu presented himself to the church; in January 1914, Dan Crawford, an African explorer, also presented himself to the congregation on his "twenty-three years among the savages of the most primitive sort."[1] In May, the month *All-Story Cavalier* magazine began the serial run of "The Beasts of Tarzan," Ed Burroughs moved his family to a five-bedroom house in Oak Park. In June, *Tarzan of the Apes* came out in book form.

Burroughs's introduction to Africa and the idea of the primitive most likely occurred in 1893, at the World's Columbian Exposition—the Chicago World's Fair—where his cavalry troop from the Michigan Military Academy performed in April, and where he helped his father display an electric automobile in the summer. During his down time, he would have doubtless visited Hagenbeck's Wild Animal Arena and Museum. Carl Hagenbeck was the world leader in the trade and display of exotic animals, and his menagerie and show at the exposition included elephants, lions, tigers, leopards, bears, dogs, pigs, goats, sheep, horses, ponies, zebras, boars, wild goats, and exotic birds. Twenty years earlier Hagenbeck had begun exhibiting indigenous people to European audiences, and his animal exhibition at the exposition shared the same space—the Midway Plaisance—with a "natural" display of various peoples, living dioramas, from Germans to Turks, Arabs, and Chinese, and finally to American Indians and African Dahomans. In *The Son of Tarzan*, when Jack Clayton's tutor complains that the boy only wants to read about Africa, he tells Jack's father Tarzan that "upon two occasions I have found him up in bed at night reading Carl Hagenbeck's book on men and beasts."[2] The book's actual title, *Von Tieren und Menschen*, was translated as *Beasts and Men*.[3]

In its spirit, Hagenbeck's book was nothing new. The second half of the nineteenth century exploded with published accounts by explorers of their African adventures, any one of which might have served as a background source for Burroughs: Francis Galton's explorers' survival manual, *The Art of Travel; or, Shifts and Contrivances Available in Wild Countries* (first published in 1855 and reissued for several decades); Paul Du Chaillu's *Explorations and Adventures in Equatorial Africa* (1861); J. W. Buel's *Heroes of the Dark Conti-*

nent (1889); and Henry Stanley's *In Darkest Africa* (1897).⁴ The hunt for an exact source is absolutely beside the point. We could list any number of other works, like the many, many volumes by Sir Richard Francis Burton. Africa and the primitive were in the air; they were the environment that nurtured Burroughs's and his audience's imaginations.

While Hagenbeck was exhibiting exotic peoples alongside exotic animals, really presenting people as animals, others were presenting primates as people. There was "a whole line of real and quite famous apes . . . living in Europe or the United States in the forty or so years around the end of the nineteenth century and the beginning of the twentieth," as Nigel Rothfels describes in his book on Hagenbeck, *Savages and Beasts*:

> Consider the chimpanzee "Consul," shown dressed in an evening suit before a tea service while holding a knife and fork on his ringed fingers [ca. 1900; published 1903]. Consider the gorilla "Miss Crowther," "interviewed" for the *Star* in London about her impressions of England during her brief residence in the fall of 1905 at the London Zoo. Consider the famous Ringling gorilla of 1921, John Daniel (also known as John Gorilla), who . . . was caught by one of Hagenbeck's agents and was raised to live as a human before being sold to the circus. Consider the gorilla John Daniel II, who was greeted at the docks in New York City in April 1924 by a welcoming committee headed by one of the most famous "missing links," the freak William Henry Johnson. Consider the almost ubiquitous tea parties for primates . . . staged in major zoological gardens up through the mid-twentieth century. Consider the many images from the period of very young apes in baby carriages and somewhat older apes drinking wine and schnapps.⁵

At least two such trained chimps were named "Tarzan."⁶ In *The Son of Tarzan*, Jack sneaks out of the house to see Ajax the "educated ape" on exhibit at a music hall. "It rides a bicycle, eats with knife and fork, counts up to ten, and ever so many other wonderful things, and can I go and see it too?"⁷ In the 1921 film version, the placard outside the venue advertises "Ajax, The Human Ape." In the first novel, the Porter party speculates that Tarzan might be "a runaway simian from the London Zoo who has brought back a European education to his jungle home."⁸

If an ape could be trained to be almost a human, what would be so astonishing about an exceptional human, raised as an ape, who restored himself to his full humanity?

~~~~~

Another source, another context, another motivation: Jack Johnson.

On December 26, 1908, Jack Johnson defeated the Canadian Tommy Burns in Sydney, Australia, to become the first black heavyweight boxing champion of the world. Decried the *Detroit Free Press*: "Are the races we have been calling inferior about to demand of us that we must draw the color line in everything if we are to avoid being whipped individually and collectively?"[9] White America, appalled and in denial, began hunting for the great white hope who would prove white physical superiority. Burroughs's literary hero Jack London, writing from ringside in Sydney, called on Jeff Jeffries to "remove that smile from Johnson's face."[10]

Jeffries, who had retired undefeated five years earlier, ran an alfalfa farm in Burbank and had built a house and opened a saloon and an athletic club in downtown Vernon, California, just south of Los Angeles and today all of twenty-six miles from Tarzana, California, a town established on Burroughs's initiative in 1930 a few years after deciding to develop much of his Tarzana Ranch land into a community marketed exclusively to whites.[11] White America implored Jeffries to fight Johnson. So did the Brits: "It is not so much a matter of racial pride as one of racial existence which urges us so ardently to desire the ex-boilermaker's triumph. The coloured races outnumber the whites, and have hitherto only been kept in subjection by a recognition on their part of physical and mental inferiority." The thought of Johnson's beating Jeffries, for this writer, was "too awful to contemplate."[12]

Nearly two years passed before Johnson and Jeffries would meet in the ring, on Independence Day of 1910 in Reno, Nevada. The *Baltimore American* conveyed Johnson's prefight nonchalance by describing him "as happy and carefree as a plantation darky in Watermelon time." Alfred Henry Lewis in the *San Francisco Examiner* labeled Johnson "essentially African," of a race that "feels no deeper than the moment, sees no farther than his nose. . . . having no fancy, no imagination" to anticipate his defeat. Similarly, Arthur Ruhl in *Collier's* found Johnson lacking the "dogged courage and intellectual

initiative which is the white man's inheritance" of "thirty centuries" of superiority.[13] On fight day, "crowds assembled in virtually every American city
as fight followers gathered all across the nation to hear the blow-by-blow
wire services accounts of the fight."[14]

Jeff Jeffries went down three times in the fifteenth round. His corner-
men stopped the fight. Across the country, racial violence ensued. Between
eleven and twenty-six people died, and hundreds more, mostly black, were
injured.[15]

On July 7, the triumphant Johnson arrived in Chicago and paraded through
crowds of thousands to his mother's house. Elsewhere in the Windy City,
Ed Burroughs struggled to feed his family. One year later, in July 1911, he
began writing his first book-length story, *A Princess of Mars*, and within a
few months his imagination turned jungleward.

Is it too far-fetched to conjecture Jeff Jeffries as Burroughs's inspiration, if
even an unconscious one? What does Tarzan promise, after all, but the great
white hope? Burroughs enjoyed prizefights, and the Johnson-Jeffries match
was one of the biggest nationwide news stories of the time, most especially
in Chicago, Johnson's adopted and Burroughs's native hometown. Perhaps
Burroughs had read and preserved in the back of his mind this December
1909 *Harper's Weekly* prefight description of Jeffries:

> [H]e stands six feet one and a half inches and in his thin serge suit weighs
> nearly two hundred and fifty pounds; yet his footfall is as light and brisk
> and sure as the step of the swiftest dancer. "Moves like a feather!" exclaims a
> hero-worshipper as he gazes in ecstasy. . . .
>
> The . . . connoisseurs are . . . intently staring at his waistline. They admire
> it. It is very brief. The man within has already worked so hard in training
> that he has burned away the surplus flesh. . . . The brilliance of his eyes and
> the glow of his clear, bronzed skin are eloquent.[16]

In a 1919 letter Burroughs provided a description of Tarzan remarkably like
Harper's description of Jeffries:

> In the first place Tarzan must be young and handsome with an extremely
> masculine face and manner. Then he must be the epitome of grace. It may be

difficult to get such a man but please do not try to get a giant or a man with overdeveloped muscles. It is true that in the stories I often speak of Tarzan as the "giant ape-man" but that is because I am rather prone to superlatives. My conception of him is a man a little over six feet tall and built more like a panther than an elephant.[17]

Don't forget the white man's superiority inherited from generations upon generations—it really is beginning to read a lot like Tarzan. Sounding uncannily like a piece of Burroughs fiction, one article explained that Johnson won because he wasn't really black, but a descendent of "a long lost tribe of Caucasians" from ancient Numidia in northern Africa.[18]

We don't know when Burroughs dreamed up Tarzan. He dated the original manuscript version as "Commenced Dec. 1 1911 8:00 p.m." But Burroughs's biographer Irwin Porges conjectures that the Tarzan idea "may have gestated for long years in Ed's mind before he scratched the first story lines on paper," perhaps as early as 1907.[19] In an unpublished autobiography, Burroughs reports that he began reading pulp fiction magazines and imagined writing stories for them while working for the Physicians Co-Operative Association in 1909.[20] During the buildup to the Johnson-Jeffries fight.

Whether Burroughs held the Johnson and Jeffries story in the front or the back of his mind is impossible to say. It is enough to use the story to provide the racist context. Burroughs's racism, however, is a trickier subject. His apologists excuse him as a man of his time. They also point out evidence of a more progressive attitude. Burroughs wrote and spoke in high praise of the African American soldiers with whom he served in the cavalry in Arizona—they were, as a group, much more competent and professional than the lazy whites. He also published in 1899 a poem called "The Black Man's Burden" as a challenge to the racism of Kipling's famous "The White Man's Burden." A common defense of Burroughs's Tarzan novels rallies around the fact that the villains are always white. Yet this argument neglects the racist logic by which the African natives aren't clever or capable enough to be villains. Like the jungle animals, they are sometimes obstacles and sometimes helpmates. Like animals and children, they serve their own interests out of innocence—evil being a human and adult capacity. Those black pygmy cannibals, who first appeared on screen in 1932, were used to spice things up, as "regular" Africans were simply too innocuous or too boringly savage. Tarzan befriends superstitious Africans in the books and films, but his superiority stands firm.

We don't need to look any further than the originating tale, "Tarzan of the Apes," for indicting evidence. Tarzan's general rule of killing only for food or in self-defense does not apply to the natives. Twice Burroughs's novel even refers to the local native village as a "plantation." He constantly belittles the blacks, both the Africans and the one African American, Jane Porter's companion and nursemaid, Esmerelda, who provides one point of the novel's comic relief: "Ah done thought it was de devil," she reports when Jane is abducted by an ape-creature; "but Ah guess it mus' 'a' been one of dem gorilephants. Oh my po' baby, my po' li'l honey!"[21]

Burroughs also conspires with his culture's association of blacks with animals, specifically primates. Burroughs fills the twenty-four novels with a menagerie of ape-creature variations, each type closer to animal or to human, never either one, a spectrum aptly accommodating the racist association. The first time we ever see one, "a great figure standing upright upon the ridge," standing "as though listening" to Tarzan's birth parents on their first darkening jungle eve, Alice Clayton gives as succinct and refined a definition as Burroughs ever manages: "No, John, if it was not a man it was some huge and grotesque mockery of a man. Oh, I am afraid!"[22] When later a tribe of blacks has captured and ceremoniously prepares to eat the Frenchman Paul D'Arnot, the scene mimics the earlier scene of the ape-creatures' Dum-Dum ritual, when they cannibalized a dead member of another clan. Darnot's captors, with "bestial faces, daubed with color—the huge mouths and hanging lips—the yellow teeth, sharp filed—the rolling, demon eyes," tear at him "with clawlike hands."[23] They take turns spearing him from the crowd, just as the ape-creatures had taken turns beating on their rival's corpse before setting upon it in a feasting frenzy. If anything, the apes fare better in Burroughs's imagination than the blacks. Both might be cannibals, but at least the apes don't torture their prey. Tarzan will himself conflate the native people with the native animals for his white audience when he introduces himself to Jane Porter and her entourage by a warning note he has left at the cabin: "THIS IS THE HOUSE OF TARZAN, THE KILLER OF BEASTS AND MANY BLACK MEN."[24] The very fact of the note, Tarzan's writing of it, further distinguishes him from beasts and blacks, as literacy in America had long been considered a signal of higher intelligence. African American slaves in the United States weren't taught to read and write because the racist system presumed that they lacked the capacity, and because the system could not risk revealing that they could, that they were fully human. More practically, of course, the system could not risk arming them with literacy.

And if you are reading a post-1963 edition of a Tarzan novel, you are reading a racially sanitized version, in which a line like "I don't chum with niggers" becomes "I don't chum with porters," and a line like "Dem niggers is sho nuf hot babies" does not appear at all.[25]

Like page, like screen: In the early movies, like the 1918 *Tarzan of the Apes* and the 1932 *Tarzan the Ape Man*, Tarzan kills blacks wantonly. At least by the latter film Johnny Weissmuller had toned down these murders, dispatching his victims quickly and quietly; Elmo Lincoln, on the other hand, after killing two Africans in extended scenes, glows with ecstasy. He also grins hugely when setting fire to the native village. For 1941's *Tarzan's Secret Treasure*, the government finally stepped in to reduce the racism, limiting "the deaths of natives . . . to a maximum of eight or ten."[26] One of the more outlandish examples of racism in the 1932 film occurs when a native porter slips while ascending the Mutia escarpment and plunges to his death, and the very white Harry Holt asks, "What was in that pack?" A half century later, Bo and John Derek were legally obligated to perpetuate this racism. Bo's autobiography supplies two examples of how MGM forced the Dereks' 1981 film to conform to the original, both examples being the gratuitous murders of blacks.[27] To the Dereks' credit, they fought back: after the escarpment incident, instead of Harry Holt lamenting the lost pack, James Parker raises clenched fist heavenward: "Why did you do that? Why?!"

~~~~~

The month "Tarzan of the Apes" appeared in *All-Story* magazine, October 1912, the first black heavyweight champion was again in the spotlight. Jack Johnson's first wife dead just over two weeks from suicide (blamed by her mother and the white press on Johnson), the thirty-four-year-old Johnson stepped out publicly with a much younger white woman fresh from Milwaukee. Lucille Cameron's mother followed her daughter to Chicago and signed a complaint of disorderly conduct against her to drag her away from

Johnson. Federal agents charged him for violating the Mann Act, a 1910 law designed to prevent the trafficking of prostitutes across state lines but written in language vague enough to be applied to consensual, nontransactional yet morally suspect sexual acts. Evidence, including Lucille's testimony, proved that she had come to Chicago on her own, having never met Johnson. The Mann Act accusation was shelved.[28]

For a week. On November 7, 1912, Jack Johnson was indicted on trumped-up charges of transporting another woman—a spiteful jilted lover—to Chicago two years earlier for the purposes of prostitution, debauchery, unlawful sexual intercourse, and crimes against nature.[29]

On December 3, Jack Johnson and Lucille Cameron married. The governor of South Carolina called Johnson a "black brute" and asked, "If we cannot protect our white women from black fiends, where is our boasted civilization?"[30] The governor of Virginia called for Johnson's lynching, the governor of New York called the wedding "a blot on our civilization," and a U.S. congressman from Georgia introduced a constitutional amendment "banning marriage between whites and 'any and all persons of African descent or having any trace of African blood. . . . It is destructive of moral supremacy, and ultimately this slavery of white women to black beasts will bring this nation a conflict as fatal and bloody as ever reddened the soil.'"[31] The amendment would not pass, nor did similar statutes proposed in ten of the twenty states already lacking such a law,[32] but the charges stuck—the trial and jury deliberation lasted a single day.[33] The court sentenced Johnson to a year and a day. The newlyweds fled to Paris.

(Where else? In Paris, thirteen years later, Josephine Baker would become a star, an African American dancer who performed to her audience's expectations of her primitive, animal sexuality. In Paris, Paul D'Arnot tames Tarzan, civilizes him, and introduces him to the world and the world to him. French is Tarzan's first civilized tongue. Paris civilizes him the way it did Baker, as her reviewers claimed:

> But she has worked hard to please us [the French]—this cannibal beauty
> with her fetish face—She is anyway too exquisite for a Negress—she
> seems to whiten as we gaze at her—By far the best possible example of
> the perfecting of the black race by its intellectual contact with European
> civilization—What a difference between the little savage of the early days

with her delirious, grotesque dances and the toned-down, refined *artiste* transformed by Paris. . . . Civilization has done its work—Josephine is from now on assimilated by the western world. . . . "Josephine est blanche . . . (Josephine is white)!"[34]

While civilization saves Baker through its cultivation, Baker saves civilization through her primitivism and its connection to the physical life from which the modern civilized white race felt it had become estranged. In the second book, Tarzan returns to the jungle by way of Paris. The cultural capital of the Old World and symbol of the Old World's degeneracy, Paris plays an apparent transitional role between savage Africa and civilized America, which disturbed America's deep racial and cultural anxieties and contributed to white America's disapproval of Baker's appeal.[35]

Where else? The musical film *Wonder Bar*, which appeared in 1934, the same year as *Tarzan and His Mate*, occurs entirely in a Paris nightclub, and includes all sorts of passionate transgressions, including suicide, murder, adultery, homosexuality, miscegenation, the exotic allure of Latin actors Dolores del Rio and Ricardo Cortez, whose dance number involves a whip, and a white male pair gone black in the form of an Al Jolson and Hal LeRoy blackface number.)

Now transport yourself almost exactly a century ago, to October, November, or even December of 1912. For two years you have followed the story of Jack Johnson's wildness—his reckless driving, his brawling, his romancing of white women. You have just been reading about his recent marriage and the accusations against him—including the *Chicago Daily News* suspect quotation from Johnson to Lucille's mother, "I can get any white woman in Chicago I want"[36]—when you pick up the October *All-Story*. Like Lucille Cameron, Jane Porter is nineteen, white, and blonde. You resume where you left off the day before: chapter 19, "The Call of The Primitive." Terkoz, a bully of an ape-like creature, has been exiled from his tribe:

> The first intimation Jane Porter had of his presence was when the great hairy body dropped to the earth beside her, and she saw the awful face and the snarling, hideous mouth thrust within a foot of her.
> One piercing scream escaped her lips as the brute's hand clutched her arm.

Then she was dragged toward those awful fangs which yawned at her throat. But ere they touched that fair skin another mood claimed the anthropoid. The tribe had kept his women. He must find others to replace them. This hairless white ape would be the first of his new household.

He threw her roughly across his broad shoulders and leaped back into the trees, bearing Jane Porter away toward a fate a thousand times worse than death.[37]

The two scenes of a big brute carrying off a young innocent could not have failed to resonate. Various articles and speeches referred to Johnson as a gorilla or an ape; a U.S. congressman called him a "big black gorilla," an "African biped beast."[38] A cartoon in the *Chicago Evening News* on the occasion of Johnson's victory over Jeffries showed a black woman decorating her room with pictures of Johnson clipped from newspapers—the woman's face and Johnson's face are those of cartoon monkeys.

The first Tarzan film, released in 1918, didn't bother disguising the racism. Instead of an ape-creature, a black native abducts Jane, a man who with his size, round face, bald head, and defiant grin looked an awful lot like Jack Johnson. An ad in the *New York Times* published the day of the opening apparently forgot the film's adaptation or intentionally committed the conflation: "SEE TARZAN'S STRUGGLE WITH THE LION—THE ELEPHANT RAID ON CANNIBAL VILLAGE—BATTLE BETWEEN AN APE AND GORILLA—ABDUCTION OF THE WHITE GIRL BY APES . . . " Back in Burroughs, the first African we meet thinks of the ape-creatures of Tarzan's tribe as "wild, hairy men."[39]

The bestiality and miscegenation story doesn't end when Tarzan saves Jane, however. Terkoz's lust for Jane thwarts our seeing the true nature of Jane's desire for Tarzan. Whatever her instincts tell her about her savior's nobility—note the irony that instincts were, according to the logic of the day, a primitive-animal-black trait—her eyes tell her body a different story. He's garbed as a black savage. He sports jet-black hair and a deep all-body tan. His hairlessness distinguishes him from the ape-creatures and asserts his conquest over hoary nature but simultaneously aligns him with the natives. At best he's a métis—his gray eyes suggest equal parts black and white.[40] Toward the end of the first novel she admits that, to him, she is a "strange girl of a strange race."[41] The locals of *Tarzan Goes to India* and *Tarzan's Three*

Challenges use the adjective "African" as a moniker for Jock Mahoney's very white Tarzan. As a very dark comic-book Tarzan declares, "To the denizens of the jungle, I am no white man."[42] We should also remember that only hours before Tarzan's birth, an ape-creature attacked the Claytons—"Screaming with rage and pain, the ape flew at the delicate woman, who went down beneath him to merciful unconsciousness"—and ends up dying atop Alice's body.[43] Ape and man after all: Is it the trauma of childbirth or ape-rape that sends Alice into delusional bliss for the next, and the last, year of her life?

Many comic-book Tarzan fans protested the darkened skin of this late 1990s Tarzan as a blasphemous capitulation to political correctness, but Tarzan's whiteness was tainted from the beginning. The original story's initial descriptions of him by Jane's party call him "brown" and even "indigenous" before Burroughs remembers to note that he is "tanned to a dusky brown."[44] (This last phrase is from Jane, writing a letter repeating the stories of those who have actually seen Tarzan—but they have not mentioned his tan. Either the comment occurred offstage, or Jane's imagination or intuition supplies the word.) Men's adventure magazines of the late 1940s through the early 1960s used the same trick with its depictions of native women, making them look like "Caucasians with Coppertone® tans" to make them more palatable to their white male consumers.[45] Tarzan actually looks like a Native American, and he very much conflated white America's anxieties over the two dark-skinned savage races sharing its landscape—Burroughs's first book refers to him as looking like "a young Indian,"[46] and in *Tarzan and the Amazons*, Johnny Sheffield's Boy, eager for his first bow-and-arrow hunt with Tarzan, quotes Longfellow's "Hiawatha" (Burroughs also wrote two novels featuring Native Americans). The adolescent appeal of Tarzan's story also marks his blackness; as scholars like Eric Lott and Nicholas M. Evans have observed, if savages are stuck in adolescence and civilized adolescents are evolving through their savagery, then white men revisiting their youth perform a subtle sort of blackface.[47]

Tanned white skin, ambiguously a marker of leisure and labor, at one time very much suggested the slipperiness of racial categorization. Conevery Bolton Valencius's study of settlers of the American West in the nineteenth century, *The Health of the Country*, establishes the racial threat feared by whites of living in the country's hotter climates: "The logic of white Americans in the antebellum period was simple. They did not belong in hot places; black people did."[48] Thus when we first meet Edna Pontellier in Kate Chopin's 1899 novel *The Awakening*, this "American" from Kentucky is sunburnt "beyond recognition"[49]—her steamy Louisiana environment, and her new intimacy with Creoles and Mexicans, awaken her impulsive, physical (sensual) self. Whether Jane Porter subscribed to *monogenesis*, the theory that all peoples derived from the same original ancestors and that living in different environments for generation upon generation effected racial difference, or *polygenesis*, the theory that different races were created for different environments, would not matter. Tarzan is either a white man conditioned "black" by his environment or a fundamentally "black" man ordained to live in the savage environment where he belongs.[50] In Burroughs's colonial Africa, miscegenation was always the context for sexual relations. When Jane entertains the fear that Tarzan has gone native, perhaps even cannibal, her fear mixes with excited curiosity: "If he belonged to some savage tribe he had a savage wife—a dozen of them perhaps—and wild, half-caste children. The girl shuddered." Does she subconsciously fantasize about the wild children he might father on her, and the savage fathering process? These are her own thoughts that nevertheless "forced themselves upon her."[51] In Jane's attraction to Tarzan the reader experiences both the erotic charge of racial transgression and the prudish rejoicing in a white-on-white affair.

Dark and passionate Tarzan saves Jane from the rapacious ape-creature Terkoz only to feel the rapacious impulse himself. In fact, Tarzan and the reader first hear Jane's scream immediately after Tarzan penned a note asserting his possessive desire for her such that he and Terkoz claim her co-instantaneously. Their desires are one and the same. After killing Terkoz, he "did what no red-blooded man needs lessons in doing. He took his woman in his arms and smothered her upturned, panting lips with kisses." She succumbs, then protests, and a confused "Tarzan of the apes did just what his first ancestor would have done. He took his woman in his arms and carried her into the jungle." Just as Terkoz had done. He ruminates: "True, it was the order of the jungle for the male to take his mate by force; but could Tarzan be guided by the laws of the beasts? Was not Tarzan a man? But how did men do? He was puzzled; he did not know."[52] White Tarzan fought Terkoz to save Jane from the black beast only to repeat the scene; this time the white

Tarzan fights to save Jane from his own black-beast self. In one cartoon, a just-sexed Jane says to Tarzan as he climbs into their tree house, "If it wasn't you Tarzan—who the devil was it?" On the other side of the tree a smiling ape climbs down.[53] Before MGM's Tarzan and Jane find their son, Cheta the chimp suggestively completes the ape-man's family.

Tarzan is half restrained white man, half rapacious black-beast. Furthermore, he only knows that he is a "Man," he only knows to question his impulses, and then he knows to imagine how a gentleman should behave, from his books. His restraint is a matter of training, of nurture over nature— he is, deep down, a salivating primitive. For Bederman, who also sees in Tarzan the savage rapist, the end of the novel "can be read as an indictment of civilization's effeminacy, an elegy for the doomed primal rapist in the civilized man," because he refrains from seizing his mate, refrains from killing Canler, refrains from revealing his identity, and thus "loses Jane to his effeminate cousin Clayton."[54] Earlier I interpreted Tarzan's selfless sacrifice as signaling his arrival into full, civilized manliness—into his whiteness. Yet also his blackness: his story follows a common trend in African American literature whereby the black hero inevitably and climactically chooses to make a sacrifice for the interest of others, a decision that proves his civilized soul.[55] So while Tarzan the white man plays black for the reader's sake, perhaps expressing the desire "not only to replace [the black body] but to obliterate it" in Susan Gubar's words, Tarzan the black man passes as white, reinforcing Gubar's claim that "racial impersonation and masquerading are a destiny imposed on colonized black people who *must* wear the white mask— of customs and values, of norms and languages, of aesthetic standards and religious ideologies—created and enforced by an alien culture" if they want to achieve legitimized selfhood.[56] James Weldon Johnson's *The Autobiography of an Ex-Colored Man* appeared the same year as Burroughs's "Tarzan of the Apes" and problematizes this logic; in Johnson's novel, the fair-skinned mixed protagonist adopts a white life of high culture out of self-interest in his refusal to sacrifice his comfortable life to help others of his race. In Nella Larsen's novel *Passing* (1929), a black woman living a very bourgeois white American life without actually passing as white disparages a woman who does pass by attributing to her such "black" traits as having "nothing sacrificial in [her] idea of life, no allegiance beyond her own immediate desires."[57]

Back in the jungle, Tarzan's mastering of his bestial desires for Jane proves his civilized whiteness. "Above all," writes Richard Dyer in *White*, "the white spirit could both master and transcend the white body, while the non-white soul was prey to the promptings and fallibilities of the body."[58] Thus Tarzan's strong heterosexual desire proves his masculinity but actually *threatens* his whiteness—for a white man to heed his lust is to go native. The 1934 film *Tarzan and His Mate* directly links male sexual desire with blackness. When the white ivory hunter Martin Arlington spies lecherously on Jane changing clothes in her tent, we see behind him a gaggle of African men peering equally intently. Arlington shoos them away. But the visual argument remains: there's something black, base, and bestial in the white man's desires. Tarzan appears and delivers Jane from Arlington's Terkoz-like lust only to carry her off to certain coitus as the screen darkens suggestively.

The trailer for the 1932 *Tarzan the Ape Man* seizes on the book's portrayal of Tarzan as sexual predator, echoing the statement Jack Johnson allegedly made to his future white wife's mother. "Tarzan knows only the law of the jungle—to seize what he adores!" trumpets the text, followed by a scene with Tarzan dragging Jane into his burrow while she kicks and screams to be let go. Followed by more text—"Many women would delight in living like Eve—if they found the right Adam!"—followed by a shot of Jane lying on the floor of Tarzan's bower, her hair disheveled as his bare torso hovers over her and she testifies, "Not a bit afraid. Not a bit sorry." So sometimes *no* means *yes*? When audiences made it to the theater they saw the promised rape's beginnings: this Tarzan doesn't carry Jane off after rescuing her, he simply appears out of nowhere and abducts her. She has no idea who he is. With the salvation context removed, just what are viewers to conclude? After all, the Motion Picture Production Code of 1930—the Hays Code— permitted the suggestion of rape. This Tarzan has apparently not mastered his body's black and bestial appetites. Burroughs's Jane, though not actually raped, to some extent relishes the prospect, as long as the rapacious beast is a handsome white man:

> Presently Tarzan took to the trees, and Jane Porter, wondering that she
> felt no fear, began to realize that in many respects she had never felt more
> secure in her whole life than now as she lay in the arms of this wild creature,
> being borne, Heaven knows where or to what fate, deeper and deeper into
> the untamed forest.

When with closed eyes she commenced to speculate upon the future, and terrifying fears were conjured by a vivid imagination, she had but to raise her lids and look upon that face so close to hers to dissipate the last remnant of apprehension.[59]

Nazi Germany banned the film exactly for its miscegenous message: "If this film were shown, in which a forest animal, an ape-like being, wooed by and loved by a woman, it could be dangerous to society. The film's content is thoroughly capable of hurting the government's attempts at racial clarification and teachings. It would work against our nation's intentions. The preservation of a healthy racial sense is vital for the state."[60] The actual couple to which they objected consisted of the Austrian-born perfect-specimen Johnny Weissmuller and the fair-skinned, blue-eyed Maureen O'Sullivan. After her "seduction," Jane insists to her father that Tarzan is white. Her father's reply speaks to the stimulating ambiguity of Tarzan's blackness and animalism: "Oh, whether they're white or not, those people living a life like that, they've no emotion, hardly human." A year later Columbia Picture's jungle-movie spoof *So This Is Africa!* included a tribe of native "savages" called "Tarzans."[61] The possibility of Mark Twain's *Pudd'nhead Wilson* (1894) as the source for Burroughs's use of fingerprinting to prove Tarzan's identity as Lord Greystoke is rather provocative, given that Twain's novel involves racial passing in both directions, a young black man as white and vice versa. Twain's novel is post-Darwin detective fiction concerned with racial origins; Burroughs's characters even wonder aloud if fingerprints can indicate a person's race.

Nigel Cox's novel *Tarzan Presley*, in imagining Tarzan brought from New Zealand to America by Jane and then becoming Elvis Presley, takes advantage of the black appeal of both men: "Tarzan [Presley] was not just the race thing but also the race thing with sex in it. What does rock 'n' roll mean but fucking?"[62] Sex with Tarzan is racially charged and transgressive even as it is safely white. He's a crossover artist, a hybrid artist, like Elvis, and Louis Prima, and Eminem.[63] Britney Spears, who based her young pop career on a persona of white blonde innocence and a dance style blatantly aping the moves of two black Americans, Michael and Janet Jackson, in 2007 went primitive by shaving her head, dying the remaining locks dark, and sporting a new tattoo, in Burroughs's own Tarzana, California (during African American History Month to boot).[64]

America the melting pot: the age of emancipation and immigration just happened to be the golden age of the cocktail (1870–1920), aptly enough an American invention, and like Tarzan initially a workingman's drink that evolved into a gentleman's libation. Burroughs even concocted a Tarzan Special: 2 oz. bourbon, 1 oz. water, 5 drops angostura bitters, 2 tsp. simple syrup, 1 ice cube: "Pour into old-fashioned glass and stir; squeeze lemon peel over top and garnish with thin slice of orange and a maraschino cherry."[65]

Burroughs can deny white sexual attraction to blacks all he wants, yet he doesn't hesitate to play with miscegenation through hybrid bestiality and the convention of the exotic allure of dark skin. The sexiest women in Tarzania, La and Nemone, are exotically dark and the figureheads of animal-human hybrid societies. La, the High Priestess of Opar, belongs to the last city of the fabled Atlantis empire, the Oparians having survived by breeding with the local ape-creatures. La is literally part human, part ape-creature (the film Oparians of *Tarzan and the Lost Safari* [1957] are simply a black African tribe). Nemone, Queen of Cathne—where nobles were called lion-men, soldiers dressed in elephant hide and lion hair, and everyone worshipped a living lion—took her own life when her lion familiar died. In *Tarzan and the Lion Man*, the character Balza, "born of genetically altered gorillas as a beautiful blonde woman with some tendencies toward gorilla behavior," is brought back from Africa by a Hollywood film crew and becomes a star.[66] With the beautiful Gonfala, Queen of the Kaji, Burroughs makes miscegenation an actuality, though still in the spirit of white superiority: "Originally [the Kaji] were blacks who wished to turn white; so they married only white men. It became part of their religion.... [and now] there is no unmixed black blood among them."[67]

The real appeal of the celluloid Tarzan's Latin American turn lay in the display of dark-haired and barely clad beauties. Their exotic appeal emanates from their ethnic difference even as it hints at while hiding the threat of black-white sex—these women are playing African natives. The films' white audience gets to have these women both ways. It can enjoy the miscegenation without acknowledgment. Tarzan is not attracted to them, so the narrative refuses to admit their appeal, yet the white male audience is asked to gawk. As for those leopard-skin costumes, as any child will tell you, when a white person and a black person marry, their children will come out with spots. Two years before her title role in *Tarzan and the Leopard Woman*, Acquanetta, the "Venezuelan Volcano," had starred in *Captive Wild Woman* as a kind of lab-produced were-ape. In the middle stage of her transformation between dark-haired lovely and rampaging beast, she appeared as a black woman.

When in *Tarzan's Peril* (1951) the cream-colored native Queen Melmendi tells the British commissioner, a man easily old enough to be her father, "You are our father, and our mother," she might as well toss a wink to the audience. She acknowledges him as her father—at least as figurative of colonial fatherland, England—and she denies her black mother—at least as figurative of her natural motherland, Africa. Or maybe she's winking at him and us to indicate his fathering with her of the boy Nessi, the only other light-skinned, English-speaking native around. (The Boy surrogates played by Manuel Padilla Jr. in the 1960s also exhibit this possibility.) Melmendi's hair also distinguishes her from the other black women—it's long, straight, coifed, and adorned with a white feather, and thus associates her with this movie's coifed blonde (white) Jane. Her white smock is almost identical to Jane's. Melmendi's whiteness qualifies her for kidnapping, bondage, leering, and threatened rape by darker African men from another tribe, and it also qualifies her for rescue by Tarzan. Jane's presence in the film deflects the erotic risk only so far. When Tarzan slips into the hut to rescue the bound Melmendi, he hesitates long enough to relish the view. Prior to his arrival, the camera had already run its gaze up her body in a scene that was censored by Hollywood's Production Code Administration for being "offensively sex suggestive."[68] The film marks Melmendi as mixed race and as a more acceptable erotic object than the more obviously African women. No wonder she's the queen—even without the commissioner's support of her obsequious regime, her superior white blood would have naturally elevated her to the top.

At the end of the Dereks' *Tarzan, the Ape Man* remake, Jane and her party are captured by the warriors of the villainous Ivory Chief. This tribe loves body paint—the natives' faces, their entire heads, are painted various bright colors. The Ivory Chief's womenfolk prepare Jane for a ritual by bathing her and painting her entirely, starkly white. As in Burroughs, the Dereks' potential ritual rape of Jane distracts us from the scene's miscegenous revelry—a celebration of deliberately colored people colorfully intermixing. Underneath the paint the story is even more obvious—these bit actors, supposedly from the same tribe, are black, Asian Indian, and white. The Ivory Chief is himself a white actor presumably playing a native but whose underlying whiteness explains his dominance. Of course, this motley tribe is savage and is punished for its sins, but only because the Dereks can't script the film any other way. They are bound by MGM's contract and by convention. Yet as with having watched any film that wraps titillating immoral behavior in a thinly moralizing package—think of how the undercover aliens capitally punish Frankenfurter for his unabashed gender-bending in *The Rocky Horror Picture Show*—our cells have duly recorded the thrill.

The painting of Jane invokes the racist white aesthetic ideal: "The physical body was an image of inner spiritual life; the beautiful body implied the beautiful soul; the ugly body, the ugly soul. Members of darker races, who could never be sculpted in pure white marble, were therefore by definition ugly on both accounts and necessarily marked by physical flaws."[69] The painting of Jane's body pure white by the brightly colored natives reflects their internalization of imposed white beauty standards. But it also makes sense to see this climactic sequence as exposing the artificiality and impossibility of that ideal—pure whiteness achievable only after a trip to the paint store, the chromatic equivalent of liposuction, boob jobs, and Botox—and the consequent racial anxiety of whites. My favorite image from the film is a photograph during a break from shooting. Still painted stark white, Bo sits eating what looks like soup. Production equipment occupies the background. On one foot, the paint on her toes has washed away.

The other way the film digs after Tarzania's miscegenous subtext centers on Jane Parker's father James's native paramour, played by Akushula Selayah. Rather than a black African or a black of African descent, they have cast a woman who looks like a Bollywood starlet (most likely she's Sri Lankan). The film gives us no reason to think that she's not supposed to be an African native, and indeed both her real name, Nambia, and James Parker's pet name for her, "Africa," insist on it. Moreover, if we ignore the actress's ethnicity, the visual logic of her skin color and features suggests that she is herself issued of a miscegenous white-black coupling. The matter-of-factness of her sexual relationship with James Parker points to the imperialist obligation of the alpha male European colonizer to acquire a native woman. His "Africa" is Africa; his renaming of her indicates the extent of colonial domination.

Burroughs protected his readers from cognizance of interracial sexual titillation. Sexual desire for a black person threatens a white person's "white" identity. It also threatens the white person's "human" identity and the entire racist system to the extent that blacks are figured as animals, and sexual reproduction admits species kinship (the real threat comes from black men and white women, because the baby can't be disassociated from the mother). Anxiety is often expressed through hostility against the embodiment of that threat: Tarzan kills black Africans and ape-creatures alike. The redirecting of sexual desire for a member of a darker race into violence is nowhere as blatant as in Burroughs's original story, when Tarzan on one of his raiding forays into a native village finds himself in a hut hearing "approaching footsteps" outside:

> In another instant the figure of a woman darkened the entrance of the hut.
> Tarzan drew back silently to the far wall, and his hand sought his knife. The woman came quickly to the center of the hut, and there she paused for an instant, feeling about with her hands for the thing she sought. Evidently it was not in its accustomed place, for she explored ever nearer and nearer the wall where Tarzan stood.
> So close was she now that the ape-man felt the animal warmth of her naked body. Up went the hunting-knife, and then the woman turned to one side, and soon a guttural "Ah!" proclaimed that her search [for a cooking pot] had at last been successful.[70]

Is it possible that Burroughs did not see that orgasmic release for what it was? Steve Neale's observation that in action films "eroticism around the male body is displaced into ritualized scenes of conflict"[71] applies here with a twist, in which eroticism around the black body is displaced not once but twice: when Tarzan hurries away first to meet a lioness and sink an arrow "deep into Sabor's loin," and then when he grapples with and kills the ape-creature patriarch Kerchak: "with a shuddering tremor, the great body stiffened for an instant and then sank limply to the ground." Tarzan withdraws his knife, the new king of the apes.[72]

And lo! There's Jane now. Tarzan's attraction to Jane is based primarily on her "snowy" whiteness, as she's the first white woman he's ever seen, and is beautiful for her whiteness.[73] Even the apes lust after white bodies such that race seems to trump gender in sex appeal: Kerchak the ape-king longs "very, very much, to feel his teeth sink into the neck of the queer animal," the "white ape" that is Tarzan's father John; Kerchak "yearn[s]" to grasp the "object of his desire," the phallic rifle of "the wonderful white ape," which took him several minutes to "bring himself to touch."[74] In *The Return of Tarzan*, a very single Tarzan has as a companion for a time Ouled-nail, an Arab girl as bronze as he, noble in her own right as the daughter of a sheik, sexy enough to be a dancing girl, and a more-than-able tomboyish traveler and hunter. She's perfect for him. But she's no Jane.

"Daddy, is he really a savage?" Bo Derek as Jane and Richard Harris as James Parker in the filming of *Tarzan, the Ape Man* (1981).

"Were I not already engaged along other lines of research, and were it possible, I should like to determine the biological or psychological explanation of the profound attraction that the blond female has for the male of all races."

GOD, *TARZAN AND THE LION MAN* (1933)

FIVE

ENTER JANE

Jane is a blonde. We forget this fact, because of all those brunettes who have played her, from Enid Markey in 1918 through Maureen O'Sullivan and even Disney's animated rendition. Only a handful of the twenty-some actresses who have played her have been blonde, most notably Brenda Joyce, the only woman to play Jane opposite two Tarzan actors (Johnny Weissmuller and Lex Barker). But Jane is a blonde-haired, blue-eyed beauty. As Philip José Farmer's "biography" *Tarzan Alive* hyperbolizes: "We have no data about her figure then, but measurements taken at a London shop twenty years later, when she had not lost or gained a pound, are: height, 5 feet 7 inches (tall for those days); bust, 38; waist, 19 inches; hips, 36 inches."[1] The casting director for *Tarzan and the Slave Girl* (1950) considered the newcomer Marilyn Monroe to play Jane, but the producer, Sol Lesser, felt that she was too much the bombshell.[2] (Though in 1952 Monroe had a prominent part in *Monkey Business*, a film with an absent-minded professor and an elixir of youth mixed by a mischievous Cheta-like chimp).

Jane gets a title role only once, with *Tarzan and Jane*, a DVD/VHS release combining three episodes from *The Legend of Tarzan*, Disney's 2001 television sequel series to the 1999 animated feature. Yet without Jane, there is no Tarzan. Civilization knows of him only because of her; he makes himself known in Africa because of her, and he abandons the jungle and enters civilization because of her. Weissmuller's Tarzan never says to O'Sullivan's Jane "Me Tarzan, you Jane"—it's Jane who points to herself saying "Jane" and points back to him to prompt him to say "Tarzan." To borrow a term from literary theory: she interpellates him. In Jane, Tarzan discovers his purpose: "He knew that she was created to be protected, and that he was created to protect her. . . . It seemed to him that no pleasure on earth could compare with laboring for the welfare and protection of the beautiful white girl."[3] The instant love and sexual longing for this American New World beauty validate his humanity, his whiteness, and his masculinity. In the first film, Tarzan in the jungle hands his knife over to Jane, who then returns it to him.[4] In a scene from the *Tarzan the Tiger* serial of 1929, Natalie Kingston's Jane sits with Frank Merrill's Tarzan holding an open book across their laps as he points to a picture of an ape with one hand and to himself with the other.

We also tend to forget how much the stories belong to her. Her dilemmas and decisions drive them forward. Should she choose him or his cousin Cecil, the acting Lord Greystoke? She faces this decision twice—first in Africa and again in Wisconsin, in the novel's final pages. There, she considers that "the spell that had been put upon her in the depths of that far-off jungle" was put upon her *by* that far-off jungle, "but there was no spell of enchantment now in prosaic Wisconsin." It occurs to her that her jungle affection "seemed . . . only attributable to a temporary mental reversion to type on her part—to the appeal of the primeval man to the primeval woman in her nature. . . . Excitement would not always mark their future relations, should she marry him, and the power of personal contact would be dulled by familiarity."[5] As Jane suspects, and as Burroughs knew, Tarzan's apishness would have repulsed her. Except, of course, for the fact that his love for her has inspired his metamorphosis. Their first kiss "seared a deep brand into his soul—a brand which marked a new Tarzan."[6] After she leaves Africa he follows her and becomes a proper gentleman—"for your sake I have become a civilized man—for your sake I have crossed oceans and continents—for your sake I will be whatever you will me to be."[7] The good girl tames the bad boy. Tarzan has always been chick lit as much as it has been lad lit. The films with Jane are chick flicks, with Tarzan obeying Jane even against his infallible instincts and judgment: "If Jane say go to moon, we go to moon," he says in *Tarzan's Savage Fury*. "If Jane say go to Waziri, we go to Waziri."

In the 1932 and 1981 versions of *Tarzan the Ape Man*, Tarzan is secondary to Jane. The films begin with her arrival in Africa; they follow her adventure into the interior, her discovery of him, and her decision to stay in the jungle with him. She is the protagonist with the majority of the screen time; he is the object of her decision. In 1981, at a time when the feminist '60s and '70s were giving way to the conservative Reagan '80s, the Dereks wanted to update the original MGM film's feminist message. As Bo's Jane tells off Harry Holt: "It's a man's world; women aren't allowed to be participants. We're here for your pleasure, not for ours. . . . I don't dislike men. I envy them. I envy your freedom. I resent not having the same." Indeed, the Dereks are using Bo's body to challenge the male viewers lured to the theater for the promise of pleasure in seeing Bo's body. The earlier film, too, appeared at a similar transitional moment, from the "New Woman" era of the early twentieth century to the Great Depression's re-entrenchment of old gender roles.[8] Edgar Rice Burroughs, Inc.'s lawsuit complaint that Bo's Jane "in sexual matters . . . is now the aggressor"[9] indicates the major difference between the two Janes, but also reveals an unsettling preference for Jane's rape in the early film.

Almost all of the films that include Jane continue this pattern. Jane always faces the difficult dilemmas, she struggles between loyalties, and the plots follow from her choices. Tarzan acts without thinking because his perfect natural nobility precludes internal conflicts. The screen Jane is a three-dimensional character; the screen Tarzan has two dimensions. Maybe just one. In *Tarzan's Revenge* (1938), Tarzan occupies the screen for ten minutes; the rest of the film belongs to a Jane surrogate named Eleanor. The major exception is the 1984 film *Greystoke: The Legend of Tarzan*, which promised a realistic restoration of Burroughs's vision. Yet this film betrays the Jane of Burroughs's first Tarzan novel and the Jane of the screen by disempowering her—this Jane makes no decisions whatsoever. This Tarzan of the manly 1980s is entirely in charge. Jane only makes it to the jungle at the end of the movie, in full skirt, to watch her man abandon her for fraternal apehood.

If Jane gets it both ways with Tarzan—European scion and American Adam, wholesome white man and black beast—Tarzan gets it both ways with Jane, too. After their marriage in the second book—his cousin William Cecil's death providing Jane the only possible honorable release from that betrothal—Jane appears in only eight of the next twenty-two books in the series, and in many of these her role is minimal.[10] Even assuming that the periods of Tarzan's life not covered in any of the novels he spends with Jane, either at the English manor or their African plantation, their marriage is strikingly convenient for him. He's married and domestic, and he's free as a tropical bird.

With the Jane of the movies, Tarzan gets it both ways somewhat differently. This Jane is fiercely independent and drably domestic. Maureen O'Sullivan played her as a spitfire tomboy, as ready and able for exotic adventure as her father, and finally free-spirited enough to turn her back on the world that created her and adores her. She is a proper lady who abjures the trappings of proper ladyship: society, money, clothes, jewelry, even a decent bed (not to mention plumbing, electricity, and medicine).[11] She gives up the creature comforts that in her day defined womanhood so that she could unite, out of wedlock, with her wrong-side-of-the-ocean man. In O'Sullivan's Jane, Weissmuller's Tarzan gets a petite vixen, particularly in their first two films. Sexual Jane persists in the later films of Tarzan's golden era mainly through the audience's memory of her. The courtship and honeymoon are over: Jane gives up bowers and nests for a tree house like you've never seen: running water, an elephant-powered elevator, a stove, and a refrigerator for the caviar. The sensual shots, the knowing cut-to-sex moments, are replaced by tenderness and sentiment. Our jungle goddess is returned to her proper sphere. She manages the house, he rules the jungle—with the occasional assertion of his ultimate authority in the roost too, such as when Tarzan barks his decision to name their found son "Boy." When she does presume a public role—when she makes a decision involving the outside world—it's always the wrong decision, the consequences of which involve Tarzan saving the day. The other white men often patronizingly admire her modern pluck, but in the end she is soundly put in her place.

Both the movies and the novels put women (and men) in their place. Burroughs's Jane never obtains the fiery independence of Maureen O'Sullivan's, despite a few times when necessity dictates she use some of the survival skills

Tarzan taught her. After *Beasts of Tarzan*, in which she returns to Africa alone to find her husband and her kidnapped infant son, Jane retreats into the background of domestic life. Otherwise, gender roles in Burroughs are rigorously conventional. After Tarzan's birth, his mother Alice, who perhaps a little unconventionally had insisted on accompanying her husband to Africa, loses her grip on reality. For the next year, before passing "quietly away in the night," she believes the family returned home to England. "In other ways she was quite rational, and the joy and happiness she took in the possession of her little son and the constant attentions of her husband made that year a very happy one for her, the happiest of her life."[12] The root of "hysteria," *hyster*, means "womb." A mother belongs in her home, sheltered from the brutal reality of the world by her husband. When Alice dies, John Clayton writes his last entry in his diary: "My little son is crying for nourishment. Oh, Alice, Alice, what shall I do?"[13] Instead of heading out after coconut milk, this great specimen of manhood, inherently devoid of the maternal instinct, falls asleep, only to awaken for the length of time it takes a charging ape-creature to kill him. The infant Lord Greystoke needs a mother, *any* mother; his real father will not do; and behind the murderous bull-ape comes Kala, still grieving over the loss of her own child and eager to nurture another. In the short story "Tarzan and the Black Boy," a pre-Jane Tarzan wants to be a father and kidnaps a native African boy. Tarzan's lack of the maternal capacity turns his project into a fiasco. He returns the child to his mother.

Even the books' independent women, the alternative heroines like the exotic La and Nemone, suffer for need of a man. For need of Tarzan. La betrays her people out of unrequited love for Tarzan, and he twice restores her to power. Nemone also falls in love with Tarzan, is refused by him, and takes her own life—literally after Tarzan's lion killed her lion, because she felt bound to it in life and death, but one wonders how much Tarzan's killing of her love, symbolized in the lion affair, led her to suicide. The most astonishing payback against women who transgress proper gender roles happens in *Tarzan and the Ant Men*. The women of the Alali stand six feet tall, are well muscled, have hairy chests, arms, and legs, and dominate the shorter, slighter Alali men. With Tarzan's help, however, the men learn to stand up for themselves—they gain weapons, learn to fight, and overthrow their women:

Now each male had a woman cooking for him—at least one, and some of them—the stronger—had more than one. To entertain Tarzan and show him what great strides civilization had taken—the son of The First Woman seized a female by the hair and dragging her to him struck her heavily about the head and face with his clenched fist, and the woman feel upon her knees and fondled his legs, looking wistfully into his face, her own glowing with love and admiration.[14]

~~~~

Women and men's "natural" roles are clear. Less clear in Tarzania, however, is the relationship between gender and nature. "Woven everywhere into the tapestry of European art and literature are seemingly an inseparable part of most philosophical and scientific texts—even embedded in the structure of European languages—is the assumption that women are closer to nature than men are," Susan Griffin has written. "The notion is not intended as a compliment. In the hierarchical geography of European tradition, not only are human beings elevated above the rest of nature, but men are closer to heaven than women. In short, the idea that women are closer to nature is an argument for the dominion of men."[15]

Traditionally conceived, women's insistent physicality—menstruation, birthing, and lactation—have connected them with "nature." Accordingly, relative to men, women are creatures of body and emotion, instinct, and irrationality; they have less control over their immediate wants, and they exhibit little capacity for forethought. In women we find the true revelation of our animal selves. The first section of Griffin's *Woman and Nature* is an amazing assembly of found (if paraphrased) historical prose, including this passage:

> (And among the lower races, it is observed, the pendulous abdomen, want of calves, flatness of the thighs, all features of the ape, are common.)
>
> And woman, it is observed, like the Negro, is flat-footed, with a prominent inclination of the pelvis making her appear less erect, and her gait less steady.
>
> That as regards his intellectual faculties, the Negro partakes of the nature of the child or the female or the senile white.

That woman's brain is smaller and the shape of her head closer to that of infants and those of the "lower races."

And it is put forward that "wherever one sees an approach to the animal type the female is nearer to it than the male." That in the *female* Hottentot one can see the monkey more clearly.

(From voyages around the globe, it is whispered, one hears stories of women mating with monkeys or bears and bearing progeny.)

Slavery is said to be a condition of higher civilization.

A woman should be an enthusiastic slave to the man to whom she has given her heart, it is declared.[16]

No wonder white American men worried about their women consorting with African Americans. Birds of a feather. The "Women's Building" at the Columbian Exposition was separate from the White City's testament to civilization and proximate to the Midway Plaisance's exhibit of the lower races and animals.[17]

Griffin's book focuses on a woman's Western ideological inheritance—much of that first section condemns Christianity's contribution to this belief.[18] The woman-nature association is, however, a more universal problem, as Sherry Ortner reminds us. For Ortner, culture opposes nature and attempts to "transcend natural conditions and turn them to its purposes." Women are seen "as being more rooted in, or having more direct affinity with nature" than men, "as representing a lower order of being, as being less transcendental of nature than men are."[19] While clear historical and possible biographical motives for Tarzania's misogyny exist, in response to early feminism (the rape urge was not uncommon in modernist fiction and film) and in Burroughs's failed marriage (per Torgovnick), we might explain misogyny not as hatred of womankind simply, but of womankind as symbol of human creatureliness and mortality. Humanity denies death and nontranscendent selfhood by dominating its most corporeal selves—its women. Today's rail-thin fashion model also joins this fear-filled hostility to what the female body has represented, a beauty standard less objectifying than abstracting (from three dimensions to two). Men can yield to their own bestial nature while symbolically conquering it by conquering her.

If men turn their mortal despair into hostility against women, logically women would direct their hostility against their own bodies. Thus the male imagination has projected a masochistic desire onto women, as Griffin has recorded, perhaps to justify its own brutal selfishness: "[It is said that] the female cell, the ovum, in the act of fecundation, being wounded, is primordially masochistic. . . . That women have a lust for pain."[20] The association of women and nature suggests that the earth also desires to be exploited.

Are women in Burroughs' stories closer than men to nature? Isn't it Tarzan the ape-man, not Jane the ape-woman?

On the one hand, the idea of linking women with nature in Burroughs sounds preposterous. Women like Tarzan's mother Alice Clayton and Jane Porter represent society and civilization. They cannot survive outside of society and civilization—Alice dies, and Jane can manage the wild only in short bursts. Such a woman embodies that which binds men to society and civilization, the muse that inspires them to commit to society, civilized behavior, and the self-sacrifice to the collective that is the very soul of social life.[21] Tarzan tames his rapacious self, gives up the jungle, and learns to behave as a gentleman, all for Jane. He sacrifices jungle life for her, and then he sacrifices her hand in marriage in order to preserve her honor after she becomes betrothed to his cousin. After all, he's the noble savage, the ape-man, the natural one ruled by instincts and physicality; his wife is the one who wants to deny their son's natural interest in beasts and the primitive. Civilization effeminizes; nature, be it the jungle, the forest, or the frontier, makes men. Ortner notes that women's association with children, those little human animals, strengthens women's association with nature; thus Tarzan the hairless man-boy (especially Weissmuller's Tarzan who pals around endlessly with Boy and Boy's near-sibling Cheta) would be the more "natural" creature. In those film versions of the ur-story in which Jane introduces Tarzan to the world through books and in Disney's case a slide show, she serves her proper role as civilization's domesticating agent (Cheta and Boy are practically siblings). In the films, Tarzan's foes frequently die at the earth's empathetic hands—drowning in quicksand, falling off a cliff, stumbling into the jaws of an alligator or lion.

On the other hand, these deaths are not indifferent accidents of nature, but nature responding to Tarzan's will. Alice and Jane can't conquer nature because they are nature. When Tarzan's parents find themselves abandoned on the African coast, John Clayton knows that he carries in his blood the might of his manly ancestors who were victorious over nature. "Ah, John," his wife Alice responds, "I wish that I might be a man with a man's philosophy, but I am but a woman, seeing with my heart rather than my head."[22] Alice again sees with her heart rather than her head after Tarzan's birth, when her devotion to her child supplants reality. Indeed, the two characters most alike in *Tarzan of the Apes* are probably Alice and Kala, Tarzan's ape-creature mother, in their absolute obeisance to the "universal" call of motherhood. The irrational denizens in Tarzania, those most ruled by passion, instinct, and immediate appetites, are animals, Africans, working-class whites, and women. The reader sees Jane's rational decision to marry Tarzan's cousin as a mistake, a betrayal of her passion, her instinct, her nature. When Jane loses her sexual vitality after the first book, Burroughs transfers the erotic energy to her two chief rivals, La and Nemone of the hybrid human-animal societies.

Moreover, we could claim, as others have and perhaps in accord with Burroughs's vision, that Tarzan doesn't thrive in nature as a child of nature, but as a child of civilization. His animalism is circumstantial and external, not natural and internal. As the story develops he does not give up his natural self; he rediscovers his true nature as the end product of thousands of years of human progress, the height of physical, intellectual, and moral fitness. He becomes a man only after his ape-creature mother Kala dies, after killing his two surrogate ape-creature fathers Tublat and Kerchak, and after killing his African doppelgänger Kulonga—only after killing the beasts of his nurture. When Jane restrains herself in Tarzan's arms, when she checks her passions, we pity her; when he restrains himself, when he checks his passions to ravish her or succumb to La and Nemone, we cheer. Burroughs's having Tarzan teach himself to read in picture books before he encounters Jane undermines the book's assertion of essential gender roles, possibly even in the matter of sexual attraction. His feelings for her have been just as conditioned by the words and pictures as his gentlemanly behavior has (if less consciously): "He had had time to recollect all that he had read of the ways of men and women in the books at the cabin. He would act as he imagined the men in the books would have acted were they in his place."[23] Tarzan the ape-man is a consummately socialized and civilized soul.

Then there's the matter of his immaculate conception.

I don't blame Burroughs for failing to formulate a clear relationship among men, women, and nature. I don't blame him because his failure reflects his age's confusion over the matter, a confusion revealing the artificiality, the constructedness, of any such connections. Burroughs wrote to entertain, working the moment to command the audience's immediate attention. So sometimes the male psyche implied by Burroughs's Tarzan novels wants his women pure of heart and above base sex, as civilization's vanguard in the nurturing of its future moral and productive citizens; and sometimes he wants them on the ground fondling his legs, as base in posture and stature as his own bestial desires. If anything, Burroughs slighted women by removing them from the equation entirely: Tarzan is nature and civilization, but Jane is just a girl.

The femme-Tarzan film genre solidly associates women with wild nature and men with taming civilization in titles like *Savage Girl* (1932), *Queen of the Jungle* (1935), *Jungle Princess* (1936), *Her Jungle Love* (1938), *Jungle Siren* (1942), *Nabonga* (1944), *Tiger Woman* (1944), *Blonde Savage* (1947), *Daughter of the Jungle* (1949), *The Panther Girl of the Kongo* (1955), *Untamed Mistress* (1957), *Eve* (1968), *Luana, Jungle Girl* (1968), *Samoa, Queen of the Jungle* (1968), *Tarzana the Wild Girl* (1972), *Mistress of the Apes* (1979), *Goliathon* (1981), *Diamonds of Kilimandjaro* (1983), and *Jane* (1985). Not to mention a number of similar characters in series with a male central character: Weissmuller's post-Tarzan Jungle Jim and Sheffield's post-Tarzan Bomba, as well as the many book and comic femme-Tarzans. In the classic femme-Tarzan plot, a white girl orphaned in the jungle is the object of a white man's quest.[24] The early examples generally do not depart significantly from the general Tarzan and jungle adventure genre in budget, plot, and appeal. And while some later femme-Tarzan films—*Sheena* (1984) and *Mara of the Wilderness* (1966), for example—are proper action adventures, the *New York Times* review for *Liane, Jungle Goddess* (1959) captures the spirit of most latter femme-Tarzan flicks:

> If you are looking for something that approximates a waking nightmare, then by all means subject yourself to "Liane, Jungle Goddess." The actors are German. The dialogue is English, out of synchronization in several accents.
> The direction is bad. The color is that of over- or under-exposed home movies. The point is pornography, conveyed by the nudity of the Liane of the title. She is a female Tarzan, found without her undershirt in the jungle. She is clothed before the picture is twenty minutes old and sent back to civilization. It's a shame.
> The film opened at about forty theatres yesterday. Another shame.[25]

For such films, viewer satisfaction did not matter; selling tickets sold everything.

The poster for *Tarzana the Wild Girl* declares that "SHE SWINGS THROUGH THE JUNGLE NAKED AS THE ANIMALS," and wittily apologizes: "SORRY: Due to the '*nature*' of this film, no one under 17 admitted without a parent or guardian." The publicity sheet calls the movie an "adult jungle film" that "touch[es] on attitudes carefully avoided in other similar movies." The sheet recommends that theaters stage a marriage ritual as a promotional device, and provides a script that includes a "'Wild Girl' primitive goddess," a "beautiful savage Negro girl," and a "captivating Chinese savage girl." Before the movie begins, an announcer introduces the three recently captured wild girls over the theater's sound system:

> Since they are still very much in their wild state, they will be brought to
> their cages in about one hour. We have recently discovered that "the Wild
> Girl" is becoming more and more civilized, day by day, and has expressed her
> desire to marry a [*sic*] eligible American bachelor. Therefore, we urge all of
> you young bachelors to sign and deposit your name at our concession stand.
> Some lucky gent will win the hand of "the Wild Girl" and will be married
> TONIGHT at break time.

The marriage ceremony is to be interrupted "by screams of fury" as the other two girls "break from their cages and grab 'the Wild Girl'" because "they don't want her to marry a civilized man." But Wild Girl fights back. "Enter squad car, screaming siren, lights flashing; patrolman throws net over the girls and hauls them off."[26] The movie hardly lives up to the hype.

It should not surprise us that the savage femme-Tarzans are a sexually aggressive lot. Raised among natives or beasts or both—the distinction is immaterial—we know with whom they learned to kiss, although we also know that they, being white, never slept with their kissing partners. So they are sexual animals and virgins. Nor should it surprise us that femme-Tarzans frequently carry a reputation, among the civilized, for controlling nature and natives with supernatural powers—not by being above nature, supranaturally, but by being so thoroughly a part of it. But they get it both ways: the natives also worship them because of their unearthly white skin. These heroines are not hard-bodied muscle heads; they have not, per Dyer, mastered their own physicality. And such a woman is never alone, never autonomously manly—

she often lives with natives and always ends up romantically attached to the white man who has come to her rescue. He returns her to civilization, conquering her natural self, or opts to live with her in her jungle paradise—a male fantasy either way.

~~~~

Tarzan of the movies sometimes wants her slaving in the tree house kitchen (but looking like she just left the beauty salon), and he sometimes wants her to drop what little clothes she wears for some skinny-dipping fun.

Weissmuller and O'Sullivan's second film as the jungle couple, *Tarzan and His Mate* (1934), reinvigorated the Hays Code office, Hollywood's self-created institution for policing itself to ensure propriety, decency, and morality (the office had been dormant since its inception). Jane's skimpy clothes, her choreographed underwater ballet in the buff with Tarzan in his loincloth, and the supposed flash of a breast when she popped out of the water brought the film to the censor's editing room. It didn't help matters that she was his mate, not his wife. Three versions of the film, with varying levels of editing, were released around the country. I am fairly sure that none of them cut the scene in which Arlington and the natives watch through the backlit tent wall as Jane changes clothes, even though the Hays Code expressly forbade "nudity in fact or silhouette, or any lecherous or licentious notice thereof by other characters in the picture."

The Hays Code office was only part of the uproar. Thousands of women wrote letters in objection, and O'Sullivan suspected that the film helped inspire the formation of the Legion of Decency, a Catholic organization founded in 1933 whose members would unite in their condemnation of "vile," "unwholesome," and "salacious" motion pictures "as a grave menace to youth, to home life, to country and religion. . . . which, with other degrading agencies, are corrupting public morals and promoting a sex mania in our land" (though the chronology suggests the culprit would have been 1932's *Tarzan the Ape Man*, with its nonmarital sex and skimpy clothes).[27] O'Sullivan displayed her anger over the ado in another interview:

Between the violent reaction of an Anglo-Saxon puritanic public because of what they termed my "nude" scenes in the first couple of Tarzan films, and the equally intolerant reaction of MGM executives, who then clothed me in virgin-white swim costumes which looked like they came off the rack at Macy's, I was thoroughly disgusted with the whole scene. . . . The fact that Olympic gold medalist Josephine McKim performed the "nude" scenes, and the fact that only her bottom really showed in the underwater swimming shots, made no difference. I was a promiscuous harlot in the eyes of many of the viewing public.[28]

Even more ridiculous were the body stockings worn by Cheta and the other chimps in compliance with the Hays Code's forbidding of any display of any sex organs whatsoever. A telling sexualizing of primates?

After *Tarzan and His Mate*, MGM cleaned up its act, covering more of Jane's skin and relinquishing the lovers' treetop bowers in favor of a proper suburban tree house. Yet the flesh appeal of the films remained—with MGM's Tarzan nearly a mute, he and Jane connected primarily through body chemistry. MGM and every other Tarzan, faux-Tarzan, and femme-Tarzan production company have known that the films owe their success to the ur-story's excuse for the exhibition of bodies—its sanction, its command really, to surrender ourselves to our unbridled gaze. "I wonder what you'd look like dressed," Maureen O'Sullivan's Jane told Johnny Weissmuller's Tarzan in the 1932 *Tarzan the Ape Man*. Early men's magazines and pinups too knew the appeal of barely clad jungle girls. I've seen vintage photos of women dressed as "jungle girls" from the 1920s, although the most famous photos, Bettie Page's "Jungle Bettie" photos, appeared in the mid-1950s. Cover illustrations of 1940s magazines like *Jungle Stories* and *Jungle Comics* loved to feature a woman bursting from her animal-skin bikini, frequently about to be saved from some animal's feasting by a Tarzan look-alike.

Of course Bo Derek was chosen for her body—or more accurately, she and her husband chose *Tarzan, the Ape Man* for her body. Tarzan speaks not a word in this film; like Bo, the actor Miles O'Keefe was chosen for his body, "the most beautiful body" she had ever seen.[29] We might playfully contend that Bo's bad acting—the exaggerated inanity of her lines characterizing Jane's innocence—mimics the acting of Johnny Weissmuller to call attention to his physicality as his only qualification for the role. Her frequent and overblown fingers-to-mouth gesture of anxiousness becomes her version of his ubiquitous, cartoonish, bepuzzled furrowed brow.

Ironically, in the context of the sexual and cinematic mores of their times, the Dereks' film was far less risqué and tantalizing than MGM's original and its sequel, *Tarzan and His Mate*. *Time* magazine contrasted the Dereks' film with the "innocently sensuous 1932" original,[30] but innocence was exactly the point of the Dereks' film. "You could say this is a sexy film," Bo said in an MGM press release, "but there is nothing lewd or obscene about it. It's pure sex, and there's a lot of nudity, but it all appears very natural." By "pure" she meant pure of heart, or *innocent*, and she was right: you might call it sexy, except that it isn't. It's downright lame. MGM's legal department cleared it for not violating the remake clause's allowance for "bring[ing] the story up to the standards and mores of the times," and, as Bo's memoir further notes, "There wasn't even a love scene in our film, just some seminudity, and in 1981 almost every film had nudity."[31] When the film appeared on HBO, it "had very high ratings," meaning a lot of people tuned in, "but very low satisfaction levels."[32] They wanted sexy sex; they were disappointed. The remake outdid the original in its innocence.

Like *Tarzan and His Mate*, the Dereks' *Tarzan, the Ape Man* found itself censored. The nearly four minutes of lost footage were, according to Bo, "only bits and pieces of nudity" determined "arbitrarily."[33] If the surviving nudity is any indication, we can trust Bo's evaluation that the cuts did not bring the film within contemporary standards of graphic sex because it never transgressed those standards in the first place. Relative to the mores of the 1930s, the Dereks were contractually obliged to make the movie more salacious, more shocking. To bring the spirit of the original in line with contemporary standards, the new film should have shown Tarzan raping Jane instead of relegating it offscreen. Instead, the Dereks transfer the rape threat from Tarzan to the villainous Ivory Chief. In the climactic sequence, a handful of the Ivory Chief's women prepare Jane for a ritual whose unspeakable nature is not spoken of, most likely a ceremonial rape. "They're washing me just like a whore," Jane plaints.

In addition to the racial message, the painting of Bo's stark naked body stark white—sometimes on all fours, sometimes on her back—matters because it remarks upon the Tarzan films' obsession with bodies, with sexual objectification at its most pernicious. This film does equalize the genders to the extent that it has already spotlighted the objectification of Miles O'Keefe's body. If the natives have transformed Bo's Jane into a perfect ivory statue, she has at least already observed that O'Keefe's mute Tarzan looks "just like a statue in a museum." Still, the ultimate focus on Bo's Jane's body must occur, for dramatic simplicity, surely; because women in our culture have traditionally been objectification's chief victims; but mostly because it sharply draws the metaphorical connection of exploitative objectification and rape.[34]

The completely objectified person becomes a statue. Bo's Jane for all intents and purposes has become an ivory carving, an abstraction for the Ivory Chief's and our pleasure. Indeed, the presumed ritual rape could instead or additionally be a sacrificial killing, the ambiguity of the ritual's nature furthering the Dereks' message. Objectification, inasmuch as it reduces a person to her body, establishes an antagonistic relationship between them, dividing the person from her body in a kind of living death. As James Parker advises his daughter to defend herself mentally from her impending fate at the Ivory Chief's hands, "You are not of the flesh. You are of the spirit. That is why you must leave your body right now. You must leave him nothing." Nothing but what he wants, anyway.

The issue is not the natural, necessary, and beautiful sexual objectification between consensual lovers (which the film struggles to achieve), but the collective appropriation, commodification, and distribution of that most intimate and private physical transaction. The sequence of Jane's public objectification resembles nothing less than a staging of a staging, with the Ivory Chief's pad consisting of various platforms and the players elaborately costumed in body paint. But the spectacle of the spectacle is exactly the point of the film's metaphorical critique of Hollywood culture specifically and modern U.S. media culture more generally.

Perhaps I give this film too much credit.

After killing the Ivory Chief and all that he represents, Tarzan joins Jane in the river to help her wash off the paint. Man and woman together undo her victimization. The solution, like the problem, involves both genders. Together, they flee into the jungle. Together they flee the spectacular nature of civilization that can't help but objectify them—they are too beautiful by far, and civilization requires each of us to sacrifice some part of ourselves to its needs and pleasures. But this Tarzan and Jane restore the primacy and integrity of honest physical being. They regain their bodies, and in the process their very souls. Eden is regained.

Yet the film finally fails to reconcile its appreciation for beauty and its objection to the objectification and commodification of beauty. How does a woman embrace her sexuality without disempowering herself to male exploitation? How can she be a strong woman retreating into a conventional protective heterosexual relationship? The film also fails to combine innocent physicality and bestial lust, though to be fair this failure comes with the Tarzania territory.

〜〜〜〜

Of his father's "very healthy libido," Johnny Weissmuller Jr. writes: "Passion? Yeah, he had that too, and when women stampeded over him he may have had his weak moments, but that did not make him a womanizer. . . . It made him Tarzan."[35] Tarzan is sex; paradoxically, the Tarzan novels and films constitute a remarkably asexual oeuvre.

After the first book, *Tarzan of the Apes*, the only sexual heat for Tarzan comes from women other than Jane, and this heat never leads to consummation. We know that Tarzan and Jane procreate once, but the absence of any children other than their son Jack is suspicious in an age long before birth control and an age in which large families were the norm. Do we really imagine the ape-man living by the rhythm method his entire life? Tarzan's absence from home and Jane's absence from the majority of the novels are also suspicious. Maybe her prediction at the end of *Tarzan of the Apes* was right—familiarity quenched their mutual desire. Jane and Tarzan of the movies, with the exception of the first two Weissmuller-O'Sullivan productions, barely cohabitate. In *Tarzan and the Trappers* they live in separate tree houses. After finding their son, according to Tarzanologist Francis Lacassin, "Tarzan always shar[es] a room with Boy while Jane sleeps in her own room";[36] and in more than a third of the fifty-two Tarzan films and television series, there's no Jane at all, including the one production overseen by Burroughs, *The New Adventures of Tarzan*.[37] The movies have rare moments, as when in *Tarzan's Greatest Adventure* (1959) a sudden cut interrupts Tarzan and Angie kissing and rolling out of frame. The next thing you know they're sharing satisfied smiles. But fast-forward to 1967, when the Jane-less *Tarzan and the Great River* ends with Tarzan and the film's requisite token white girl shaking hands good-bye. One of the most sexual scenes of any occurs in

Tarzan and the Hidden Jungle (1955), when Gordon Scott's Tarzan bathes the thighs of an unconscious Vera Miles's Jill Hardy, and she squirms and moans suggestively. When she revives and covers her thighs with what's left of her khaki culottes, we are not fooled into thinking sex has been prevented.

The easy explanation for the asexuality in the case of the movies is their audience. These are family movies, children's movies, PG movies—indeed another reason for Tarzan's waning appeal for adults around the late 1960s and early 70s might involve the movie's inability to compete with the emerging new standards of graphic nudity and sex in mainstream productions (including television). The movies' asexuality, however, also follows that of the novels. The original *All-Story* story bore the subtitle "A Romance of the Jungle," the term "romance" indicating a genre based on adventure and courtship. Sex and sexuality did not belong in public discourse—it barely belonged in private discourse. Joan Burroughs recalled that her father, who began dictating his stories in the 1920s, "never dictated love scenes. This seemed to embarrass him and all such scenes were transcribed from the Dictograph."[38] It's hard to imagine what love scenes in the Burroughs canon could have possibly provoked such chagrin; it's even harder to imagine what it was like to live in that sexual climate. The sexual tension that until only very recently has characterized American teenage life—the tension of never achieving physical intimacy, of never talking about sex, of having the entire business abandoned to the individual's imagination—in Burroughs's day characterized much of adult life. Naturally, it characterized his novels.

America's historical discomfort with human sexuality brought Leslie Fiedler, in his classic account of American literature, *Love and Death in the American Novel* (1960), to the supposition that "Perhaps the whole odd shape of American fiction arises simply . . . because there is no real sexuality in American life and therefore there cannot very well be any in American art."[39] For Fiedler, the American hero thus becomes a loner, like the protagonist of James Fenimore Cooper's nineteenth-century Leatherstocking novels, Natty Bumpo, "a law unto himself." This prototypical hero "is the deliverer, the rescuer, the man who arrives in the nick of time—but only to deliver the ingénue into the arms of someone else."[40] In order to arrive in the nick of time, such a hero must enjoy total freedom to be where he needs to be when he needs to be there. His commitment to freedom precludes commitment to anything else, especially a wife. And thus the problem, as defined by Fiedler: "In an age of Romance, what can one do with the hero who, *in essence and by definition, cannot get the girl?*"[41] At the end of Burroughs's original story, Tarzan doesn't get the girl; he leaves her in the arms of, to finish Fiedler's line, "a stuffy and genteel young man of the proper station in life to marry the kind of young lady . . . worthy of being a heroine," all without surrendering true romance.[42]

Then, unexpectedly, the Tarzan story saw instant success. Its readers demanded more, and they demanded that Tarzan get the girl. Steven D. Utley believes that Burroughs had wanted to give up the Tarzan character shortly after the couple's marriage in the second book. Burroughs's next story, *The Eternal Lover* (1914), introduced their domestic bliss with their son Jack at their African estate. The opening scene, in which the Tarzan family entertains Barney Custer and his sister Victoria, only serves to launch Barney and Victoria on their adventures. "[Q]uietly and contentedly married," writes Utley, "the trials of the first two novels behind [them], the Claytons were obviously trying to take a last bow." But Tarzan wouldn't go away. His readers and Burroughs's financial obligations demanded more. A few years later, struggling with how to reconcile a married man with the conventional American lone hero, Burroughs even tried to kill off Jane. His editors balked, and the body in *Tarzan the Untamed* (1919) that Burroughs originally named as Jane's now only *might* have been hers, burned beyond recognition. Her possible survival, which Tarzan learns by novel's end, gave Burroughs a starting point his next novel, *Tarzan the Terrible*, in which our hero tracks her down and saves her.

By leaving Jane at home, Tarzan is a loner hero of the standard American variety and also a properly married gentleman who, luckily enough, uses his marriage as the excuse for not becoming entangled with the sexpots he encounters. For Fiedler, Natty Bumpo cannot marry because marriage "stands for the loss of freedom" and "would have meant in short a kind of *emasculation*, since the virility of Natty is not genital but heroic."[43] Tarzan's virility is also heroic, but his marriage of convenience provides the illusion of genital virility, too.

Tarzan of the movies dealt with the Jane problem exactly as Burroughs had. MGM killed Jane in the first draft of *Tarzan Finds a Son!*, the fourth

Weissmuller-O'Sullivan feature, but fan outcry in response to a news release forced the production team to shoot a new ending. Now she impossibly survives the spear plunged in her back. Otherwise Hollywood simply dropped her out of the picture without bothering to kill her and frequently without bothering to explain her absence or even to mention her, as if she never existed. As producer Sy Weintraub explained his decision to ditch Jane for *Tarzan the Magnificent*, "A bachelor figure is a lot more exciting than a man who comes swinging home through the jungle every night to tell his little woman what's been happening during the day."[44] Bachelorhood—sexual freedom—sells.[45]

Yet Burroughs grew up in the nineteenth century, with Tarzan debuting in his creator's thirty-seventh year and during cinema's infancy. His world would not be Weintraub's—Weintraub and his Hollywood ilk had no trouble talking about love scenes. Burroughs had more to reconcile than Tarzan as lone hero and married gentleman. He also had to reconcile the two parts of Jane: the primitive woman who responds lustfully to her discovery of her primitive (albeit aristocratic) man, and the proper woman destined for gentle wifehood and motherhood.

In the nineteenth century's cult of the lady—or cult of true womanhood, or cult of domesticity—the woman as wife and mother was idealized as the moral, spiritual, and cultural center of the home. The angel of the household charged with civilizing her husband, she was "less driven than a man by sexual passion, more given to restraint and delicacy, and a creature of love rather than lust. Purity came naturally to her, whereas a man constantly struggled to subdue his animal instincts."[46] In other words, if it's true that Western civilization long associated women with nature and sinful passion and physicality and devilry, at some point another notion took hold. (The transformation of women from wild creatures to domestic angels converged with two related transformations: that of nature, from the devil's den to God's weekend sanctuary, as the American frontier shrank and vanished; and that of American Christianity's, from its focus on God and fear to Christ and friendship.)[47] For Fiedler, this radical shift by the middle of the nineteenth century preserved the fear of passion by turning contempt for the woman as evil temptress into idealization of her as asexual, spiritual guide. Men could still fear passion and the strength of their own sexual desires, but they could now do so while esteeming their women. The ideology "simultaneously disowns sex and glorifies women."[48]

Fiedler does not completely explain this shift. Maybe the culture was responding to early feminism's assertions of strength and moral fortitude, either as a way of honestly respecting the woman or as a way of keeping her in her place in the home. Maybe men finally recognized that for centuries they had been projecting their lust onto women, blaming them for the temptation of their own bodies; maybe men had begun to acknowledge and even romanticize the animal within themselves. Or maybe the woman-as-beast-and-devil view and the woman-as-saint view simply reflected two different cultural responses to a conflict that has always dogged us: the desire for transcendent love and for physical love, and their apparent irreconcilable opposition. Jane is Tarzan's "golden-haired divinity" . . . whom "he was as near to worshipping . . . as mortal man ever comes to worship."[49]

Another Burroughs contemporary and a fellow Chicagoan, Sherwood Anderson, in his story "Respectability," explored the problem of, in Fiedler's formulation, "the use of women as symbols of piety and purity" leading to "misunderstandings" when "the sentimental view came to be accepted as quite literally true" and "was imposed upon actual women as a required role and responded to by men as if it were a fact of life rather than of fancy."[50] Set in the 1890s, the story dramatizes the plight of a man taught to worship his wife as a spiritual and asexual ideal. As Wash Williams describes his marriage, "I loved her. . . . There in the dusk in the spring evening I crawled along the black ground to her feet and groveled before her. I kissed her shoes and the ankles above her shoes. When the hem of her garment touched my face I trembled. When after two years of that life I found she had managed to acquire three other lovers who came regularly to our house when I was away at work. I didn't want to touch them or her. I just sent her home to her mother and said nothing."[51]

Burroughs inherited this tradition but conceived of Tarzan during still another transformation of the cultural concept of the love and lust relationship. As Jonathan Ned Katz has described the moment, the mutual exclusivity of "pure love and erotic desire" began to give way, around the turn of the twentieth century, to the suspicion and indeed "revelation" that "sexual lust and spiritual love could merge in one attraction."[52] Ernest Becker also sees the modern godless world transforming the creaturely act of sex, through pure and everlasting love, into the means to meaningful existence. The romantic solution permits one's corporeality to serve as the very means of its own transcendence. Through the immortal love of couples like Tarzan and Jane, a person attempts to deny that he is "a mere fornicating animal like any other."

Perhaps the linking of spiritual love and procreative sexuality responded to the immigrant and racial threat as a means of increasing the white population, or to the new interest in defining and containing homosexuality. With heterosexuality a legitimate spiritual path, homosexuality is not just bestial, but sinful in its refusal of the proper path. Whatever the case, the perfervid turn-of-the-twentieth-century commitment to marital procreative sex—Katz records that in the United States the criminal prosecution of any other sexual act "*increase[d] strikingly*" from the 1850s to the 1890s[53]—presented something of a puzzle. The dogma of procreative sexuality unequivocally exposes the biological necessity of heterosexual intercourse at the very time when sex through romantic love was being employed to transcend biological being—in having sex we confirm our creaturely, mortal selves.[54] So another solution to the problem of sex as a reminder of our animal selves is to avoid it altogether; Tarzan the ape-man would require celibacy to defy his animal self and his mortality. This too is an old idea, as Susan Griffin has reminded us: "And the old texts read that where there is death there too is sexual coupling and where there is no death there is no sexual coupling either."[55] Mastery of the physical world demands mastery of one's own physicality—an asexual Tarzan is a direct descendent of Galahad, the knight whose purity earned him the Holy Grail and transcendence to Heaven thereupon. The long-held belief that intellectual and physical achievement required that a man not spill his energy elsehow persisted into Burroughs's day.

Burroughs manages his quandary by basing Tarzan and Jane's marriage on an initial intense physical attraction and passion, but also on her immediate repression of it and her inspiration for his repression of his immediate desires, followed by a lifelong asexual partnership. After than couple's initial lust for one another, the Tarzan novels defer to separation of the two kinds of love. This deference is most blatant in Tarzan's rejection of La of Opar. Raised in Africa and with a little ape-creature blood in her, La had much more in common with Tarzan the ape-man than did Jane. Their primitive, sensual selves made a more sympathetic match. But he says no: "Tarzan extended a bronze hand and laid it upon her slender, tapering fingers. 'You have always possessed my heart, La,' he said, 'up to the point of love. If my affection goes no further than this, it is through no fault of mine nor yours.'"[56]

For Jane, the whiteness that is the source of her angelic beauty presents this same nasty sexual dilemma, because "the means of reproducing whiteness"— bestial sexuality—"are not themselves pure white."[57] That Jane once found her inner-primordial woman and lustily embraced Tarzan suggests that Burroughs and his generation could never completely surrender their sexual hopes to the asexual cult of true womanhood; Burroughs the atheist would have accepted primitive womanhood over the spiritual kind (a product of the prim Gilded Age and then the Jazz Age, Burroughs would give us asexual Jane and later have an affair with a much younger woman). Sadly, blonde Jane must reproduce her and her husband's ideal whiteness; she must also preserve the integrity of her whiteness. She conceives their son and never again taints herself with sex.

~~~~

Instead of sexual love, we get an endless orgy of violence. Burroughs's frequent use of the rape threat indicates just how thoroughly his novels confuse sex and violence: "One industrious critic has counted 76 rapes in the books Burroughs wrote in the first four years of his career and time did not slow down his pace."[58] His Tarzan's refusal of his impulse to rape Jane demonstrates his animal virility and his civilized mastery, his whiteness. Paradoxically, Weissmuller's Tarzan's offscreen rape of Jane might be read not as violence against Jane, nor even as Tarzan's uncontrollable lust, but as his mastery of the physicality she represents; in raping her, he controls his sexuality and asserts his superiority.

Often, and even beyond the clear references to rape, sex and violence in Burroughs go hand in hand. In a single sentence, Burroughs relates Tarzan's killing of Terkoz, the ape-creature who has abducted Jane, with the flowering of sexual desire: "When the thin knife drank deep a dozen times of Terkoz's heart's blood, and the great carcass rolled lifeless upon the ground, it was a primeval woman who sprang forward with outstretched arms toward the primeval man who had fought for her and won her."[59] Two books later,

Tarzan's son Jack-Korak in a strikingly similar scene kills the ape-creature threatening his female jungle companion Meriem, and suddenly, for the first time, he feels sexual desire for her.[60] The language of both scenes conflates sex and violence: whereas Tarzan's phallic knife plunges into Terkoz and "drank deep a dozen times," Jack-Korak forgets his own knife as "Rage and bloodlust such as his could be satisfied only by the feel of hot flesh between rending fangs, by the gush of new life blood against his bare skin, for, though he did not realize it, Korak, The Killer, was fighting for something more compelling than hate or revenge—he was a great male fighting another male for a she of his own kind." He kills the beast by clamping down with his teeth on its "pulsing jugular."[61]

A more telling confusion of sex and violence occurs earlier in *The Son of Tarzan*. Stalking a presumed black native with murder on his mind, the young Jack-Korak instead discovers the girl Meriem, "a little nut brown maiden" with "wavy, black hair," a "shapely knee protruding from beneath her garment," a "rounded cheek," a "piquant little chin," and a "slim finger." Both Korak and Meriem are prepubescent—neither can even imagine intercourse. Korak the Killer's curious observation of the girl mixes his murderous lust with his incipient sexuality:

Korak, momentarily forgetful of his bloody mission, permitted the fingers of his spear hand to relax a little their grasp upon the shaft of his formidable weapon. It slipped, almost falling; but the occurrence recalled The Killer to himself. It reminded him of his purpose in slinking stealthily upon the owner of the voice that had attracted his vengeful attention. He glanced at the spear, with its well-worn grip and cruel, barbed head. Then he let his eyes wander again to the dainty form below him. In imagination he saw the heavy weapon shooting downward. He saw it pierce the tender flesh, driving its way deep into the yielding body. He saw the ridiculous doll drop from its owner's arms to lie sprawled and pathetic beside the quivering body of the little girl. The Killer shuddered, scowling at the inanimate iron and wood of the spear as though they constituted a sentient being endowed with a malignant mind.[62]

Like a penis. The cover of *All-Story Weekly* in which the story first appeared presents an equally ambiguous image: Meriem leaning back into Korak, her hand on his furry toga, looking away from him, and Korak with raised spear, his spear and his eyes aimed downward—at some jungle threat, or at Meriem herself?[63]

One explanation sees the violence as an expression of the characters' and audience's sexual frustration, which brings to mind the abundance of bondage scenes in Tarzania, those bound bodies begging for release. A second explanation for such confusion is as an expression of the misogynist extreme of conventional man's-world sexism especially during a period in which women were clamoring for respect, career opportunities outside the home, and a public voice.

Tarzania's women seem to enjoy the prospect and the act of being raped—to enhance the male audience's pleasure in the fantasy, to suspend its conscience. *Nabonga*, an early femme-Tarzan film, portrays a woman longing to be raped. In this jungle adventure starring former Tarzan actor Buster Crabbe, the white villainess, having been jilted by her white villain partner who suddenly only has eyes for the girl raised in the jungle by a gorilla, releases the gorilla from a cage. The villainess then runs away from the gorilla, but several times stops to look back, as if making sure he is following her. She finally falls down. She sits up and looks up—the great black beast moves in—the camera goes black. The next thing we see is the woman's bare leg, cocked at an angle, as the gorilla walks away. The plot says he killed her; the images say he ravaged her, by invitation. In the femme-Tarzan film *The Diamonds of Kilimandjaro*, a manly hunter declares that women fantasize about being carried off by apes, and in *Golden Temple Amazons* the femme-Tarzan is herself raped before killing her rapist.

We are supposed to be titillated by the near-rapes in Burroughs, and to the extent that his narratives require us to imagine the rapes actively, to the extent that we do imagine (or almost imagine) them, we become complicit. Indeed, Tarzan and his son Jack-Korak fall in lust with their women in the context of imagining (or almost imagining) their rape by ape-creatures not unlike themselves. The rapacious apes in films like *Nabonga* aren't just apes, and aren't just surrogate Africans and African Americans; they are also white men's bestial selves—it's as if white men needed confirmation that women actually desired their ugly hairy horny selves.

A less belligerent explanation, I would offer, focuses on the stories' juvenile setting, characters, and appeal. Pre- and early adolescent youth don't understand sexuality such that Tarzan and his readers might share boyhood's general dislike for all things girly—the no-girls-allowed tree house clubs, the fear of cooties. These youngsters do, however, understand physical force, and forceful and intimate physical play. Pre-adolescents tumble and wrestle and grab and giggle, behaviors not entirely surrendered when they become young adults. So we could interpret Tarzania's juvenile confusion of violence and sex as an expression, or reflection, of a very natural, standard juvenile confusion. Intimate roughhousing is as close an analogue to sex, as close a path to learning about that sort of physical intimacy, as they know.

Cheta and Tarzan (Herman Brix/Bruce Bennett).
The New Adventures of Tarzan (1935).

SIX

MONKEY BUSINESS

Stimulating juvenile roughhousing most usually takes place between two boys. You see where this is going: to the potential of the homoerotic, even if an innocent homoeroticism, in presexual intimate play, as evoked by and experienced in Tarzania.

The convergence of hyper-masculine performance of the heterosexual variety with the potential sexual pleasure of two men tussling and swapping sweat is made manifest in Philip José Farmer's Tarzan parody, *A Feast Unknown* (1969). Every time the Tarzan character gets in a fight, he gets an erection, ejaculating with the killing blow. In the novel's climax, he squares off with his chief rival. They have already torn away one another's testicles when the Tarzan character grabs his opponent's manhood: "The penis, amazingly, was still huge and hard, though it was deflating. It twisted like a spigot in my grip; he screamed; I yanked with all my strength; the flesh tore like a piece of silk; the member, spurting blood at one end and jism at the other, was in my hand and before his face." Tarzan lets it go, positions himself behind the other man, and puts him in a full nelson, his own penis "still hard and throbbing" and now "up against his buttocks." When he snaps the other man's neck, he "spurted over him" before blacking out.[1]

Farmer shows what Tarzania insinuates: hyper-masculinity and homoeroticism are not mutually exclusive. One cover for Farmer's book shows two bare-chested men locked in intimate melee while a nearly naked woman (and a huddle of ape-creatures) watches. She is their excuse, and she directs our gaze to them as well. Such male rivalry is the very stuff of René Girard's theory of male rivalry, mimetic desire, and the monstrous double, whereby the male-to-male relationship precedes either man's desire for the woman. Girard's theory served as the springboard for the idea of the homosocial continuum proposed in Eve Kosofsky Sedgwick's study of Victorian men, according to which the relationships between two people of the same sex fall along a continuum with "straight" and "gay" on either end, very nearly abstractions, and most affections and interactions falling in between.[2]

The thousands of items on sale daily at the online auction site eBay under the keyword "Tarzan"—generally around 2,000, though I've seen over 10,000—frequently include photographs tagged as "gay interest." Most of these are shots of a Tarzan actor, especially Johnny Weissmuller, striking a particularly languorous pose; the item description for one of these taunted potential bidders by declaring that "no self-respecting queen" can live without it. I've seen a photo of an anonymous effeminate man hanging out barely attired on a tree limb, a "happy beefcake ADONIS w[ith] TARZAN swimsuit GAY INT 30s photo," and an "Abercrombie Sexy Beefy Tarzan in Waiting gay AD Poster" showing a naked young man sitting with his buttcheek on a tree house rail. Another item carried this description: "This is another great old photo from one of my late gay uncle's photo albums. It is a picture of Wallace Holden, also known as the boxer Kid Wallace. He also doubled as a stunt man for Johnny Weissmuller in the Tarzan movies. The photo was taken in the 1930's." In it a very slight young man wearing only shorts strikes a boxing pose. An item of a Tarzan actor in action announced itself as "GORDON SCOTT FIGHTING HOMOEROTIC PHOTO."

Adulatory exhibitions of the male body have a difficult time maintaining the integrity of heterosexual manhood. Just as in the early 1970s photos of Weissmuller and other Tarzan actors in magazines like *After Dark* that appealed to gay men without directly acknowledging this audience, in

Burroughs's day images of Eugene Sandow and other musclemen were consumed by some men for their erotic appeal.³ The context for Sandow's performances was the fifty years of women's bodies displayed under "the thinnest of pretexts" of " 'living sculptures,' 'tableaux vivants,' and 'model artist' shows."⁴ Sandow had inserted himself into a feminine tradition. In discussing Weissmuller's 1932 screen Tarzan, Barbara Creed argues that the film "constitute[d] him as the sexual object of the camera's voyeuristic gaze . . . a place which is conventionally that of the 'feminine.' "⁵ Feminized displays of manhood for other men, at a time when effeminate generally signified gay, would have meant that Tarzan's display of himself as one big vein-popping muscle for a mostly male audience would hardly be any different.

Fredric Wertham made this observation back in 1953, in his widely read book *Seduction of the Innocent.* Wertham's argument exaggerated the negative influence of comic books on juvenile behavior, and his inclusion of homosexual activity alongside sadistic violence against women was misguided, but he and the pre-adolescent and adolescent subjects of his study all recognized how the "muscular male stereotype" worked as "the object of homoerotic sexual curiosity and stimulation." Wertham's major example came from a "popular comic," and it looked a lot like Tarzan, with a "well-filled loin cloth," long hair, suntan, and "a bare dagger coquettishly fixed in front of one hip." These comics also included "art nudes" of men in their various advertisements, images "which correspond to the athletic male art nudes appearing in certain magazines for adults so often collected by homosexuals."⁶

The increasing public recognition of the homoerotic risk in presenting a well-muscled, nearly naked male body might have led, in 1957, to the deliberate heterosexualizing, in *Tarzan and the Lost Safari*, of its bachelor Tarzan's appeal, when two female characters ogle at Tarzan bathing in a small waterfall. "I like the way it ripples," one of them says as water rolls over his torso. Then, after he catches a fish with his bare hands, "I'll bet he does *everything* well." The tactic backfires: looking through these women's eyes we occupy their feminized position and, if we are men, a homoerotically charged one. Images of idealized masculinity effeminize the audience by insisting upon a difference, a gender gap, between the screen's manly ideal and the lesser creature: the slouching, limp viewer. Such films insist upon the imaged man's heroic virility, which the passive viewer happily receives. For much of the twentieth century, anxiety over masculine deficiency often translated into anxiety over sexual orientation. Moreover, in Burroughs's day watching *any* movie meant that the viewer participated in a commercial leisure culture at odds with manly values of work and self-restraint.[7]

The period from 1890 to 1920 saw an assertion of masculinity in the face of a number of threats. With the concomitance of the industrial age, the closing of the American frontier, and the flight from rural to urban life, American men found themselves working in offices and factories, tied to clock and desk and assembly line, no longer outdoors moving their bodies, and no longer their own bosses—it's the factory boss in Charlie Chaplin's *Modern Times* who reads the Tarzan comic and issues orders to his bare-chested foreman. The post-emancipation rise of the New Negro and the great influx of immigrants during this period also challenged the "native" white man's ability to command wages and maintain ownership of what he perceived as his nation. This was the age of the short-haired, pants-wearing New Woman, who asserted her rights to self-determination through suffrage, higher education, employment, and the bachelorette life. This period also saw a reconsideration of homosexual acts such that what had been behavior that any man could practice without gender anxiety became a characteristic of homosexual identity.[8] The new inflexibility of gender identity and the hostil-ity toward practitioners of the homosensuous were symptomatic of the larger general cultural response to the various threats to American manhood.

Even Jesus Christ underwent this reassertion of masculinity, as early as 1880 with Thomas Hughes's book *The Manliness of Christ* and continuing with Carl Delos Case's *The Masculine in Religion* (1906), Jason Pierce's *The Masculine Power of Christ* (1912), Harry Emerson Fosdick's *Manhood of the Master* (1913), Bruce Barton's *A Young Man's Jesus* (1914), and Warren Conant's *The Virility of Christ* (1915), plus the hymnal *Manly Songs for Christian Men* (1910). This Jesus was not slender, soft, and doe-eyed, but large, muscular, and vigorous—Barton's book in particular portrayed Christ as a veritable Tarzan down to the sense of humor and the sexual magnetism despite a fundamental celibacy.

The Tarzan movies have always given us the masculinity associated with midcentury America: the strong talk-is-cheap man. Burroughs objected to the infantile grunt-speech of most screen Tarzans, because his hero was a polyglot of languages real and invented. Yet even his Tarzan never wasted precious seconds or spittle on words for their own sake, and he looked down upon those who did. The irony, of course, is that Tarzan's wordlessness turns him into a voiceless object; he assumes the classic role of the silent, gazed-upon woman. Scenes in which we see Jane lose her clothes distract us from his permanent lack of clothing. The more recent Tarzan actors have defied Burroughs's telling insistence that his hero not be pretty: "Tarzan must be young and handsome with an extremely masculine face and manner. . . . I conceive him of having a very masculine face and far from a pretty one."[9] The Tarzans of Miles O'Keefe, Joe Lara, Wolf Larson, and Travis Fimmel are all very pretty and trim boy-men.

I also wonder about the homoeroticism and general gender-bending of femme-Tarzan movies. *Tarzana, Luana,* and *The Diamonds of Kilimandjaro,* for example, show their femme-Tarzan characters studying a naked woman in the group that has come to find the wild girl. These movies intend for us to see the femme-Tarzan's awakening into heterosexual womanhood, but the fascination she shares with the male audience for the other woman's body tells another story. As the male viewers share her gaze, they identify with her, inhabiting her body and her potentially natural homoerotic curiosity as their own positions intermingle. The script on the *Tarzana* sheet for the marriage gimmick specifies that the other savage girls are "extremely jealous"—they must be caged, and even then their jealousy motivates them to break out and intervene in the ceremony. A poster for the Italian release of this film shows two jungle women, one Caucasian blonde and one dark-skinned "other," wearing next to nothing and holding hands.

This homosexual intimation caters to the infamously pervasive male fantasy of being a party to woman-on-woman sex. Yet if the femme-Tarzan films entertain and make money only by the display of bodies, if they do carry a homoerotic appeal, and if the chief body in question is a version of Tarzan, we might reverse-imagine the male homoeroticism of Tarzan. We might also reverse the association of women with nature and say that Tarzan's association with nature effectively effeminizes him. The cover text for three representative lesbian pulp novels—"They hid their claws under nail polish!" "Where women became as beasts," and "THE SAVAGE STORY OF A PRETTY TEEN-AGER ENTICED INTO FORBIDDEN PRACTICES BY OLDER GIRLS!"—is matched in bestial-primitive spirit by the cover text of a male gay pulp: "A PAGAN OF THE WILDS TRAPPED BY CIVILIZATION."[10] Indeed, in Burroughs, Tarzan's thirst for knowledge and his restlessness to leave his garden render him a new Eve, not a new Adam.

Burroughs created Tarzan during an era one historian has dubbed the age of the bachelor: "In 1890 an estimated two-thirds of all men aged fifteen to thirty-four were unmarried, a proportion that changed little through the first decades of the twentieth century. In cities the proportion was higher still, forming the basis for a flourishing urban bachelor culture that included a growing gay subculture."[11] Tarzan the bachelor is free to be an erotic possibility for the women *and men* he rescues. According to John Kasson, through "boisterous play and aggressive competition, bachelors could enjoy a continuity between boyhood and manhood. They played or watched sports and reveled in contests of physical skill and decisive triumph," especially wrestling.[12] We should perhaps not be surprised that Burroughs's Tarzan is an expert and constant wrestler who discovers and masters the full nelson on his own—that is to say, naturally.

Both Tarzan's heterosexual commitment to Jane and then his renunciation of her, for her honor and her well-being and for the social order, undermine his masculinity. He surrenders manly independence; and his self-sacrifice, as Burroughs has already established through women like Tarzan's two mothers Alice and Kala, is a feminine, maternal trait. His relinquishing of Jane also allows him the pretense of mature social manhood while permitting him to wallow in the murky gender swamps of adolescence. To be a bachelor is also to be a juvenile. In terms of gender identity, adolescent boys are literally boy-men, sexually able and, in appearance and gender development, as androgynous as they will ever be. Burroughs's "Tarzan of the Apes" trailed J. M. Barrie's book *Peter Pan* by one year. As Steven Cohan argues in *Masked Men: Masculinity and the Movies in the Fifties*, the decade deliberately contrasted young male stars like Montgomery Clift and Marlon Brando with standard, older manly men like John Wayne to display the younger protagonists' defiance of gender conventions. These "boys who are not men" opened the possibility of behavioral deviance from the manly norm as well.[13] The youthful look of Burroughs's Tarzan despite his advanced age was no accident, just as Johnny Weissmuller's filled-out, more mature body in the later Tarzan films worked against the role and, for some moviegoers, made the actor and those films something of a joke. As the eternal boy-man, Tarzan is stuck at the prime stage of sexual confusion, before one's gender identity gets sorted out. Most boys experience heterosexuality—experience "women"—initially in the company of another boy or boys through collaborating imaginations, for example, huddled proximately in sleeping bags looking at contraband porn. Still-forming juvenile sexuality is a slippery business, a slipperiness in which our experience of Tarzan participates. Burroughs's svelte young Tarzan is acutely aware, in studying his stronger, more able, and hairier brother apes, that he is "different."

~~~~~

I want to take a moment to offer an example of how Tarzan, for boys and young men, can enable the expression of both heterosexual masculinity and homoerotic stimulation without contradiction. The example comes from an essay published in one of the several Burroughs and Tarzan fanzines from the pre-Internet days. The following is a close reading of a piece of writing never intended to be closely read. In interpreting it as one might a fictional passage, for what its language suggests, I am interested in and can truly only speak to the character of the implied writer, not the actual one.

First, the author recalls his childhood discovery of Tarzan as a practically ecstatic epiphany:

> And then IT HAPPENED! I looked across the aisle at Patrick Seitz. He also was reading a book behind his school book. I leaned across the aisle and took a peek. Wow! An electric chill went all the way down my spine to the tips of each big toe! I later decided it was one of the *grand* moments of my life. A double spread illustration partly covered the page Patrick was reading. A group of great apes were taking off for the jungle, while a giant white man had dropped down (from somewhere) on the back of a panther, and clinging tightly to its back, with his head tucked behind its neck, he was pushing a knife under its left front leg toward its heart. I could tell instantly that this was *my* kind of story!

That prepubescent homoeroticism wiggles here might seem ludicrous, except that the rest of the essay bears it out.

After comparing himself to Tantor the Elephant, Tarzan's most intimate and constant friend, the author next declares that he "was ready both psychologically and physically to take him on as my hero." But he very deliberately distances himself from the mass of anxious weaklings drawn to Tarzan's fantasy of masculinity, to those who—for certain imaginations—tend to the effeminate, possibly the gay. His attraction to Tarzan "was not for the usual reasons," he says: "Tarzan fans all over the world, almost without number, want to be like Tarzan. Why? It is because in countless cases, they are weak, lack courage, often get pushed around, feel that someone else or some outside force is directing their lives, and that they are being strangled by the restrictions of modern civilization." The language again points to a potential homosexuality, to a child whose sexual orientation is strangled by social norms.

When he declares his feeling of "immediate kinship" with Tarzan—"He became something of an ideal for me because I believed I was already very much like him"—he means that he and Tarzan share a fundamental masculine physicality. Like Tarzan, this boy was big, strong, fast, athletic, and handsome. His entire life he cultivated his resemblance to his Uncle Leslie, "who was tall, blonde, and handsome and built like an ideal Tarzan." The author's masculinity, however, did not stand as indisputably as all that:

> When I was born my Mother wanted a girl. She was very disappointed when I turned out to be anything but. . . . In spite of all this my dear Mother, against the protests of my Father, continued to rear me like a girl. I was taught to be kind and gracious and never fight back. I was taught to love everybody. . . . When I was four, and large as a six year old, I was still wearing dresses like a girl and had never yet had a haircut.

"Mollycoddle" is Tarzan's son Jack's word for the girly mamma's boy he fears becoming, the word "molly" dating back to around 1700 in England as a term for effeminate men who practiced sodomy.[14] Luckily for our author, his uncles undertook to cultivate his manliness on the sly out in the barn, teaching him to "box, wrestle and dodge," to "live with pain" and "not to cry":

> Considering the sweet and kind treatment of my Mother, the feminine clothes I had to wear, the long golden hair which came down to my shoulders, and various other peaceful training which I was given in large doses, my uncles looked ahead. They were somewhat like the Old Testament prophets. What they saw ahead for me was trouble. Their forward vision indicated to them that when I got out into the real world, including school, I would have trouble from boys who might be inclined to say unkind things to me.

One instance of such trouble occurred in Sunday school:

For example, when Calvin . . . remarked during class that I looked like a girl, I walked slowly around the table and practiced my "bear-hug" on him. It worked. Our teacher Miss Sadie attempted unsuccessfully to pull me off Calvin. She didn't make any progress. When I was ready I loosed him. . . . . Miss Sadie whom I liked very much was very put out with me, but I explained to her that though Calvin was my friend and I liked him, he had brought this trouble on himself and that it was for his own good that I had taught him this small lesson.

The world, the boy learned early, "was not always sugar and spice." That this teasing about looking like a girl and his bear-hugging of a boy he liked took place in Sunday school speaks to the sexual conflict. For no apparent reason, the author assures us that, Tarzan aside, "the great influence of my life has been my basic and fundamental faith in God." He never missed Sunday school, morning and evening Sunday services, and Wednesday night prayer meeting. "Even then I was trying to reconcile the gentle teachings of the church as compared to the rather straightforward approach taught by my uncles." These brothers' contribution to his upbringing amounted to an attempt "to undermine the fine Christian training and profuse feminine influence of my Mother"—the same woman who dressed him as a girl until late in his childhood. Thus he associates his gentle, loving religion with effeminacy, an association challenged by his uncles' "*straight*forward" masculinity, but also an association shared by the larger culture. The turn-of-the-twentieth-century's restoration of a manly Jesus was a response to this association, and even a century later we still have not quite surrendered it.

"But back to that purpose and motivation in my uncles' training," the essay closes: "What they were really doing was establishing in me an attitude. An attitude of readiness. The idea of being prepared for whatever might happen. In fact it was essentially the same concept as 'Be Prepared' the motto of the Boy Scouts of America. This is a great motto and has been a part of my life, just like Scouting has been." The explanation of his uncles' purpose dodges the real issue. They taught him to fight as a response to and deterrent against teasing by his classmates for being girly; they might also have been genuinely worried about their queer nephew and undertook to steer him straight. There's possibly something up with his connecting his uncles' wrestling lessons with the Boy Scouts and with his lifelong love of this notoriously—however inaccurately—homoerotic, pedophilic organization. His adoration of his "Mother" also plays to stereotypes of gay men.

But I go too far. I don't mean to "out" this man—no doubt he grew into an unconflicted heterosexual. He must have overcome any apprehensions about the relationship between churchgoing and gender in view of the fact that he later committed his adult life to a career in the ministry. The story's significance, for my purpose, stems from the fact that he brings in Tarzan as a critical figure in his journey from prepubescent sexual ambiguity to settled adult identity. In vicariously experiencing Tarzan's ideal body and intimate grappling with foes, he found his means of incorporating the homoerotic within his burgeoning heterosexual masculinity.

As for Burroughs, it is interesting if likely irrelevant that he was the youngest of four boys—five including Arthur, who died at twelve days, a year before Ed's birth—and that youngest sons have a higher propensity to homosexuality: "for each additional brother that precedes him, a boy's chance of growing up to be gay increases by a third."[15] Girard's mimetic desire is suggestive, with the affection for the older sibling preceding the mimetic attraction to girls as modeled by the older sibling. And for the record, as you'll recall, I'm the youngest of three sons. I remember looking at contraband porn at sleepovers in the basement of a boy with three dreamy sisters, two slightly older and one slightly younger, asleep in their rooms upstairs. They were pretty and petite, and he, huddled proximately in his sleeping bag, looked just like them.

~~~~

For a more literary approach I turn, briefly, to Leslie Fiedler's *Love and Death in the American Novel*. Fiedler's book is astonishing in its application to Tarzan, such as the analysis of the gothic romance tradition in American literature,[16] yet it never mentions the hero Fiedler had read about and play-acted as a boy, and with whom he liked to shock his highbrow university audiences by citing Tarzan's status as America's most predominant literary creation worldwide.

In Fiedler's eyes, American culture has suffered from an embarrassment over sex and a hostility toward women; a fetishism of violence, autonomous manhood, and eternal childhood ("a world doomed to play out the imaginary childhood of Europe"); and a guilt-ridden relationship with nature and the indigenous population, both of which it has idealized and destroyed. This singular combination led to a penchant in the nation's fiction for a *hierogamos* between two male characters: "Yet there is a relationship which symbolically joins the white man to nature and his own unconscious, without a sacrifice of his 'gifts'; and binds him in lifelong loyalty to a help-mate, without the sacrifice of his freedom. This is the pure marriage of males— sexless and holy, a kind of counter-matrimony, in which the white refugee from society and the dark-skinned primitive are joined until death do them part."[17] Fiedler's major examples are Cooper's Natty Bumpo and Chingach- gook, Melville's Ishmael and Queequeg, and Twain's Huck Finn and Nig- ger Jim. The book insists that these companionships are sexually innocent: "pure."[18]

Tarzan, in fact, fits Fiedler's scheme better than any actual pair because the *hierogamos* exists in a single body. He isn't just Tarzan; he is Clayton-Tarzan, white man and dark buddy. Burroughs's creation enacts the quintessential American "plot" detailed by Fiedler without the homoerotic threat. Tarzan solves Fiedler's problem. Tarzan, not Jane, is Tarzan's beard.[19]

In RKO's *Tarzan and the Huntress* (1947), a teenage Boy enjoys a compan- ionship with a local native king's son, Prince Suli, a pretty youth who proves to be rather defenseless and effete. Another film, *Tarzan the Magnificent* (1960), has a rather suggestive pairing of a white riverboat captain and his African first mate—their boat is their joint domicile, and the mate must avenge his partner's murder. The faux-Tarzan book series *Bomba the Jungle Boy*, instead of absenting the native partner, splits him into two characters, white Bomba's faithful darker sidekicks Gibo and Wafi. *The Jungle Twins* comics of the early 1970s split the white partner into the twins Tono and Kono, pairing them with their sometimes sidekick and "foster brother" Bakali. In the first issue, Bakali swears a marriage-like oath to Tono-and-Kono that "our hearts are as one—faithful to death!"[20] "Brothers of the Spear" ran in the back pages of Dell's Tarzan series from 1951 to 1971, making it one of the longest-running and most successful of these back-page series. It featured two faux Tarzans, Dan-El and Natongo, a white man and a black man, two usurped kings romping together in the jungle. But for the color of their skin, the two men look like identical twins—the same bodies, the same cheek- bones, the same pageboy haircut. One early episode finds the two sharing a bed, where they discover a rifle hanging on the wall:

"It's the heaviest wood I have ever lifted—and hard! And curiously carved, too!"

"It is hollow! Look at this end!"

"Oh! Here is something that moves a little—"

BOOM![21]

Needless to say, neither one is hurt. In the next frame, their host draws back the curtain to check on them to reveal the pair on the bed on hands and knees, looking naked, surprised, and guilty. Dan-El and Natongo's backdoor exploits clearly continue America's literary tradition of the ambiguously gay duo, implicating Tarzan along the way.[22] These several examples of adolescent pairings—even of late adolescence—speak to the innocent intimacies and to the curious sexuality of boys together becoming men (of whatever sexual orientation). They echo the story of the anonymous Tarzan fan described above.

To be sure, Fiedler's is not the last word on this subject. Julie Ellison has argued, for example, that white male affinity for the racial other aided the early development of global capitalism by establishing sympathetic relationships and thus "trustworthiness in the intricate network of exchange."[23] As noted earlier, the tragic irony of escapist frontiersmen and colonialists like Natty Bumpo and Tarzan—especially Tarzan of the movies—is their enabling of civilization's expansion through contact, trade, and exploitation of the native population and the natural resources. Several critics have written about the deluge of black-white buddy films of the 1980s. For Cynthia J. Fuchs, such films attempt to closet the gay subtext of male bonding narratives by directing the viewer's focus on racial difference. Yvonne Tasker agrees and further suggests that these movies serve to reinforce white heterosexual masculinity; the real hero in these buddy movies is always the white man, whereas the African American male, as Robyn Wiegman writes, "assumes the emotional, feminine sphere" so that the films reinforce the same old story while providing the pretense of inclusion and equality.[24] Tasker's term *musculinity* refers to the emergence in 1980s films of extreme displays of musculature on men's and women's bodies; Tasker's insight on the androgynous and gay intimations of muscular women-heroes, of the blurring of gender display and behavior, can be extended to the men these women so thoroughly resemble. It wasn't until the 1990s that a television show took Fiedler's rustic marriage and Tasker's musculinity out of the closet, albeit in the relatively safe form of quiet lesbianism, in The WB's *Xena: Warrior Princess* (the actress who played Xena, Lucy Lawless, later played Tarzan's aunt in The WB's *Tarzan*).[25] The 1980s also brought us the two most thoroughly re-imagined Tarzan films in decades, *Tarzan, the Ape Man* and *Greystoke: The Legend of Tarzan*, thoroughly re-imagined except anyway for their apparent fundamental loyalty to traditional narratives and values, to the story of Tarzan's origins and his naturally triumphant, heterosexual, civilized white masculinity. Yet these films could not expunge Tarzania's legacy of homoerotic anxiety, perhaps of homoerotic delight. Indeed, the very act of returning to the origin story perforce returned them to the moment of anxiety and to the predating and contributing cultural forces.

~~~~~

Fiedler's men belonged to the American frontier, where men could be men together, intimately if innocently, unhindered by social institutions. In real life, too, according to Katz's *Love Stories*, men pursued intimate relations with one another—or at the least were imagined to do so, and were pursued by the law for doing so—out there, on the plains, in the mountains: "Americans' quest for union via sodomy, buggery, and the crime against nature—or the allegation of such a quest—followed the westward movement of the frontier, roughly mirroring the nation's expansion from sea to shining sea,"[26] and then even farther.

The movement of sodomy and buggery prosecutions from the American West to Hawaii around 1860 connects the frontier with more exotic locales (as would the Tarzan movies in the next century, when North American deer and squirrels frolicked in darkest Africa, and when the native African "look" sometimes suggested a native American one, as with the mohawked man in *Tarzan's Fight For Life* [1958]). In 1893, Frederick Jackson Turner famously declared the frontier closed, the end of an era. Published in the years surrounding Turner's speech, Teddy Roosevelt's four-volume *The Winning of the West* (1889–1896) also depicted the frontier as the site where American men established their (white) nation and their (white) manhood. The perception of the closed frontier, true or not, meant that men had to imagine new proving grounds for themselves and their nation. They turned overseas, to Puerto Rico, Cuba, and the Philippines. A decade later, a private citizen again, Roosevelt explored his manhood by traveling across the ocean, in his mind back in time, to Africa.

In September 1869, only a few years after the Hawaii sodomy cases, Charles Warren Stoddard published "A South Sea Idyll," a story loosely drawn from his own trip to Hawaii. According to Stoddard's unnamed hedonistic white narrator, on his unnamed South Sea island "there were no temptations which might not be satisfied." He immediately meets Kana-ana, an androgynous sixteen-year-old boy with a "round, full, rather girlish face; lips ripe and expressive," whose smile "was of that nature that flatters you into submission against your will." As the story continues, Kana-ana declares them best friends and tells the narrator to "come at once to his house, and there live always with him." The narrator, at this point "actually hating civilization— feeling above the formalities of society," decides "to be a barbarian." He becomes a barbarian in the arms of Kana-ana: "taken in, fed, and petted in every possible way, and finally put to bed, where Kana-ana monopolized me, growling in true savage fashion if anyone came near me. . . . I didn't sleep much . . . I think I must have been excited."[27]

I am reminded of Tarzan's ethnic orphan companions from the 1960s movies whose neocolonial presence revisits the pervasive European reportage of pederasty among colonial natives and between European men and native boys. In the faux-Tarzan *Forbidden Jungle* of 1950, Tawa the jungle orphan is dainty, he prances about like a girl, and he loves hearing from his new manly white hunter "friend" about Broadway shows. More pointed is the outpost scene in the "realistic" *Greystoke* and its not-at-all-subtle suggestion that white European working-class male colonialists anally abuse the native boys.

Tarzan audiences that didn't notice the colonial connotations of such relationships might have wondered in light of Wertham's *Seduction of the Innocent*, a sensation when it appeared in 1953 for, among other things, pointing out the homoerotic bent of Batman and Robin's dynamic duo. In *Tarzan Finds a Son!*, MGM wanted to kill Jane so that Boy could play Robin to Tarzan's Batman in future films. Tarzan's underwater scenes with Jane in the earlier Weissmuller-O'Sullivan films clearly expressed the grace and beauty of the couple's relationship as lovers. When Boy replaces Jane in the watery trysts, we cannot ignore the sexual undercurrents. (O'Sullivan's pregnancy is irrelevant; a double had always done the swimming scenes.) During Jane's absence in *Tarzan's Triumph* and *Tarzan's Desert Mystery* (she's back in Europe), "father" and "son" bed down together; once, in *Triumph*, they wake spooning, with limbs fully entangled (and Cheta on the bed, too). The presentation of orphaned Boy as Tarzan's son mimicked a popular tactic among nineteenth-century American men of disguising the nature of their intimate relationship with other men by referring to them by kinship terms, as Katz's book frequently observes. In the colonial context, the name "Boy" recalls the use of that term as a general moniker for all male natives—especially the domesticated, passive ones, the ones who at least metaphorically shared the white man's bed and received his authorial rod.

Situating homosexual practice in exotic overseas places did not begin with the closing of the frontier; Americans did not simply transfer their imagination's locus. Such tropical places had already, over the longer history of European exploration and colonialism, been established as homoerotic hotbeds; by "the late nineteenth century, a widespread belief circulated in Europe that homosexuality (and other sexual deviance) was endemic in the non-European world."[28]

Europe's reputation for colonial homosexual adventure would have played interestingly in the United States at the time dominated by the nostalgia for the lost American man-making frontier. Effete overcivilized European men already bore a certain gender stigma—sodomy was both a savage practice and a *vice aristocratique*.[29] In 1842 a New York City paper, the *Whip*, began a sensational series exposing the city's sodomitic side. Among this "beastly crew," the paper assured its readers, were "no Americans, as yet—they are all Englishmen or French," for such "horrible offences" were "foreign to our shores—to our nature they certainly are."[30] For an American audience Tarzan the Englishman whose first civilized tongue is French is in quite the gender pickle. While each of his two selves, noble and savage, counters the other's intimation of sodomitic desire, his two selves also make him doubly vulnerable. Jane's wish that her first suitor, Tarzan's cousin William Cecil Clayton, "were only a plain American gentleman" troubles his gender when Burroughs later tells us that because "Clayton was an Englishman" it took him a moment to figure out the manly remark Jane refrained from making.[31] White civilization conferred supreme manliness even as it, in Imamu Baraka's words, "trained [white men] to be fags";[32] while blackness too signified either masculine potency or effeminate inferiority.

Rudi Bleys's *The Geography of Perversion: Male-to-Male Sexual Behavior Outside the West and the Ethnographic Imagination, 1750–1918* charts in ruthless detail the history of the West's employment of male-to-male sex as characteristic of the natives of the Americas, Asia, Oceania, and North and Sub-Saharan Africa. From a sign of moral depravity contributing to the justification of conquest and redemption by Christian civilization to an inherent marker of race and racial development by Burroughs's day, sodomy functioned consistently as "a parameter of 'civilization.'"[33] The fear that European men might go native in this fashion contributed to the permissive approach toward "heterosexual unions based upon concubinage and prostitution" with native women "as a 'necessary evil'" to prevent sex between men.[34] Beyond its impressive assembly of European accounts of native sexual practices, Bleys's book argues that we cannot understand the construction of modern homosexuality, really a domestic concern, without accounting for the profound influence of the colonial experience. The definition and classification of strict hetero- and homosexual identities in the latter half of the nineteenth century "occurred simultaneously with the first, systematic attempts to define and classify human diversity according to the principles of race"[35]—simultaneously and concertedly: the new formulations of gender and race were mutually supportive responses to European and American sexual and cultural anxieties. As an embodiment of this joint response, Tarzan the métis man-boy's heterosexuality is equally anxious, equally pregnable.

Burroughs and his contemporaries inherited a strong legacy of associating homoeroticism with so-called primitive and exotic environments and peoples. However vaguely, this legacy contributed to the audience's experience of Tarzan. Bleys's book documents two other Western explanations for male-to-male sexual acts in primitive societies relevant to Tarzan. Some commentators perceived intimacy between men as operating conjointly with misogyny, a thesis that resonates with what we've already explored (and which Wertham contended). The other explanation Bleys refers to as *tropicalization*—the notion that atavistic behavior including sexual activity is determined through interaction with the environment.[36] The fear of the tropicalization of Europeans living in these areas intensified in the latter half of the nineteenth century and fits with the racial anxiety faced by Americans settling the torrid South in this same period. The tropicalization threat to Tarzan's sexuality surely festered between the lines.

At the World's Columbian Exposition of 1893 in Chicago—which Burroughs frequented—the presented contrast between white civilized achievement and nonwhite primitive life emphasized the presumed relationship between race and gender. The exposition displayed manly white accomplishment in the White City and exhibited the uncivilized races at the World's Museum in the Midway Plaisance: "What an opportunity it was here afforded to the scientific mind to descend the spiral of evolution," trumpeted the *Chicago Tribune*, "tracing humanity in its highest phases down almost to its animalistic origins."[37] The voyeuristic descent from the White City to the West African Dahoman village traced humanity from its manliest height to its effeminate source. According to the *New York Times*, "The Dahomey gentleman, (or perhaps it is a Dahomey lady, for the distinction is not obvious,) who may be seen at almost any hour ... [is] clad mainly in a brief grass skirt and capering nimbly to the lascivious pleasings of an unseen tom-tom pounded within ... There are several dozen of them of assorted sexes, as one gradually makes out."[38]

The manly white voyeur would have gotten it both ways, simultaneously relishing the fantasy of returning to such a "natural" state and his vicarious erotic experience of a polymorphous perversity—of sex every which way with every which partner—while pridefully asserting his racial and gender superiority and his proper, restrained sexuality. The Freudian sense of *polymorphous perversity* refers to the infant's experience of sensual stimulation by a variety of physical contact beyond the usual adult erogenous fare. The different uses of the phrase work within the post-Darwin, Freudian ontogeny-phylogeny correspondence. If individuals regressing to infancy move toward polymorphous perversity, so too must the human species as it regresses. "Condemned to perpetual childishness" as Susan Gubar has described them,[39] people of African descent were condemned (and envied) for having the gender innocence, the gender fluidity and mischievousness, of youth.

When Josephine Baker became an overnight phenomenon in Paris in 1925 by flaunting on stage the exotic, erotic primitivism imposed upon her, reviews questioned her gender, echoing the *Times's* comment on the Dahomans.[40] Her famous banana skirt invited both men and women to bend over and either climb inside or gobble her up. Gubar's book *Racechanges* recalls that Baker in her acts wore "boyishly short, cropped hair ... daringly exposed [her] fashionably small breasts," and "often appeared in public dressed in men's clothing."[41]

Gubar and others have written extensively about how the white discourses defining blackness and homosexuality overlapped. Racial confusion and racial play signified gender confusion and gender play.[42] Indeed, the two prevailing images of black masculinity in the nineteenth and early twentieth centuries—the feminized, subservient "boy" and the hypermasculine rapist—stir the homoerotic (bottom and top), and Tarzan's blackness serves both.

Perhaps following Freud's linking of "primitivity and homosexuality,"[43] rental libraries often placed gay novels in the "colored section"; some speakeasies and dances catered both to interracial and homosexual romances (and interracial homosexual romances); and gays reputedly enjoyed African American music. Sites known for homosexuality were in and around Chicago's Black Belt and New York's Harlem.[44] Nineteenth-century minstrelsy shows, largely performed for northern urban audiences but rooted in the rural South, also combined performances of racial and gender crossings, with "in its most elaborate form . . . a blackened, cross-dressed white male minstrel portraying an ultrafeminine prima donna female impersonator."[45] The simple and standard performances of white men as black men offered an "appreciation of black male sexuality [that] could always slip into homoerotic desire," as Eric Lott has written.[46] Desire can manifest as identification. Blackface becomes a symbolic act of a white man's entering and possessing a black man's body and his becoming the castrated, feminized black man.[47] It also potentially shared in the fancied mingling of wildness, perversity, and the American frontier.[48]

Trudier Harris's *Exorcising Blackness* and Robyn Wiegman's *American Anatomies* see the castration accompanying many lynchings of black men, along with lynching's excuse as punishment for the purported raping of a white woman, as indicating a white male fixation on the black man's genitals such that the lynching becomes a homophobic as well as a racist act. Emasculated by his own vision of the black man's hypermasculinity, even envious, appreciative, and desiring of it (on one or more levels), the white man literally and finally gets his hands on the fetishized black penis. Lynchings become "a grotesquely symbolic, if not literal, sexual encounter between the white mob and its victim," or in Tarzan's case between Tarzan and his several African victims, especially his first, Kulonga "the '*archer*,'" whose arrows Tarzan desires, with whom he identifies, a "sleek thing of ebony, pulsing with life."[49]

Mixing of racial and gender crossings on stage continued in the South well into the 1950s.[50] But it was in the 1960s that the South saw its most "strident, organized resistance to queer sexuality" in conjunction with its resistance to the Civil Rights movement. White civil rights activists were characterized as both racial and sexual perverts. Some "right-wing radicals. . . . implied, as did more and more observers, that the proponents of racial justice harbored deviant sexual practices that went beyond interracial heterosexual intercourse to include interracial homosexual intercourse."[51] Tom of Finland, the Norman Rockwell of male gay erotica, gave us his Jack of the Jungle three-issue comic book series in the late 1960s, with this faux-Tarzan frequently getting it on with native men. The resurgence of Burroughs's Tarzan in the 1960s— the reprinting of the novels and the new life they breathed into Tarzan of the comics, film, and television—could almost be said to have played an organized part in the straight white male resistance to the civil rights and the feminist and gay movements of that tumultuous decade—just as he first appeared during the turn-of-the-century's chaotic era of racial and gender anxiety and has again resurged during the turn-of-the-millennium's new threats to white heterosexual sovereignty by the growing Hispanic population and the increasing likelihood of real acceptance of and rights for gay Americans.

~~~~

The Columbian Exposition's hand-in-hand descent toward the least manly and most animalistic humans, along with the co-locating of the native human exhibit with Hagenbeck's wild animal shows in the Plaisance, prompts another line of inquiry into Tarzan of the Ape's sexual ambiguity.

Katz devotes much of *Love Stories* to the pre-twentieth-century link between homosexuality and bestiality. Legally and culturally, sodomy, buggery, and crimes against nature could have and did refer to either act, and more: "Judicial practice and tradition constituted a bestial/sodomy connection, a historically specific association of human-beast mating and men's anal intercourse with other humans."[52] The logic involved the racial superiority of white civilization's transcendence of bestial physicality as well as the cult of true womanhood's idealization of sexual purity as spiritually essential: "All sexuality was animalistic and bad. Even the 'natural' intercourse of human males and females had to be redeemed by marriage and procreative necessity."[53] Especially if the "urge to perform sodomy," between two men or a man and an animal, "was not thought of as restricted to a particular, small minority of Americans" but "considered a general propensity of all fallen humans," an animalistic urge plain and simple. The modern construction or invention of homosexuality transformed it from a physical, animal act available to anyone to a condition of character, of individual psychology, such that we cannot account fully for this construction—and the era's recommitment to spiritual heterosexuality—without acknowledging the anxiety Darwin stirred about humanity's animal nature. In brief, this construction permitted humanity to deny its creatureliness. (It's important to note that this discussion about the "nature" of homosexuality refers only to the understanding of the dominant culture, not the experience of individuals).

But not so fast, not so easy: Frank Norris's 1899 novel *McTeague: A Story of San Francisco* presents a very crude, Tarzanian paradigm of natural gender roles and animalistic heterosexual love, whereby a man seeks to ravage a woman and she seeks to be ravaged. It also contains one moment of male homosexual anxiety: McTeague and his male friend Marcus "took a great pleasure in each other's company, but silently and with reservation, having the masculine horror of any demonstration of friendship."[54] In historical context, the novel's insistence on the bestial nature of male sexuality necessarily evokes the potential for male same-sex desire. The two men will become fierce Girardian rivals, getting in more than one physical contest over a woman.

Tarzan, a product of the generation undergoing this reconception, has it both ways. He kills beasts, after all, kills the apes Darwin claimed as our ancestors; yet his intimacy with them, deep in the dark jungle, plays to the earlier understanding. Nineteenth-century America was still mostly rural and agricultural, and relative to New York City or Boston, uncivilized. In sparsely populated areas not far removed from their frontier days and reputations, available female sexual partners for men were more rare, so the presumption and equivalence of male-male and male-animal sexual activity made practicable sense.[55] Bestiality, especially ape-human couplings, figured into the European imagination of the wild parts of the globe as well,[56] and Bleys specifically connects colonial sodomy with bestiality and animalistic behavior. The most striking example comes from Sir Richard Francis Burton's report of 1845: "Karachi ... supported no less than three lupanars or bordels, in which not women but boys and eunuchs, the former demanding nearly a double price, lay for hire." The boys demanded the higher price because, according to Burton, "the scrotum of the unmutilated boy could be used as a kind of bridle for directing the movements of the animal."[57] The plethora of movie publicity shots and comic book photo-covers in which Tarzan and Cheta strike a romantic pose comes to mind. In the Boy-less films, Cheta plays Robin to Tarzan's Batman; in Jane's absence, Cheta fills in, as Tarzan and chimp frequently snuggle up in their overnight bower. One of the female leads in *Tarzan and the Lost Safari* (1957) flirtingly accuses a bachelor Tarzan of being Cheta's mate. We might wonder too what that dapper bachelor in the ithyphallic yellow hat was doing in his apartment with that rule-breaking, curious chimp named George he abducted from Africa.

As we've seen, Tarzan's instinctive rapacious desire toward Jane is identical to his ape-creature brother Terkoz's, and in the nineteenth century the courts occasionally considered rape the legal equivalent of bestiality.[58] So we see the bestiality when the ape-man grapples with animals, especially ape-creatures, *and* with Jane. In *Tarzan's New York Adventure* (1942), an African American janitor named Sam—short for Sambo?—finds himself talking on the phone with Cheta, to whose chimp-speech he responds, "You ain't getting fresh with me, is you colored boy?" (That same year that same actor, Mantan Moreland, had another moment of amorous confusion, this time with a gorilla, in *Law of the Jungle*. What an apt coincidence of the colonial and the domestic co-construction of race and sexuality.) Tarzan in *Tarzan and the Leopard Woman* (1946) wrestles a hirsute fellow named Tongolo the Terrible, supposedly a native despite being played by a Caucasian professional wrestler, King Kong Kashey. In *Nabonga* (1944), when the voluptuous young virgin raised by a gorilla tells the white hero that she enjoys looking at him and repeatedly asks him to sleep in her cave—the cave she has presumably shared with the gorilla—he refuses. She tells him he ought to go sleep in the trees with the monkeys. This is the same film in which the foreign-or-part-native girl, Marie, frees the gorilla from a cage and leads him on to an ambiguous murder-or-ravishment scene.

Tarzan's first love, as we know from "Tarzan's First Love" (1916), was an ape:

Teeka, stretched at luxurious ease in the shade of the tropical forest, presented, unquestionably, a most alluring picture of young, feminine loveliness. Or at least so thought Tarzan of the Apes, who squatted upon a low-

swinging branch in a near-by tree and looked down upon her. . . . his intel-
ligent, gray eyes dreamily devouring the object of their devotion. . . .

Of course Kala had been beautiful—one's mother is always that—but
Teeka was beautiful in a way all her own, an indescribable sort of way which
Tarzan was just beginning to sense in a rather vague and hazy manner.[59]

She was "a wondrous thing" and "the most desirable thing in the world."[60]
That Tarzan eventually talks himself out of loving Teeka—"Teeka is an
ape. . . . Tarzan is a man"—does not negate his genuine desire,[61] a desire that
actually challenges Tarzan's innate sexuality by offering itself as a matter of
social conditioning rather than biological hardwiring.

The bestiality in the Burroughs stories and the old movies is exploded in
the Dereks' production. If in 1932 MGM's Cheta helped Tarzan with Jane
by tearing off a piece of her clothes, in the 1981 film chimps follow suit. Two
chimps and the orangutan watch when the unconscious Tarzan becomes
the first man Jane has ever touched; they have, in fact, helped prepare him
by helping her bathe him in river water (oddly foreshadowing Jane's pre–
ritual-rape ablution). A few minutes later, when Tarzan pulls her into his
bower, a chimp nuzzles her, kisses her, and holds her hand, quieting her scared
whimpering. Tarzan and Jane don't make love until the end of the movie, yet
the chimp's comforting very much plays a role in her long seduction. Finally,
in the scene in which Tarzan first touches her breast, Jane considers losing
her virginity to him while unpeeling and eating a banana handed to her by
a member of this scene's chimp audience. She soon enough offers a bite of
her banana to her jungle crush. The film's censored footage included a chimp
kissing Jane's breast and an encounter between Bo and an orangutan named
C.J., a scene Bo called "really sweet and cute."[62]

The movie's most sexual scene involves Tarzan, Jane, and C.J. The credits
roll past as these three frolic and grab and heave and twist and laugh, switch-
ing between the threesome and the possible twosomes, now one on top, now
another, now the orangutan between Jane's legs, now Tarzan behind and
atop the orangutan, now the orangutan atop Tarzan atop Jane. In the film's
final visual moment, after all the credits have rolled, C.J. has thrown off Jane
and grabs Tarzan's crotch. With miscegenation not quite as explosive in the
early 1980s as it was in Burroughs's time, the film's animalistic polymorphous
perversity focuses on its day's gender threat to the social order. The sexually

ambiguous and childish chimps and the orangutan kiss, fondle, and nuzzle both Tarzan and Jane, on the one hand recalling innocent pregendered youthful physical play, but on the other hand engaging in transgendered sexuality. The movie's climactic fight between Tarzan and the Ivory Chief is nothing less than a homoerotic entanglement. These two all-but-naked men don't strike each other with club or fist—they hug and squeeze in slow motion. At its slowest moment, the Ivory Chief, with his painted face and cherry-red lips, stands holding Tarzan, Tarzan's arms thrown wide, his head back, and his legs wrapped around the larger man's waist. The minimal perceptible movement resembles the ebbing jerks of orgasm. The chief's red hair and grunting sexuality connect him with the orangutan, as does the fact that he takes the part played by a gorilla in the 1932 original. This Girardian tussle and the later one with Jane, Tarzan, and C.J. use Jane as merely the excuse for the two males to have at one another.

The feminized position of Weissmuller's Tarzan has nothing on that of O'Keefe's. This ape-man finds his body stroked, he lies around stretching it out, and he struts his stuff like he's on a catwalk or an exotic dance club stage. Jane constantly redirects the male audience members' gaze from herself to Tarzan; it's Jane who tells us he's "more beautiful than any girl" with his long legs, thin wrists, natural curls, cheekbones, even the softness of his muscularity. This Tarzan we read in the context of this Jane, who spends the film asserting her manly independence by defying social expectations. He is the voiceless object to whom she offers *her* banana. He is the native on whose passive body Jane the patriarchal colonizer goes primitive—like her father ladling water onto his sleeping African lover, Jane dribbles water onto her unconscious African lover. As feminized as Tarzan is with respect to the camera and Jane's aggressiveness, and given her estimation of his feminized beauty as well as Bo's billing as "the most beautiful woman of our time," the couple also flirts with female homoeroticism. We see such a flirtation again when the Ivory Chief's women wash Jane, breasts and hands and butts and water everywhere, a slumber party fantasy par excellence. Did the lawsuit complain about the "'rubbing of breasts' that takes place when she is 'leaning on all fours'" because of its evocation of the moment's bestial nature?[63] One scholar's summary of theorized causes of homosexuality from "the late 18th century to the early 20th century" includes "regression to a prehuman era when the hindquarters were the primary visual stimulant," and Wertham asserted that the "fetichism" of "girls' buttocks" in comic illustrations "may have a relationship to early homosexual attitudes."[64] One of Josephine Baker's signature moves, on all fours or with bent knees gyrating her bottom at her audience, would have added to her gender-bending image.

The Dereks confront the film's male audience members who have come to see Bo with the undeniable visual appeal of O'Keefe. "'He just has this glorious, glorious, fucking body,' enthuses John. 'Nobody can deny his body—man, woman, dog, priest or anything. You've got to flip over this guy's body.'"[65] If you are a straight man and you find yourself enjoying watching Jane run her hand down Tarzan's belly and along his groin, you who like her have never touched a man before, and then hear her telling you that touching him is very nice, your heterosexual world has very likely just been rocked. Film theorists have long recognized that one of cinema's chief pleasures (and complexities) is the simultaneous identification with multiple characters, their dilemmas and often contradictory perspectives and desires. So, according to Tasker, "popular cinema affirms gender identities at the same time as it mobilises identification and desires which undermine the stability of such categories."[66]

It's also possible to read Jane's father's obsessive hostility toward Tarzan as homophobic. James Parker's cultural training demands that he aggressively repress the faintest homoerotic inkling toward any man who holds his gaze or imagination a second longer than the man ought. His exaggeration of Tarzan's size feels like obsessive curiosity: "One hundred feet tall!" Parker's repeated insistence that Tarzan is an animal simultaneously struggles to stifle the erotic potential and to justify shooting him while admitting the age's conflation of bestiality and homosexuality. The film reenacts colonialism's prophylactic concubinage against male-male unions by using Parker's native mistress to protect him and us from his subversive desires. His death makes perfect sense: Parker, on his back, is impaled by a tusk shoved into him by the Ivory Chief. Parker's self-destructive repression has destroyed him. He wraps his hands around the other man's ivory phallus, an act he can permit himself only in his last moments.

A New Yorker cartoon from 1934—the year of MGM's censored heterosexual Tarzan and His Mate—deliberately plays with the homoeroticism of Tarzan's wrestling with apes, though probably with unintentional reference to the bestiality-homosexuality link. As Tarzan holds an ape in a headlock, the movie director calls up to the actor in the ape-suit: "You're not supposed to smile, Mr. Leary. The jungle-man is slowly tightening his viselike grip."[67] A Tom of Finland black-and-white drawing, presumably from the Jack of the Jungle series, parodies the bestiality-homosexuality association: in it, a sailor drapes his arm around a Tarzan look-a-like, whose hand tugs at the sailor's penis while his pet lion licks the sailor's testicles.

~~~~

The foundational Tarzan scene looks a lot like the cover for Farmer's *A Feast Unknown*, as Tarzan wrestles Terkoz while Jane looks on. Male readers watch with Jane, admiring and maybe even desiring the muscles on that great big penis of a man. When Tarzan kills Terkoz by having his knife drink deep the rival's blood, they drink, too. "SEE beast-clawed leopard men prey on fellow-humans!" titillates a movie poster for *Tarzan and the Leopard Woman*. I would like to speculate that the cannibalism omnipresent in the plots of Tarzania texts is male homoeroticism, displaced. That the anxiety of men being eaten by men substitutes for the anxiety of, well, men being eaten by men.

This confusion of appetites, of killing and consuming and fornicating, along with the confusion of species, races, and genders, fits the West's projected polymorphous perversity of primitive (and juvenile-infantile) life. Bleys provides several examples of European writers who associated sodomy with cannibalism and even human sacrifice, including Montaigne's famous essay *Les Cannibales*.[68] Moreover, the 1890s saw a number of American court cases debating whether oral-genital sex acts qualified as sodomy or as crimes against nature. Until 1897, the courts condemned such acts but did not expand the legal definitions to accommodate them. By 1897, however, an Illinois court did, ruling that "the state's criminal code did indeed proscribe 'other forms' of the 'crime against nature' than 'sodomy or buggery,' including the crime of putting a penis in a mouth.[69] Josef Danilowatz's cover art for Stefan Sorel's critical study *Tarzan the German-Eater* (*Tarzan der Deutschenfresser*, 1925) depicts Tarzan holding hands with a black man while standing over a supine German.[70]

The new determination of oral-genital sex as a crime against nature, linked in the spirit of the law with sodomitic intercourse between two men or a man and a beast, brings a new dimension to our discussion. Cannibalism and its threat pervade Tarzania as one of the markers of the uncivilized, the savage, the animalistic. Tarzan's first moment of civilized restraint involves rejecting cannibalism, after he has killed Kulonga, the native who killed his ape-creature mother, because he has learned from his books that they are both men. Two books later, when two Russians kidnap Tarzan and Jane's infant son to deliver him to a tribe of African savages, the parents' greatest fear is that their child should become a cannibal (in *The Beasts of Tarzan*). Indeed, the only whites to practice cannibalism in the Tarzan novels are villains, including a muti- nous crew of working-class sailors. The movies only sometimes employ the word "cannibal." Still, the dialogue, visuals, and plotlines strongly suggest the practice—all those skulls, ritual sacrifices, and large fires. Audience expecta- tion meant that the filmmakers did not need to do much to show what these black savages were up to. Advertisements, product descriptions, reviews, and later discussions use the terms "savage" and "cannibal" interchangeably, even when the jungle film itself makes no explicit reference to cannibals. Sometimes "headhunter" appears. As in the novels, cannibal and savage are synonymous; cannibalism is how Tarzania distinguishes savage from civilized (as civilized whites, even Tarzan, commit murder). Most perniciously subtle is the opening music for the first five MGM-Weissmuller films, an eerie instrumental titled "Cannibal Carnival."

As for associating cannibalism with sex, the Dum-Dum ritual of Tarzan's fellow ape-creatures, in which they feast on the body of an ape-creature from a rival tribe, Burroughs calls a "savage orgy." The Oparians drinking the blood of their sacrificial victims takes on strong sexual undertones, even homosexual ones—the sacrifice might be performed by a female high priest- ess on a male victim, but the drinking of the vital fluid falls to the apish males. The language of eating has always served the language of copulating; the metaphors of cannibalism and sex have always collaborated. The white anthropologist in another jungle film, *Slave of the Cannibal God* (1978), has per Fiedler a young male native companion who we later learn is the son of a cannibal tribe's chief. Telling another white man about his time with the cannibals, the anthropologist shouts, "You don't forget the taste of human flesh!" He has never told anyone about his experiences with the cannibals because he has always been "too afraid, too ashamed," and now he wants to return in order to destroy every last one of them.[71]

Following Franz Fanon, Susan Gubar points out how the focus on mouths and eating in white representations of blacks, and "comments about cannibalism," project "white fear of black retaliation, white dread of being gobbled up by black people." She quotes a minstrel song that confuses the two appetites, and she notes white male performers in blackface with exaggeratedly large lips turn the black man into "the engulfing, cannibalistic female," and his clichéd gustatory insatiability is "like that of an infant or an animal or a woman."[72] The white man's own role-playing of the imagined bestial, womanly oral hunger of black men could very much express the conflict between their desires and their homophobia, a conflict perhaps also expressed in the reported stuffing of the castrated genitals into the lynched black man's own mouth. It is therefore not insignificant that after Tarzan lynches his first African man, to his own eyes a very virile youth like himself, he admires the other's "sharp-filed teeth" and prepares to eat him:

> How may we judge him, but what standards, this ape-man with the heart and head and body of an English gentleman, and the training of a wild beast? . . .
> Of a sudden, a strange doubt stayed his hand. Had not his books taught him that he was a man? And was not "the archer" a man, also?
> Did men eat men? Alas, he did not know. Why, then, this hesitancy? Once more he essayed the effort, but of a sudden a qualm of nausea overwhelmed him. He did not understand.[73]

Freudian infantile, oral-stage polymorphous perversity includes the pleasures of devouring and tasting and is perhaps primarily those pleasures, an idea reinforced by the pygmy cannibals of such films as the original *Tarzan the Ape Man*, *Tarzan's Greatest Adventure*, and *Greystoke*. Burroughs's *Tarzan and the Ant Men* gives us another conflation of cannibalism, gender reversals, bestiality, and childhood. Smooth-skinned and sleek Tarzan, waiting in a cave to be raped by a hairy manly woman-creature, must first face off with the woman-creature's kids, "fully aware of their cannibalistic intentions": "The males did not attack him at once, but busily engaged themselves in fetching dry grass and small pieces of wood from one of the covered chambers, and while the three girls, one of them scarce seven years of age, approached the ape-man warily with ready bludgeons, they prepared a fire over which they expected soon to be broiling juicy cuts from the strange creature that their hairy dam had brought them."[74]

Even more bizarre is "The Nightmare," one of several stories from *Jungle Tales of Tarzan* relating incidents from Tarzan's youth. A famished Tarzan has eaten the flesh of his "best" friend Tantor the elephant straight from the cannibals' cooking pot after they finished their feasting "orgy."[75] That night Tarzan has his first dreams. In one, Histah the snake wears the face of the old native man whom Tarzan murdered and then dropped into the cooking pot after emptying it of its elephant flesh. The dream image is hungrily phallic and maternally ripe:

> It was indeed quite preposterous, yet he saw it with his own eyes—it was nothing less than Histah, with the head of the old man Tarzan had shoved into the cooking pot—the head and the round, tight, black, distended stomach. As the old man's frightful face, with upturned eyes, set and glassy, came close to Tarzan, the jaws opened to seize him. The ape-man struck furiously at the hideous face, and as he struck the apparition disappeared.[76]

The next dream isn't a dream, but Tarzan hasn't yet learned to distinguish between dreams and reality. "Bolangi was glowering at him from red-rimmed, wicked eyes. . . . Tarzan found his knife, but he merely fingered it idly and grinned in the direction of the approaching gorilla. . . . [with its] magnificent dark coat glistening with life and health."[77] Grinning and admiring the gorilla's virility while fingering his surrogate phallus?

"[P]uzzled by the strange passivity of the hairless ape," the gorilla "paused an instant with his jaws snarling close to the other's throat" as a new idea occurred to him. He threw the ape-man over his shoulder, and sped deeper into the jungle[78]—as Terkoz and then Tarzan had done with Jane. When the ape-boy finally succeeds in twisting out of the other's arms, "the dream gorilla . . . seized him once more and buried great fangs in a sleek, brown shoulder." Pain tearing into him, Tarzan concludes that "Asleep or awake, this thing was no longer a joke!" So "[bi]ting, tearing, and snarling, the two rolled over upon the ground" until Tarzan's "blade plunged to its goal."[79] While "[s]ome of the red life-blood crimsoned his fingers," Tarzan tries to discern "[h]ow much of all that had happened in his life been real and how much unreal." In the end, he decides he "did not know what was real and unreal; but there was one thing that he did know—never again would he eat of the flesh of Tantor, the elephant," who had made one peculiarly intimating appearance in the first book: "With Tantor, the elephant, he made friends. How? Ask me not. But this is known to the denizens of the jungle, that on many moonlit nights Tarzan of the Apes and Tantor, the elephant, walked together, and where the way was clear Tarzan rode, perched high upon Tantor's mighty back." ("There is," as Fiedler describes their series-long relationship, "something deeply sensuous and wholly committed in the caresses of Tarzan and the half-blind Tantor: a tenderness he never quite manages with women.")[80]

It's all here—Tarzan's eating his companion's flesh from the cooking pot of orgiastic cannibals; his stuffing the man he murdered into the cannibals' cooking pot; the symbolic equivalence of the elephant and the man, and the androgynous oral-sexual dream involving the murdered man; and the gorilla's carrying off Tarzan and biting into the boy's sleek, brown shoulder. There's the gender ambiguity of Tarzan—hairless, slender, and idly awaiting the advance of the big hairy gorilla-creature, at a time in history when the condemnation of homosexuals, the very definition of the true homosexual, focused on the passive, effeminate (boyish), receiving partner. There's the bestial and the sodomitic. There's the dreamscape's Freudian expression of unconscious desire and the wakeful adolescent's unresolved confusion.

"The Nightmare" is not the only time Tarzan finds himself in the "passive" position. In *Tarzan and the Ant Men*, three more-or-less human women-creatures who might as well be men in their muscularity and their hirsuteness vie for sexual possession of Tarzan. That this possession amounts to rape we know from one of the woman-creature's treatment of another male-creature she has brought in from the wild slung over her shoulder and then drags by his hair into her envaginating cave. "He scratched and bit at her, trying to escape, but he was no match for his captor." When she later drags him out of her cave, he is referred to as "her new mate" and her "snarling spouse" still "protesting" as she drags him, "powerful fingers entangled" in his hair, from the cave to the corral.[81] Nor can we erase the image of La of Opar, nearly naked as she prepares to plunge her knife into a naked Tarzan bound to a sacrificial altar.[82] If images of bound women lead the imagination to their potential sexual penetration and cannibalistic victimization, the many images of a tied-up Tarzan should also suggest as much. Indeed, as Katz and others have demonstrated, at the turn the century the general imagination still conceived only the passive, bottom, penetrated partner as the gay one—a conception that permitted European colonizers to bugger African and Asian "boys" without doubting their masculinity, and a conception we see even today. In Annie Proulx's "gay cowboy" story "Brokeback Mountain," the more masculine Ennis, the penetrator in the only graphic sex scene between the men, doesn't lust after men in general, only after Jack; whereas Jack, the penetrated, Jack "Nasty" as Ennis's wife dubs him, seeks homosexual encounters wherever he can. Wherever he can is mostly Mexico, so that the story reinforces the association of homosexuality with non-Anglo settings. Ennis's sexual restraint and his positional superiority mark his white masculine mastery over his bestial body: Ennis is the penis of this pair.[83]

Graham Robb's *Strangers* recounts the potential identification of gay men with depictions of an androgynous, passive, suffering Jesus Christ: "The sacred and tender love of one's fellow man, the love of the young, naked, bleeding god," one 1896 textbook explained, "fills Uranists [. . .] with understandable enthusiasm." In the early twentieth century, some of Carl Van Vechten's photography "emphasizes the shared pain, pressure, and fetishization of ostracized white and black gay men," or perhaps of white gay men and blacks of any sexual orientation. A pair of his photographs, one using a white man and one a black man, take advantage of the traditional iconography of Saint Sebastian by linking it with Christian martyrdom and African American lynching: "The staging of his sanctification usually features a beautiful, naked youth whose flesh is riddled with arrows in a scene that extends suspense by protracting suffering; the mixture of pain due to phallic penetration and pleasure in transcendence made Sebastian a particularly resonant prototype of the ecstatic torment of supreme erotic experience." Gubar's language is also that of masochism, a sexuality that for Gaylyn Studlar is an infantile fantasy of Freudian oral-stage development, is "triumphantly bisexual," and is the position and pleasure of the moviegoer. While Tasker recalls the many images of the white phallic film hero suffering torture in the 1980s, "the boundaries of his body repeatedly violated, penetrated in a variety of ways," Gubar reminds us that deviant and sadomasochistic sexuality, for Americans especially, bears the "iconography of slavery."[84]

Oral-genital sex aside, we again see homosexuality, bestiality, bondage, and primitivism in *Tarzana the Wild Girl*'s publicity sheet. Before coming to the theater, the three savage girls of the marriage ritual, with their implied homoerotic bond, "lived literally like animals" and are currently handled "by a wild animal trainer." One photo still from the movie shows Tarzana, with her Tarzan-like dark locks, tonguing a chimp. The caption reads: "A girl growing up in the wilds of North Kilima-Njaro necessitates her finding companionship where and with whom she can"—a circumstantial or situational bestiality reminiscent of male colonial homosexuality (or worries thereof). Wait: Maybe we can connect this publicity stunt with oral pleasures, as the script requires that theaters locate the girls' cages and the ceremony by the concession stand.

And this: In the animated adventure *Madagascar* (2005), four animals from the New York City zoo have found themselves on the Madagascar coast, among them two male best friends, Alex the lion and Marty the zebra. One night Alex dreams of raw steaks like his keepers fed him back in the zoo. The steaks float down to him, he swims in them, in a direct allusion to and using the same music as the erotic rose dreams from *American Beauty*, that 1999 film with a strong homosexual dimension. Alex wakes up with his tongue lapping Marty's haunches.

"What are you doing?" asks Marty, voiced by the African American comedian Chris Rock. Alex, in the white comedic actor Ben Stiller's voice, pretends to resume counting Marty's stripes: "Thirty black and only twenty-nine white. It looks like you're black with white stripes after all. Dilemma solved." Up in the trees, two lemurs watch. One has earlier dismissed the four newcomers as "pansies," an opinion he reconfirms to the other: "You see, Maurice, Mr. Alex was grooming his friend. He's clearly a tender, loving thing. . . . Look at him. He's so cute!"

The next time we see Alex and Marty they are cavorting together across the open savannah. "You just have to let out that inner lion," Marty encourages Alex. "Who's the cat?" They cavort more, and Alex does discover his inner lion. "Let's go wild!"

"Now you're talking!" says Marty. Then the two of them share a tandem vine swing à la Weissmuller and O'Sullivan's Tarzan and Jane.

I am not insisting that every mention of cannibalism carries unconscious coding of sodomitic bestiality, or that we must translate every fantastic ritual sacrifice into a gay oral sex all-night blowout. By Burroughs's time cannibalism had long been a staple of the West's imaginings of primitive life. But we can't ignore the confluence of the primitive, cannibalistic, animalistic, and polymorphously erotic—polyerotic? polysensual?—in Tarzania.

Nor can we ignore that, its regressive primitive correspondence aside, polymorphous perversity is by definition an intrafamily affair.

"Tarzan's Mother Meets Hollywood Monkeybusiness." Mrs. Elizabeth Weissmuller, her son Johnny, and "Baby" the chimp. Set of *Tarzan and His Mate* (1934).

SEVEN

ALL IN
THE FAMILY

One Burroughs novel, *The Son of Tarzan*, jumbles it all together: adolescence, miscegenation, homosexuality, bestiality, and cannibalism, plus one: incest.

That Tarzan's young son Jack is repeatedly caught with Carl Hagenbeck's *On Beasts and Men* "in bed at night" gathers in significance when we recall Hagenbeck's world famous exotic displays of "primitive" peoples and his interbred hybrid animals—like the lion-tiger "liger," the puma-leopard "pumapard," the tiger-leopard "Tigard," the zebra-horse, and the shetland pony–mule—and when we later discover Jack cavorting in bed with Akut the ape.

Jack first meets Akut after sneaking out of the house to see the educated ape perform on stage. Seeing Jack in the audience and recognizing in him the features of his old jungle companion Tarzan, Akut goes to him in the middle of the show:

A broad smile lighted the boy's features as he laid his hand upon the shaggy arm of his visitor. The ape, grasping the boy by either shoulder, peered long and earnestly into his face, while the latter stroked his head and talked to him in a low voice. . . . . He seemed troubled and not a little excited, jabbering and mumbling to the boy, and now caressing him, as the trainer had never seen him caress a human being before. Presently he clambered over into the box with him and snuggled down close to the boy's side.

Like son, like father: When Tarzan and Akut reunite backstage, in *The Son of Tarzan*, "the man stroked the beast's head. . . . Strong within him surged the jungle lust that he had thought dead." He exorcises that chummy lust by calling up the image of Jane as a woman—it's her gender, not her humanity, that he verbalizes—of his community, and his hetero-normative nuclear family: "And then came another picture—a sweet-faced woman, still young and beautiful; friends; a home; a son."[1] One can easily imagine a gay man in that day and age choosing such a life instead of living according to his actual sexuality.

Hungry for more, Jack disobeys his parents and visits Akut in "the little room" the ape shares with his owner, the villainous Paulvitch. "As the boy entered he saw the great ape squatting upon the bed, the coverlets of which were a tangled wad of filthy blankets and ill-smelling quilts." Akut heads toward Jack, but his owner "order[s] the ape back to the bed." At this point in the story we have learned that Paulvitch has recently survived "ten years of hideous life among the cannibals of Africa," where he became as bestial as a white man can, a base savage to Tarzan's noble one. Jack pays Paulvitch in order to play with Akut, and Paulvitch "left him alone with Akut much." Once, while talking with Tarzan, Paulvitch "could scarce suppress a smile . . . since scarce a half hour had passed since the future Lord Greystoke had been sitting upon the disordered bed" with Akut.[2] Is it possible that Burroughs did not recognize this portrayal of Paulvitch as pimp, sleeping with his property and selling the latter's services to another?

Events ensue, Paulvitch is killed, and Jack and Akut flee England aboard a steamer bound for Africa with Akut disguised as Jack's invalid grandmother. "Outside the[ir] cabin—and none there was aboard who knew what he did in the cabin—the lad was just as any other healthy, normal English boy might have been."[3] So inside the cabin he was not normal, doing things nobody knew, such as having sex with a bull ape in drag as his own grand-mother.[4]

Once in Africa, Jack goes primitive under the tutelage of the avuncular ape-creature Akut and takes the ape name Korak as the pair becomes another version of Fiedler's paradigm. They soon rescue a young girl from her kidnappers, a French girl so tan that the darkly tanned Jack presumes she is Arab. The three become a family, and gradually the boy and girl think of themselves as brother and sister apes. Indeed, with her black hair and dark skin, Meriem could very well be his sister, more Adam and Eve than Tarzan and Jane ever were. In a scene repeating Tarzan's saving of Jane from Terkoz, Jack-Korak saves Meriem from the unnamed ape-creature king of a clan kin to Akut, and thus Jack-Korak's kin, too. Jack-Korak wrestles the other ape-creature while Meriem looks on, our gaze joining hers, our thirst quenched when Jack-Korak bites down on the patriarch ape's jugular.

His eyes bouncing between the ape's dead body and Meriem's live one, Korak feels sexual desire for the first time. Meriem, on the other hand, "underwent no change" and "still loved him—as a sister loves an indulgent brother." Then with "a new light in his eyes" he "laid a brown hand upon her bare shoulder. . . . crushed her to him. . . . and then he bent and kiss[ed] her full upon the mouth." Meriem still doesn't come around, though the passage is hazy: "It was very nice. Meriem liked it. She thought it was Korak's way of showing how glad he was that the great ape had not succeeded in running away with her. She was glad too, so she put her arms about The Killer's neck and kissed him again and again."[5] The 1920 film version does not equivocate, as Meriem tells Jack-Korak, "you don't seem like my big brother any more."

Later, when the two are separated, Meriem is taken in and raised into young adulthood by white African plantation owners as their own child, a husband and wife whom she knows as "Bwana" and "My Dear," and whom the reader instantly identifies as Jack's parents Tarzan and Jane. Thus Jack and Meriem become human-world siblings as well, Burroughs having twice now brought them as close to that condition as possible. The jungle couple eventually reunites, falls in love, and marries. There's even a hint of oedipal incest in their relationship, as when young Korak first spies little Meriem, she is mothering Geeka, her doll of "ivory head" and "rat skin torso" and generally "disreputable appearance"—an unmistakable effigy of himself.

Only after watching Meriem's "maternal" attitude toward the doll that is his likeness does the language of Jack-Korak's gazing turn sexual. In the later scene, after returning Korak's kisses, Meriem takes the doll from where he has tucked it in his belt, "kissing it as she had kissed Korak."[6]

~~~~~

In Tarzania, miscegenation and gender-bending are pervasive titillations because they are, culturally speaking, acknowledged and occasionally practiced. To go fully savage, however, one must violate culture's foundational taboo.

In *Forbidden Partners: The Incest Taboo in Modern Culture*, James B. Twitchell challenges the idea of "incest avoidance" as an "instinctual" behavior. Though "transgressions are punished as if they were *unnatural* acts," they are in fact "*uncultural* acts." Like Freud, Twitchell sees incest, not its avoidance, as the true human tendency. Indeed, "incest avoidance" is "the primary step in the transition from animal to human culture" because traditionally "the exchange of women, far more than any other human interchange, links families and provides the basis for producing surplus and social harmony." The incest taboo ensures virginity and thus guarantees the "equal value" of the exchanged women, prevents rivalries among men over sexual ownership, and precludes questions of legitimacy.[7] Otto Rank's exhaustive survey *The Incest Theme in Literature and Legend: Fundamentals of a Psychology of Literary Creation* (published the same year as "Tarzan of the Apes") observes that literary treatments of the Cain and Abel rivalry find the biblical account unsatisfactory. "Rather than portraying the conflict as arising over the brothers' love of God, writers have often portrayed it as centering on the brothers' love for their parents, especially their mother," when the baby Abel replaced Cain at Eve's breast. Rank also cites certain Judeo-Christian traditions in which the two brothers compete over conjugal rights to their sister[8]—who else could Cain's wife be? So he went out from the land of Nod, *knew* his wife (not *met* her), and gave birth to the rest of humankind.[9] It's conceivable that incest—ambiguously brother-sister or father-daughter—was Adam and Eve's true sin, the act that engendered civilization from out of the garden.

Barbara Creed describes the 1932 Jane Parker as treating her father "like a doting but impotent 'husband,'" then details the film's introduction of this relationship:

Jane arrives unannounced to find him gazing lovingly at her photograph. Their reunion is like that of two long-lost lovers. Jane says: "From now on I'm through with civilisation. I am going to be a savage just like you." He looks her up and down, approvingly: "Attractive. Mighty attractive." The oedipal connotations of the scene are most clearly stated when Jane undresses in front of her father while he sniffs at the scent of her clothes. . . . When Jane's father realises his daughter is clad only in a scanty negligee, he becomes embarrassed and moves away. Jane says: "Darling, don't be silly. You're not embarrassed by me! Why you bathed me sometimes and very nearly spanked me too." Jane looks directly into the mirror/camera as she removes her make-up while her father, sitting behind her, also peers into the mirror. It is as if father and daughter were looking directly at the audience while engaged in their intimate discussion. The barely repressed sexual mood of the scene threatens to become explicit but at that point we hear the sound of drums and cut to a long sequence where we see a gathering of African tribes who have come together to trade.[10]

James and Jane retreat outside to inspect the Africans in a scene that for Creed deflects the eroticism from incestuous desire to miscegenous desire, from the unspeakable to the merely unpermitted. Repression is achieved. Instead of contrasting the desires, however, I see a telling conjunction. As Creed herself writes, the appearance of the natives "gives a visual dimension" to Jane's remark to her father that she wants to abandon civilization and become a "savage" like him—I would add, to go native with him incestuously. In March of 1864, the *New York World* newspaper warned that "the logical outgrowth of the extravagant negrophilism" that supported black-white miscegenation might lead to the acceptance of "incest, or any other abomination which the progressists have not yet dubbed with a euphemistic name."[11]

Not surprisingly, the 1932 film derives its intimation of incest from Burroughs, where, for example, Jane's father refers to his dead wife as his "other Jane," and where Jane thinks Tarzan (rather than his father) is coupled with his mother in the locket miniature around his neck.[12] In the 1918 silent film, Tarzan and Jane's first tryst includes this title card: "As Kala, the Ape, had comforted his childish fears, so Tarzan comforted the woman he loved." The scene thus mixes maternal and romantic love while also figuring Tarzan as an ape (as Kala so Tarzan) and reversing genders. Philip José Farmer recognized the incestuous possibilities of the Tarzan ur-story and wrote them into his own story, "Extracts from the Memoirs of 'Lord Greystoke'":

I was not completely weaned until I was about six years old. . . . [My foster ape-mother] had suckled me for a far longer time than any infant of the tribe was suckled. . . . I would have seen the whole tribe dead before I would have given up the delicious and warm and cozy feeling of suckling. In fact, if I had been big enough and strong enough, I would at that moment have scooped up my mother and run away with her into the forest. And I suppose that if I had been that big and strong, I would have mated with her. There was a diffuse element of sexuality in this suckling. At least, I always got an erection when I suckled.[13]

Farmer's Lord Greystoke links the Oedipus complex with narcissism: "The Oedipal situation seemed to me to be a universal phenomenon. . . . My attitudes came about because of the similarity of [Freud's] familiar situation and mine. I had a mother who was the center of my universe. Or, at least, the only other center of which I was aware."[14]

Having fixed on the oedipal drama, Farmer sees the obvious father-son rivalry in Tarzan's relationship with his ape-mother Kala's mate Tublat as well as with Kerchak, the ape tribe's king and patriarch, who according to Farmer also desired Kala.[15] Farmer's *A Feast Unknown* features a Tarzan character born of the union of his mother with her husband's brother (potentially an act of revenge for the promiscuity of the brothers' mother, and so a displaced oedipal event); a character accused of raping his cousin, accused by his half-brother who happened to be their cousin's lover, a woman who eerily looks like the half-brothers; and a character engaged in a bizarre violently homoerotic (or homoerotically violent) entanglement with his half-brother who might as well be his twin.[16] Another textual riffing on Tarzan also invokes mother-son incest. Nigel Cox's *Tarzan Presley*, in which Tarzan comes to America and becomes Elvis Presley (who died before stardom), has Tarzan sleep with his mate Jane's mother, toying with the reader's knowledge of the real Elvis's rumored eerily close relationship with his mother. And *Greystoke*'s Jane and Disney's Kala, Tarzan's mate and his ape-creature mother, merge in the body of Glenn Close, the actress who provides their voices.

Beyond the oedipal circumstances of Tarzan's ape-creature childhood, Burroughs's "Tarzan of the Apes" gets after the incest threat when Terkoz carries off the "hairless white ape" Jane "away toward a fate a thousand times worse than death."[17] Terkoz, the son of Tublat and Kala, is Tarzan's ape half-brother. When Tarzan arrives on the scene to rescue Jane, Terkoz "jumped to the conclusion that this was Tarzan's woman, since they were of the same kind—white and hairless—and so he rejoiced at this opportunity for double revenge upon his hated enemy."[18] At some level Terkoz must have associated Jane with Tarzan's "kind" before Tarzan appears; the thrill at raping his half-brother's woman (and thus his kin, too) is now as much about incest as anything else—about his own transgression of the incest taboo and his forcing that transgression upon his brother's woman.

Just as Terkoz's foiled miscegenous rape of Jane distracts us from Jane's miscegenous attraction to Tarzan, his foiled incestuous rape distracts us from the incestuous dimension of Tarzan's attraction to her. Because Jane is more his kind than any other female he has encountered, she might as well be his sister (or cousin). Disney's Tarzan and Jane are a dark-haired, blue-eyed, pointy-faced pair. Burroughs titles the chapter of Tarzan's first sighting of her "His Own Kind," and in the next chapter Tarzan uses that very phrase when thinking about her, and he does not mean simply her whiteness.[19] Indeed, had she been his sister or cousin, his initial attraction to her would not have been diminished. I suspect this is one reason Burroughs made her an American: to repress the incest threat. A British Jane would have to be, like Tarzan, a member of the nobility—Burroughs's obsession with the purity of bloodlines points incest-ward. But she hails from the American South,[20] a fact she tells us, and so from the region most akin in feudal spirit to the Old World, and the region with the nation's most incest-obsessed literature (for one thing, incest was built into the slavery system, as slaves were forced to sleep with kin, and white men slept with their own daughters). And toward the end of that first novel, Jane, as Tarzan's cousin's fiancée, isn't exactly nonfamilial.

Compared to other action genres, jungle movies feature a disproportionate number of father-daughter and brother-sister pairs. From 1932 onward, the Tarzan films have propagated Burroughs's subtle incest theme. *Greystoke: The*

Legend of Tarzan (1984) is the ur-story film most faithful to the sibling incest prospect, as its Tarzan and Jane are actually cousins. We first see Jane as a little girl on the steps of the Greystoke castle the evening before her unborn cousin's parents sail for Africa (so she's also an older woman), playing with a toy ape. Like Meriem's rat skin doll, this beastly toy prefigures the little girl's bestial adult love. RKO's *Tarzan and the Leopard Woman* (1946) gives us a villain "family" that mirrors Tarzan's with Jane and Boy. It's never made clear whether Dr. Lazar and the leopard woman (whose "BEAUTY VEILS HER LUST FOR BLOOD," according to an advertisement) are siblings or lovers and so could very well be both, and Boy's counterpart is her little brother Kimba.

In the films, Boy is and isn't Tarzan's son; their subtexual relationship is and is not incest. *Tarzan Finds His Son!* also has it both ways through Boy's actual identity: when his relatives come looking for him six years later, we learn that he is a Greystoke, the nephew of the second Earl of Greystoke, to be precise. None of the prior MGM Tarzan films ever established Tarzan himself as a Greystoke—Boy is Tarzan's relation only indirectly, and only to those who know their Burroughs (not to mention all those other orphan boys in the movies, to whom Tarzan or another man acts in loco parentis). MGM's Boy had an earlier incarnation, the Bobby Trevor character who along with his older sister survives a shipwreck to become a mini-Tarzan in *Tarzan the Mighty* of 1928. In this Jane-less film Bobby's sister Mary is the romantic interest, and the actress who plays her, Natalie Kingston, would in fact play Jane opposite the same Tarzan actor, Frank Merrill, in *Tarzan the Tiger* the following year.

In *Tarzan Escapes*, Tarzan wanders into a tent and lets his gaze linger a bit too long on Jane's comely cousin. *Tarzan and His Mate* sounds a minor oedipal note when Jane gives Tarzan a bracelet her father used to wear: "I want you to wear it always," she says. When Dorothy Dandridge's Queen Melmendi tells the British regional commissioner, a white man old enough to be her father, "You are our father, and our mother," and the only other light-skinned English-speaking native around is a small boy who might well be her son, one has to wonder if the commissioner fathered the boy with his own daughter. The commissioner's response compounds the incestuous potential: "Then perhaps that gives me the right to talk like a Dutch uncle."[21]

A minor character in *Tarzan's Greatest Adventure* (1959), the riverboat captain Dino, has been recently released from a fifteen-year prison sentence for killing his father. In the story's present, his obsessive protection of a locket with a picture of his mother borders on the homicidal. He dies after a panther claws his face and he stumbles into quicksand, his incestuous desires in the form of Mother Nature literally swallowing him up, his dead hand reaching out of the quicksand toward the locket hanging on a branch. As Tarzan and his companion Angie stare at this scene, jungle music from a pygmy cannibal tribe breaks their gaze.

If colonialism can be characterized as a paternal system, such that sex between colonizer and colonized figures incestuously, it can also be characterized as cannibalistic, in as much as one people feeds off another. (It could have also worked the other way, with the fear of native cannibals reflecting a very real European fear of native subjects empowered by feeding off the Europeans—fear perhaps of the métis orphan as the literal incorporation of the white body into the racially other one and a blurring of kinship distinctions.) The linking of incest and cannibalism is important because I suspect that if in savage Tarzania cannibalism can sometimes signify homoeroticism, it can also signify incest.[22] The title pair of one of the earliest of jungle adventure films, 1915's *Jungle Lovers*, are raised as brother and sister before falling in love and the girl's capture and near-sacrifice by a cannibal tribe. And it's while kissing Meriem in the film version of *The Son of Tarzan* that Jack-Korak gets speared by a cannibal. Dino's mother-love and the pygmy cannibals in *Tarzan's Greatest Adventure* bring together oedipal incest and infantile cannibalism in a way Freud would have appreciated. Freud classifies breastfeeding—the first stage of human desire that obtains sexual confusion via the Oedipus complex—as "oral or as it might be called, cannibalistic pregenital sexual organization," during which "sexual activity has not yet been separated from the ingestion of food," as both activities aim for "the incorporation of the object"[23]—the edible oedipal. As to cannibalism's regressive implication, the spoof *Kid in Africa* drops child actors playing white adults in a cannibal cooking pot.

Freud gives us another way of looking at cannibalism and incest, a way that directly connects with the idea of defying culture to go primitive. The oldest instinctual wishes "are those of incest, cannibalism, and murder," writes Freud in his 1928 tract on religion and culture, *The Future of an Illusion*. "With the prohibitions [against] them culture began, who knows how many thousands of years ago, to detach itself from the primordial animal condition of mankind. To our surprise we have found that they are still operative, that they still form the kernel of the hostility to culture. The instinctual wishes that suffer under them are born anew with every child."[24] Freud's earlier work, *Totem and Taboo* (1913), had established the seminal chain of events leading to the prohibitions against the three ancient instincts and hence to the creation of culture (it appeared the year after "Tarzan of the Apes").

The following discussion demands a slight preamble. Not only does it draw on one of the most fanciful of Freud's theories, but it also applies that theory to the Dereks' *Tarzan, the Ape Man*, for many Tarzan fans the most embarrassing of the films. Bo received a Razzie worst actress award for her Jane, and the film does not yet rank as a cult classic. I do not mean to employ either to validate the other. Whatever we think of them, Freud's primal horde and the Dereks' film operate within the larger issue of incest and evidence its deep significance. (Indeed, it's interesting to wonder if a century's worth of Tarzania helped keep Freud in business. If Becker is right, that Freud wisely found sexuality and the parent-child relationship fundamental to the human psyche, but unwisely wove them into the family drama complex instead of seeing in sex and in the child's existence—for the child and the parents— the inescapable fact of our dying animal selves, might we read Tarzania's intimations of parent-child incest in terms of Freud's confusion?)

"From the habits of the higher apes Darwin concluded that man, too, lived originally in small hordes in which the jealousy of the oldest and strongest male prevented sexual promiscuity."[25] Freud calls such a social body a "primal" or "father" horde, whose patriarch horded all the women for himself. One day his sons, who had been denied access to their father's many mates, rebelled. They killed him and ate him: "Now they accomplished their identification with him by devouring him and each acquired a part of his strength."[26] But the father they had hated so much they had also "loved and admired," so that when the "suppressed tender impulses" reasserted themselves, the brothers felt remorse and guilt: "What the father's presence had formerly prevented they themselves now prohibited. . . . They undid their deed by declaring that the killing of the father substitute, the totem, was not allowed, and renounced the fruits of their deed by denying themselves the liberated women. Thus they created the two fundamental taboos."[27] The incest prohibition had practical reasons besides: without it, the brothers would steal one another's mates and the new social entity would self-destruct (exogamy also forced clan expansion). For the same reasons, solidarity and survival, the new social entity, the "brother clan," expanded the prohibition against killing the totem to include fratricide.

Knowing that these instincts need outlets, the members of the brother clan prevent chaos by ritualizing their expression: "Thus we have the clan, which on a solemn occasion kills its totem in a cruel manner and eats it raw, blood, flesh, and bones." Following this ritual is a short period of "loud festival gaiety accompanied by the unchaining of every impulse and the permission of every gratification."[28] Again Freud gets fuzzy. The ritual totem feast permitted the collective killing and eating of the totem, thus satisfying the murder and cannibalism instincts, but what about incest? I doubt the clansmen had group sex with the totem; I doubt too that the post-feast festival permitted sibling mate-swapping and risked the inevitable anger and violence.

Burroughs has similar difficulty incorporating incest into his ape-creature tribe's ritual, the Dum-Dum, "unquestionably" the forerunner of "all the forms and ceremonials of modern church and state." The first Dum-Dum Burroughs describes celebrates the kill of an ape-creature from a different tribe. After reenacting the kill by beating the creature "to a mass of hairy pulp," Tarzan's tribe commences its feast. Because the victim comes from a different tribe, the ritual is not technically murder or cannibalism. These, like incest, are kinship-restricted.[29] One doesn't kill, eat, or fuck one's own. As for the incest and parricide of Freud's original event, among the many reasons for holding a Dum-Dum is the death of an ape king. And at this particular Dum-Dum, Tarzan and his stepfather Tublat clash when Tarzan gets some choice meat. Tublat goes mad, first setting his fangs upon women and children, then turning his rage toward Kala, his mate and Tarzan's mother; Tarzan saves her by killing him, plunging his knife "a dozen times into the broad breast."[30] Tarzan's killing of his foster father and the preying upon the mothers perhaps points oedipally, and Burroughs does call the ritual an "orgy." And later, after Tarzan's knife drinks the blood of his half-brother Terkoz, Tarzan and his kindred hairless white ape mate (Jane) spend their first night together at the murderous, cannibalistic, oedipal Dum-Dum site.

If Freud and Burroughs had trouble formally fitting incest into their rituals, not so the Dereks. The unknown intended ceremonial fate for Bo's Jane at the Ivory Chief's hands might as well be or include her devouring. The novels' preoccupation with and the earlier movies' presumption of cannibalism apply, especially given the blatantly derivative status of this ritual from *Slave of the Cannibal God* (1978), a film that also culminates with body-painted tropical women hand-painting a bound blonde with a body nearly identical to Bo's, this one belonging to John Derek's second wife, Ursula Andress.[31] The Ivory Chief sits up, stretches, and tugs at his belly as if he's about to pull up to the table. The white paint is the perfect touch, because it allows her to be symbolically kin to the Ivory Chief and his tribal family. He can experience the thrill and power of transgression without actually transgressing: if he rapes her it's "incest," if he eats her it's "cannibalism," if he kills her it's "murder." Painted ivory, Bo's Jane becomes the surrogate totem for the Ivory Chief's clan. He and his minions can satisfy all three instincts on her body. The ivory tusk is phallus, knife, and tooth. The film's merging of the tabooed trinity into a single ritual realizes the spirit of Freud's story as Freud himself could not.

In the end, however, cannibalism and murder fail to define for Tarzania the truly primitive. For one thing, cannibalism and murder are trite devices, bits of narrative sensationalism to which we have dulled. More significant, of course, is the fact that civilized people—whites—kill and eat other people, kill and eat their own kind of people, in Tarzania. Tarzan himself murders all three of his kind: whites, blacks, and ape-creatures. For a story to tantalize the repressed savage within, cannibalism or murder will not do. Tarzania's unconscious obeisance of the incest taboo attests to that instinct's psychic dominion. The incest instinct in the novels and films achieves its power from its invisibility.

~~~~~

How ironic that Edgar Rice Burroughs, Inc.'s lawsuit complained about the 1981 *Tarzan, the Ape Man*'s "suggestions of sexuality" between father and daughter.[32] For its oedipal content, the film obeyed its sources, the 1932 original as well as the subtext of Burroughs's tales.

In the original film's closing sequence, James Parker, fatally wounded by the cannibal pygmies' gorilla in a womb-like pit, dies in the elephant graveyard. As Creed concludes, Jane is now "free to mate with Tarzan and to enter into what might be described as a 'natural' rather than a 'civilised' couple. Jane is freed from the dictates of oedipal desire—a desire which lies at the heart of the construction of the patriarchal form of the family."[33] Creed's insight rightly restores conversation of that film's plot to Jane's development, though it does not sufficiently explain her attraction to Tarzan. More significant is the neglect of James Parker—perhaps reflecting Freud's own theory's shortcoming. Focusing on the daughter's desire for the father ignores his erotic attraction to her. The father becomes a mere symbol, no flesh-and-blood character at all, and it is this problem—essentially a problem in storytelling—upon which the Dereks have seized. James Parker is their film's center, its tragic hero.

This Jane falls for Tarzan because he is and is not a version of her father; he allows her and us the thrill of miscegenation and incest without anyone's being wise to it. Richard Harris's James flirts with being a savage by living in Africa as a trader and explorer, and by having conjugal relations with a native woman. He even saves Jane and the rest of their party by talking down a rogue elephant, as Tarzan might have done. If Jane aspires to savagery just like her father, she too would want a jungle mate, especially after discovering Tarzan and learning how intractably civilized her father is—simply following in his footsteps won't take her where she wants to go. He remains English through and through—his expedition processes with a bagpipe accompaniment as well as his own rendition of "Chariots of Fire." In Freudian terms, one could characterize Jane's fascination with Tarzan as a reaction-formation, or the denying of desire through redirection to its opposite. In this case Jane represses her desire for her father by pursuing a man who is, to all appearances, utterly unlike her father.

Yet Tarzan and James Parker aren't that different after all. Tarzan abducts Jane, but does not rape her. He is just savage enough. Both men strive for an embodied pastoral ideal, equal parts savage and civilized. They also both appear to be self-made men, as the film makes no reference to their parentage. The audience knows that Tarzan the nobleman is more civilized than James, and perhaps the audience knows that in 1910 James the Irishman would have borne the popular association of the Irish with the lower races. In Britain, for example, illustrations of the era pictured simian Irishmen akin to U.S.

portrayals of black Americans. Leading his expedition under a white flag sporting a green cloverleaf, this James Parker was half-beast before he ever landed in Africa.[34] Jane duly follows in her father's footsteps, longing for a man just like her father and nothing like him at all.

The intimate scenes between Tarzan and Jane always include James. When Tarzan becomes the first man she has ever touched, a voiceover of her father calling her name as he hunts for her cuts to him as he proclaims, "Jane, Jane, Jane, she's so goddamned beautiful!" Nor can Jane divorce her sexual imagination from her father. As she presents her body for Tarzan's inspection (in the scene with the bananas), she addresses her absent father. Alluding to sleeping in Tarzan's bower the night before, "James Parker," she says, "you were wrong: I'm still a virgin. . . . James Parker, you might be right. He might want me. . . . James Parker, it's wicked I know. But I hope you're right." But the only thing that explodes is James Parker's gun, the scene climaxing with her calling out his name: "James Parker!"

At this age Jane should have left the oedipal stage far behind. In addition to their lack of erotic charge, two other elements of these scenes indicate Jane's psychosexual immaturity: the banana she eats while sexually sizing up Tarzan, and her annoying finger-to-mouth gesture in his presence. The banana exhibits Jane's lingering "cannibalistic pregenital sexual organization" that does not distinguish between eating and sex and that Freud sees in breastfeeding; her compulsive fingers-to-mouth gesture is, like thumb sucking, a "relic of this constructed phase of organization . . . in which the sexual activity, detached from the nutritive activity, has substituted for the extraneous object one situated in the subject's own body."[35] Bo Derek's painfully exaggerated acting calls attention to the Freudian gesture, just as these tepid scenes between Jane and Tarzan put in relief the most arousing scene in the film, the one between Jane and her father inside his dining tent—a womblike space for her nourishment even as his eyes eat her up.

Jane is the spitting image of her mother, Elizabeth. We first see James Parker when he wakes up, rolls over, and kisses an old sepia family photo of himself, Elizabeth, and baby Jane, with Bo Derek unmistakably posing for the Elizabeth figure (rewriting the locket scene in Burroughs). He first sees Jane when she arrives by boat through and framed by the pilothouse window, like the photo of her mother:

"Oh my God. Elizabeth."

"I'm Jane."

"Jane." He pauses. "Where's my cannon?" After another pause, he shouts over his shoulder, "Find my cannon! Bring it to me immediately!" He turns back to Jane: "I know who you are."

The last line he delivers as if trying to convince himself, or trying to convince her, that he won't again confuse her with her mother, the cannon at once phallic expression and violent suppression. That evening at his dinner table he abandons the effort. Jane has confronted him with his abandoning them when she was a year old, and has told him about Elizabeth's recent death. James is not curbed. "So frail. So very fragile," he says softly, meaning Elizabeth but taking in Jane with his eyes. He studies Jane's cheek with his fingers. She allows it. Do her cheeks glow from the firelight, or flush from his touch?

"God how I loved you."

"Her. You loved her."

"Yes. But you are her."

"I am not."

Her eyes, her body, belie her resistance and her declared hatred. Her words fail to convince not because of Bo's bad acting, but because of Jane's. The head and body send this supremely conflicted woman different commands.

Their next lengthy exchange by firelight finds him pressing the right buttons. Having introduced the legend of Tarzan, he shifts the larger-than-life possibility from Tarzan to Jane:

"I indulge myself a full one hundred percent. You do the same thing. Enjoy your beautiful time on earth. Turn yourself into a god, and then you will not have to look for another."

"A goddess?"

"Why not?"

Encouraging her to enjoy herself 100 percent with him, to become a goddess to his god, he encourages her to transcend petty inhibitions of the human world. A world bound to the morality of artificial gods. Illusions, Freud called them. The instinct prohibitions apply to the totem clan members, not to the totem godhead. He wants his Mount Olympus on earth.

(Immortality: Perhaps this Tarzan film, MGM's version, and MGM's impulse three films later to ditch Jane for Boy recognize without recognizing it the impossibility of, the deep dissatisfaction with, the achievement of extracorporeal significance through romantic love. Fictional flirtations with parent-child incest signal a transition from transcendence through a partner to transcendence through children by commingling the two paradigms as one fades and the other emerges. Our selfish genes smile.)

The earlier interpretation of James's homophobic hostility toward Tarzan yields here to a reading of violent jealousy of Tarzan rather than himself as the object of Jane's affection. "You don't find me a very pretty sight, do you?" James asks Jane before caressing her cheek. In light of his desire, the line stabs differently. And the Ivory Chief's role as James Parker's homoerotic id yields here to his role as James Parker's incestuous id. Both are red-haired patriarchs, and elephant ivory is both men's totem. James's quest for ivory leads to the Ivory Chief. It leads him to his ivory-painted daughter. If Jane does on some level respond erotically to her father, and if we accept the association between James and the Ivory Chief, the film subscribes to the Freudian-derived idea that "the infant girl wishes to be eaten, devoured by her father, that later she wished to be beaten or whipped by him, that young girls dream of rape, that the grown woman wishes to be pierced"[36]—and certainly a male viewer would need her masochism in order to justify his pleasure. James's telling her to leave her body to calm her before the Ivory Chief rapes her actually helps the Ivory Chief by beseeching her to give up her resistance:

"Jane, I see Aphrodite, and she's not half as beautiful as you are . . . Who do you see, Jane?"
"Oh god, who do I see? I see Zeus."

The seduction is complete; they have achieved Olympus, Aphrodite to his Zeus, she his immortal daughter and lover with whom he fathers Eros. Painted white, she's also her mother's ghost. The film ends here: if ritual mediates between the utterly wild and the civilized, if it imaginatively reenacts the first act of collective control over wildness, then ritual is as close as a civilized person can get to crossing over, to crossing back.

To be killed by the Ivory Chief's phallus is to die as a consequence of his self-destructive incestuous desire, though he doesn't actually die until after consummation, when his naked daughter bends over him, their bodies visually connected at the waist by the ivory tusk. Her ivory paint renders her both his daughter as the product of his ivory phallus and also his mother as the embodiment of his totem. They kiss on the lips. He has achieved his life's desire; he can die. He gets what he wants. Jane gets what she wants: symbolic sex with dad, oedipal patricide, emotional reconciliation, and life with Tarzan—and if the classic Tarzan films are any indication, as part-maternal, part-sisterly, and part-romantic companion, her Wendy to his Peter Pan. The audience gets what it wants: Tarzan and Jane together, as they must be. Everyone gets what they want, and the audience is none the wiser for the film's satisfying of our murderous, cannibalistic, and incestuous longings. Better, safer, to scoff the film away.

~~~~

The cut to Tarzan swimming to the rescue in between Jane's lines "who do I see?" and "I see Zeus" supports an argument that, as in the 1932 film, James Parker's death symbolizes Jane's graduation from the oedipal stage and her ability to love free of her father's spirit as Tarzan becomes Zeus to Jane's Aphrodite. The eros between them results from his role as her father-protector and lover. Indeed, her father conveyed her here—he led her up the narrow vaginal channel to the Inner Sea, where she splashed alone in the spume, Aphrodite herself, when all of a sudden a lion attacks and all of a sudden Tarzan appears and saves her. At film's end, Jane's lips, painted Irish green by the Ivory Chief's girls (which her dying father points out to her and us after they've kissed), further signify how her father has colored her erotic life. This *Tarzan* is James's story because he drives the plot, and it ends with his death. Like Conrad's Kurtz, he is a tragic hero fatally flawed in his submission to the primitive. James aspires to the primitivism of the Ivory Chief, a white man commanding his horde according to his impulse and instinct.[37] Like a beast. The ape-king of a primal horde.

Parker wants to live uninhibited by laws, mores, or conscience. He's jealous of Tarzan, the man he aspires to be—indeed, he calls himself *bastard* and *son-of-a-bitch* almost as much as he does Tarzan. With the cannibalism instinct overcome and the murder instinct sometimes gratified, only the incest instinct quickens the primitive within. Does he feel the incest urge because it is the route to the primitive ideal? Because it is taboo? Does he idealize the primitive as the route to his incestuous fantasies? Or more simply perhaps, does his near-primitive jungle lifestyle nurture his dormant incestuous nature?

The film further establishes incest as a form of going native by associating his daughter with his native paramour. Nambia is young enough to be his daughter, who with her light skin she might even be. That James names her also signals a parent-child relationship; moreover, his name for her, "Africa," connects his incestuous desire with his primitivist aspiration, as the colonial paternalism he enjoys means that sex with a native is necessarily incestuous, metaphorically speaking. Visually, both Nambia and Jane wear white throughout the film (Africa initially her bedsheets), and both women have their white garb drenched with water—Nambia by James with a ladle in bed, and Jane by Jane with a bucket in a tree, simultaneously positioning herself as her father's lover while asserting her independence from him. (Or from any man. There are colonial implications, too, as the native needs a white man to baptize her, but the patriarchal white woman can do it herself.) Both women are kidnapped by the Ivory Chief. James's ladle for Nambia becomes the cups revolving on a wheel used by the Ivory Chief's minions to bathe Jane.

The film also makes mother figures of both women. James Parker's primitivist vision of living by impulse and instinct, uninhibited, is the dream of restoring himself to the center of the universe—of returning to the mother's breast. The closest James can come to sleeping with his own mother is to sleep with Jane, who approximates the oedipal relationship by satisfying the incest criterion and the motherhood criterion—to the extent that James imagines Jane as her own mother, to the extent that James imagines Jane as his own mother, all three women coalesce into the idea of womanhood, of motherhood; and to the extent that the absence of any mention of his father amounts to narrative parricide. In both versions of the film, though especially in the original, Jane "mothers" her father. In the Dereks' film, before Jane's arrival, James has been playing out this drama on Nambia's body. As

"Africa," she is the mother country, the source with the womb-like Inner Sea; as a native woman of color, she represents his savage ancestry; as James's mate, she is Jane's mother, as Jane mutters to herself on meeting her ("my mother . . . ").[38]

If replacing her mother allows Jane to become a self-made woman, sleeping with one's own mother allows James to be his own progenitor (and if the two seek narcissistic self-perpetuation, logically they should couple their genes with the nearest genetic set). The fantasy of the self-made man, an individual without legacy or baggage, is the narcissistic orphan fantasy of early adolescence, maybe even of the perpetually adolescent America—the American Adam. This James Parker wants to regain his lost youth. His regression fantasy involves becoming his own daughter's lover by way of Jane and Nambia-Africa and returning to the womb by way of three surrogate mother figures: Jane-Elizabeth, Nambia-Africa, and Africa itself. For Freud the incest instinct marks the precivilized cultural state just as the oedipal desire marks the individual's earliest sexual state (both states marked by the confusion between cannibalism and sexuality). By sleeping with his mother, he can be a sexual adult and also a baby. Farmer's Tarzan-parody *The Feast Unknown* constructs its bizarre conflation of incest, murder, and cannibalism around a secret organization providing its members an elixir of perpetual youth with a ritual that involves literally eating each other's genitalia (they grow back!). The character "God" in Burroughs's *Tarzan and the Lion Man* eats people to stay young.

This James Parker needed an actor who could boast of total self-indulgence and look frustrated; they needed someone who could rejoice, "I wallow in me!" and look bored. It needed Richard Harris. "You don't think my father just plain enjoys his own image?" Jane challenges Harry Holt, the expedition's photographer. Jane is right: her father likes to strike poses. He also must be the top dog. Parker could never emulate Tarzan; he could never live alone. His flavor of narcissism feeds on others reflecting his persona back to him—he aspires to be Freud's "stronger man," the one who can live "in the sense of his own interests and instinctual impulses" only because he rules.[39] He is more self-indulgent Ivory Chief than "white ape." Nor is it a coincidence that this supreme narcissist should harbor both homoerotic and incestuous urges, as both have been considered by early theorists and the popular imagination as narcissistic affairs. When James and Jane connect via the phallic ivory tusk, we can unite his desires: Jane's "masculine" behavior throughout the film, her transformation into a phallic tusk, and her position on top of him with him remaining the penetrated one, lets the scene go both ways.

The intersection of homoeroticism and incest expresses the commingled sensualities of all transgressive longings in the indulgent world of imagined primitivism. *Slave of the Cannibal God*, the film on which the Dereks' based their climactic sequence, adumbrates homosexuality between the anthropologist and his native sidekick and sibling incest between Ursula Andress's character and her brother. The entire story hinges on the joint consummation of their (materialistic) desires, and the film's one sex scene puts them in bed together by association. She is transgressing by committing adultery at the same time he is transgressing by committing miscegenation, and the same native woman initiated both couplings (by seducing the brother and by providing the aphrodisiac, catalyzed by her own saliva, to Andress's character)[40]—and played by the same actress who later plays Nambia-Africa. The film's title in Great Britain neatly lumps together its pansexual perversities: *Primitive Desires*.

Burroughs's *Tarzan and the Foreign Legion* gives us a male character once paired with another under the label "misogynist"—which, as we've seen, might have been construed as code for "gay"—who later falls in love with a young woman who herself once spent years dressing and pretending to be a boy, and whom he calls "sister." The film *Forbidden Jungle* has the Fiedlerian pair of the white hunter and the prissy faux-Tarzan Tawa, but also two teasings of incest, between Trader Kirk and his adopted native daughter, and between that young woman and Tawa, her foster brother and Trader Kirk's grandson. The last image we see of the young siblings, perched on a tree branch with a chimp, replicates standard publicity stills of Weissmuller's Tarzan, his current Jane, and Cheta. By casting white brunettes as native African women except for the one African American playing the woman abducted by a gorilla, the film ensures that we look elsewhere besides miscegenation for its primitive transgressive sexuality.

Then we have Dan-El and Natongo, the Fiedlerian pair who are, per the comic's title, "Brothers of the Spear," and who but for their color look like identical twins. The other comic series duo, the *Jungle Twins*, is similarly incestuously and homoerotically suggestive. Their Fiedlerian native "other" is their foster brother, and though he only joins them occasionally, the twins themselves are inseparable. On one cover we see the two of them riding an elephant, but take the elephant (Tarzan's Tantor?) out of the picture, and we see one brother riding his identical twin as a volcano erupts in the background. The identical twinship of both comic book couples reflects the presumed narcissism behind their proclivities. Burroughs's own *The Tarzan Twins* has two youths, Dick and Doc, born on the same day to identical twin mothers, who themselves look identical but for their Fiedlerian coloring: one has shock black hair, the other bright blond. The two boys almost become the main course for a cannibal feast. An illustration for the 1963 Canaveral Press edition shows them dreaming of Africa together in bed.[41] Indeed, it's with his ape-brother Terkoz, prior to Jane's arrival, that Tarzan discovers the full nelson. Tarzania's innocent, presexual coupling between related boys fits many young boys' actual experience of first entertaining ideas of sexuality and gender (Jonathan Katz and John Howard both record instances among rural boys of sexual attraction and behavior through childhood bed-sharing with brothers, cousins, and close family friends).[42] Such narratives combine adolescence's sexual confusion with its familial confusion, when those of us fortunate enough to have been raised in a family feel torn between separation and integration, and first scrutinize the very idea of family—a non-issue in orphan literature, a genre that nullifies the incest threat while risking it with every romantic encounter, because one never knows.

When Tarzan battles Terkoz in their potentially bestial-homoerotic tangle ostensibly for possession of Jane, it is as ape half-brothers. The foundational scene also foreshadows Tarzan's much longer rivalry for possession of Jane with his own cousin (a narcissistic reflection of the two Lord Greystokes). Tarzan's sexual desire for Jane might follow from William Cecil's and Terkoz's, following Girard's theory of mimetic desire whereby one man desires a woman only because the man he wants to wrestle with does. Burroughs's first Tarzan novel possibly suggests as much; he renders his later reenactment of this moment in blatantly Girardian terms, when Jack-Korak comes to want Meriem sexually only after killing the ape-creature who abducted her and, upon reflection, understanding its intent. Mimetic desire might also be behind the lust of Bo Derek's Jane for Tarzan. This gender-defying New Woman wants to colonize his body because the man in whose footsteps she follows does—her father, her rival, her incestuous desideratum. In this Girardian triangle, Tarzan becomes the passive female between the two alpha males; in this triangle, homoeroticism obtains among all three.

Incest and homoeroticism finally merge in the foundational scene of all Girardian rivalries, Cain and Abel's rivalry over their sister. Perhaps she does not appear in the biblical account, not to hide her incestuous marriage to Cain, but because she was always beside the point. Tarzania's endless replaying of the primal rivalry allows us to fantasize about being the conquering brother, but it also has us entertain for ourselves the other possibility, our own most likely possibility: the fate not of the one who survived and so can return in memory, but of the one who did not.

~~~~~

Richard Harris's James Parker wants to die. Though apparently moving oppositely and in denial of mortality, regression fantasies are always also death fantasies. One longs for the unindividuated, undifferentiated state, for effortless and peaceful existence. One must go past even the womb—James must travel beyond the Inner Sea, to the elephant graveyard. So when he arrives at the Ivory Chief's place and sees dead elephants in the river, he reaches out and touches one of the Ivory Chief's "daughters" and smiles. He's a happy man, about to die.

Individuation in one sense is a desire to chart one's own course to death, to die in one's own way. Death too becomes a way to relieve the burden of individuated selfhood, to achieve continuity of being with other beings, a desire felt most strongly by the most individuated.[43] This James Parker resists death and embraces it, dying in his own idiosyncratic fashion. He becomes a self-made man who never acknowledges his own parents' existence, a man who defines himself against cultural imposition by defying God and entertaining the incest instinct, yet simultaneously a man who relieves himself of his selfhood by merging it with the already merged selves of his daughter, her mother, his mother, his "other" daughter and mother Nambia-Africa, and his other selves in Tarzan and the Ivory Chief. The regressive urge to infantile polymorphous perversity, to undifferentiated sexuality before sexual maturation, attempts to defy "the curse of arbitrariness that the body represents" in its assignment of sexuality and our general helplessness against the biological fact of ourselves.[44] The fantasy of polymorphous perversity is at once a retreat into our precivilized, creaturely, natural, and sensual past, and an attempt by the thoroughly civilized imagination to transcend nature, to defy creatureliness. Yet this film's mishmash of gender and sex symbolism goes beyond polymorphous perversity to the real goal of artless primitivism—the relieving of the burden of selfhood by dissolving all distinctions among selves, the relieving of the burden of selfhood by longing for the continuity of death. Tarzania's general confusion of genders, races, species, and kinship reflects its adult audience's desire for escapism, not simply from the daily grind of living, but from living itself.

"Tarzan and Tarzan, Jr." Tarzan (Johnny Weissmuller) and Boy (Johnny Sheffield) stand over Jane's grave in a scene cut from *Tarzan Finds a Son!* (1939).

It was impossible to believe that that perfect body, so
filled with triumphant life, could ever cease to harbor the vital
spark—as soon believe that immortality were dust.

JANE PORTER, "TARZAN OF THE APES" (1912)

EIGHT

ENDINGS

Tarzan: The Broadway Musical, Disney's stage version of its animated film, debuted on May 10, 2006. The reviews were savage. The *Washington Post* titled its review "Fumble in the Jungle" and opened with the line, "You Tarzan. Me looking at watch." The *New York Times* called it a "giant, writhing green blob with music."[1]

Like Disney's *The Lion King: The Broadway Musical* (1997), this Tarzan production is a young kid's show capitalizing on children's unceasing fascination with animals that can talk and sing, its set characterized by the *Times* review as "a super-deluxe day care center." Even more than with *The Lion King*, without whose success this Tarzan would never have been made, its appeal to adults derives entirely from the pageantry, not the story. Today more than ever Tarzan lives solely for children; fewer adults than ever bother with him except as family entertainment. Yet I can't even say with confidence that he lives as potently for children as he once did—it's the animals' antics, not Tarzan's ontological dilemma, that kids relish.

Even then there are questions. The *Times* reviewer notes that the toddlers in the audience "kept straying from their seats." According to the *Post*, the acrobatics are fine, but it's no Cirque du Soleil, and the "little ones . . . will fidget during the leaden dialogue scenes." Some online postings from viewers have complained that the violence is too much for children. The *Post* review offers that despite the swinging and singing stuffed animals and the cloying positive messages, the show perhaps appeals most to "a slightly older demographic: girls who once swooned over Simba and his 'Circle of Life' menagerie and who now, at 13 or 14, are ready for a more adult crush" (the topic here echoing the old ontogeny-phylogeny correspondence).

To whom does this Tarzan speak? To whom does any Tarzan speak at all?

⁓⁓⁓⁓

In the fall of 2003, The WB tried to revive Tarzan for a new generation only to announce the television show's cancellation before season's end. "Despite the considerable amount of money and effort we put into marketing *Tarzan*," explained Paul McGuire, senior vice president of network communications, "it really didn't ignite a mass audience the way a show must in today's multi-cluttered TV universe."[2] The failure of The WB's *Tarzan* is especially striking because the show obviously targeted younger young adults—early teens and preteens—the very age group that had constituted Tarzan's core audience from the beginning (despite his popularity among adults in its early years). The show apparently intentionally targeted the generation who only a few years before had fallen for Disney's *Tarzan*—in one scene from the series premier that also anchored the opening credits for each episode, a squatting Tarzan, partially turned away from us, whips his head over his shoulder to face us. It's a nearly exact duplicate of a move made by Disney's hero. Travis Fimmel, The WB's Tarzan actor and a male model, was to be the adult crush for that generation of girls, adding a healthy audience of girls to Tarzania's dependable boy viewership. The WB also updated the story by transplanting Tarzan from Africa to New York City and making Jane an independent, professional woman—a cop, in fact. In each episode we got a Tarzan fantasy and a police drama all in one. And the villain was, to use the slang, "the man": the balding, advanced-middle-aged head of the all-powerful Greystoke Industries and, of course, Tarzan's uncle. What else could a young audience want?

The WB's *Tarzan* was certainly better than the inane, endlessly recycled family and twenty-something-singles sitcoms inflicted on us every evening. One problem may have been that the male-licorice strategy backfired: girls didn't pay attention because Tarzan was and always will be a boy's thing, and in the meantime the show did not hand out sufficient eye candy for the boys. This red-haired and fair-skinned Jane was undeniably pretty and sported the pert, slender white body that our culture demands, but she simply wasn't sexy enough for prime time's impossibly high standards (think Teri Hatcher in *Lois and Clark*, or Sarah Michelle Gellar in *Buffy the Vampire Slayer*), and being an urban professional, she never stripped down to jungle threads.

As a modern-day cop, this Jane's an anal, hyper-rational rule follower. Her partner, on the other hand, works by gut instinct, breaking the rules when he feels he must. He's black, naturally. But after Jane falls for Tarzan, she becomes the wild one flying by hunches. She becomes more intuitive, unpredictable, unruly, and heroic than her partner. Like Burroughs's racially superior Tarzan, this Jane out-blacks the black man, out-savages the savage, out-apes the apes. These subtle racist taunts offer another possible reason for Tarzan's decline: with the racist appeal of the early years no longer available, and with a consuming audience no longer almost entirely white, Tarzania has not yet figured out how to manage the racial issues sensitively. Disney's 1999 animated version solved the problem of depicting native Africans by not depicting them—Disney's Africa is an animal-only community. The blacks have been erased; the brutes have been exterminated. Disney's *Tarzan* also catered to its white audience by modeling the title character's movement through the trees, sliding along branches, after skateboarding, an almost hopelessly white sport. Can you imagine a new Tarzan film indulging white youth's fondness for African American music as Tarzan struts through the jungle to a gangster rap or hip-hop soundtrack?

Earlier I contended that the loss of Tarzan's iconic status occurred alongside the end of American neocolonialism. A corollary theory would be that Tarzan's demise spells the end of the American century, of the American empire—his brief turn-of-the-millennium upsurge was checked by the film actor Brendan Fraser's coincidental performances as the title character of the Tarzan parody *George of the Jungle* in 1997 and the neocolonialist Alden Pyle in *The Quiet American* in 2002. (Pyle dies. In fact, he is dead before the film begins.) Another corollary is that Tarzan's brand of masculinity, the brand I associated with neocolonial and neoconservative certitude, finally lost its power over us. From the 1970s through the 1990s, with occasional exceptions, Hollywood rendered its brawny adventure heroics wryly—think of Harrison Ford as Indiana Jones. For Tarzan to poke fun at himself would be to admit something in him at which we can poke fun, a flaw, a breach, a defect, a source of insecurity—just the sort of thing his school of masculinity does not tolerate. Having a pretty face and a trimmer physique does not give Tarzan a more sensitive, lighter soul. Maybe The WB's Tarzan failed because it lacked any sense of humor about itself, and today's young audience cannot brook such earnestness.

By debuting with a fully grown yet not fully mature Tarzan, the series missed the child Tarzan at the heart of the original and perhaps missed its target audience's nostalgia. Perhaps the "real" primitive survivor series *Survivor* undermined any improbable Tarzan survival tale. The urban setting could have worked against the show, too. This Tarzan refuses to return to the jungle, because in the jungle he is utterly alone. But because the WB's Tarzan rejects the jungle, Greystoke Industries, the very soul of U.S. material-corporate culture and city life, wins. The savvy young viewers perhaps sensed the fundamental contradiction of a show villainizing material-corporate culture created and sponsored by that very material-corporate culture. Burroughs's Tarzan always returned to the jungle, and the several Tarzan-in-the-city films never worked. Wild freedom can never survive civilization—just as anthropologist Alexander Sokolowsky speculated in 1908 on the deaths of gorillas "within days of their arrival in Europe. . . . from deep sadness, even melancholy, stemming from their tragic realization of their destiny."[3] With no more blank spaces on our maps, with Internet cafes in the Congo, Tarzan cannot survive. The human-or-ape question that beleaguered Burroughs's generation has been replaced by the human-or-machine question that fills so many movie screens today. (Even if the "new" question is really just a way of avoiding the old one, a way of running away from the answer that is now assured, a way of fantasizing about a different means of mastery of the physical world, of our physical selves, our mortality. Consider, for example, ethical arguments over the technology of gene manipulation and cloning as only indirectly addressing the unsettling ontological issue.) Tarzan's superficial messages of neocolonialism and freedom and whiteness and heterosexuality confront a world today far more complex than his simple-minded, simple-bodied figure can manage.

Maybe youth, maybe the adolescent psyche itself, has changed too much for Tarzan to appeal to today's adolescents. Maybe he cannot compete with cell phones, computer games, and Internet porn. Maybe The WB's *Tarzan* simply wasn't entertaining enough, wasn't distracting enough from our lives. Which is to say, from our deaths. As Vincent Canby summarizes the 1978 German film *Jane Bleibt Jane* (Jane Is Jane Forever), about a crazy old woman deluded into believing herself Jane, "the film's real subject" is death.[4] I am reminded of the phenomenon of people who take up gardening very late in life, as if reacquainting themselves with the earth to which they will shortly return. Reading and watching Tarzan, we meet again our animal-mortal selves even as we pretend to conquer nature and preserve our eternal adolescence.

~~~~

"The lion was doped and tied up," recalled Elmo Lincoln, the Tarzan of the 1918 original film: "I was supposed to jump on his back and stab him with a knife, but they gave me an old butcher knife to use and the damn thing broke when I tried to stab it." The next day, the crew doped the lion again, and Lincoln killed it with a filed-down bayonet.[5] A stuffed Old Charlie the lion was on display for the film's premier run at the Broadway Theater in New York City.[6]

Kamuela Searle, a Hawaiian native who had previously appeared in Cecil B. DeMille's *Male and Female*, a "tale of a low-born butler and a high-born lady shipwrecked on a desert island," played the part of Jack-Korak in the 1920 serialized *The Son of Tarzan*.[7] In the climactic scene, Tantor the elephant rescues Jack-Korak from a burning stake, carries him to safety, and drops him, still bound to the stake, on the ground. According to legend, Searle suffered fatal injuries in this short fall. Burroughs, who witnessed much of the filming, may have had his own explanation for the accident, which most likely did not result in Searle's death. In *Tarzan and the Lion Man*, the two actors starring in a Tarzan-like production worry about their director discovering their off-screen romance:

"He's got a nasty temper, and there's lots of things a director can do if he gets sore."

"In a picture like this he could get a guy killed and make it look like an accident," said Obroski.

She nodded. "Yes. I saw it done once. The director and the leading man were both stuck on the same girl. The director had the wrong command given to a trained elephant."[8]

For my money, Searle was the best screen "Tarzan" we've ever had.

On July 15, 1921, during the filming of *The Adventures of Tarzan*, "three lionesses broke loose from the trainers and attacked and seriously mauled five actors, who were dressed like Arabs. Louise [Lorraine as Jane] and Elmo [Lincoln as Tarzan] were on the set at the time, but escaped injury; however, several cameras and the day's footage were destroyed, and two of the renegade lions had to be shot to be subdued. Another report had Elmo Lincoln being mauled by a lion during the filming . . . serious enough for him to be laid up for several weeks."[9]

According to James Van Hise, the lions "seen killed" in *Tarzan and His Mate* (1934) "were killed in reality to make it look good for the camera."[10]

"Death, as it must to men and apes alike, came last week [March 1938] to a famed chimpanzee—Hollywood's Jiggs.

"Imported from the Belgian Congo, Jiggs was brought up by Mrs. Jacqueline Gentry to eat at the table with the family, to use the bathroom, to ride in an automobile, to play with the children next door. One thing he refused to do, however: sleep in a blanketed bed. One night last fortnight he slept outside in a storm, three days later died of pneumonia. Paramount planned (but failed) to send a delegation of famed actors to watch Jiggs buried in his silk-lined coffin. A Christian Science funeral was read at his service.

"As an actor Jiggs was the most tractable animal ever filmed. He earned as much as $100 per day with Johnny Weissmuller in Tarzan pictures, with Crooner Crosby in *Doctor Rhythm*. In his last film, *Her Jungle Love*, with Dorothy Lamour, his hind parts proved too brilliant hued for Technicolor.

The studio tried tights, but Jiggs tore them off. Finally Cosmetician Max Factor succeeded in toning down the offending spots."[11]

Two people died during the filming of *Tarzan and the Mermaids* in 1947. One, a Mexican crew member, was crushed by a motorboat.[12] The other man received more attention. Angel Garcia, a stunt double for Weissmuller, died "making Tarzan's climactic dive from the highest cliffs, his body crushed on the rocks."[13]

W. S. "Woody" Van Dyke Jr., the director of *Tarzan the Ape Man* (1932), committed suicide in 1943.

On March 19, 1950, Edgar Rice Burroughs died of heart failure alone in the night. Legend reports that he was found with the Sunday comics in his hand. He had apparently been reading the Tarzan strip.

Elmo Lincoln died in his apartment near Paramount Studios on June 27, 1952, of a heart attack. He was sixty-three. One obituary reported that he played Tarzan "at the age of 18," when in fact he was twenty-eight.[14]

"On September 27, 1962, Skippy, age thirty-four, the chimpanzee cinema co-star of Tarzan, died at the Griffith Park Zoo in Los Angeles. When he passed away (he refused his breakfast although he did not appear to be in any pain), he was the oldest chimpanzee of its kind in the United States, equivalent to one hundred years in the life of a human. Skippy retired in 1939. He never married and there were no survivors, nor was there a funeral. (Records do not show if anyone from ERB, Inc. shed a tear at his death.)"[15]

Dorothy Dandridge died on September 8, 1965, of a drug overdose. "In case of my death—to whomever discovers it—Don't remove anything I have on—scarf, gown or underwear—Cremate me right away—If I have anything money, furniture, give to my mother Ruby Dandridge—She will know what to do."[16]

Around the same time—a couple of weeks into the filming of *Tarzan and the Great River* that had begun in late August 1965—a chimp named Dinky bit and tore open Tarzan actor Mike Henry's jaw. "It took twenty stitches to put my face back together. I was in a 'monkey-fever delirium' for three days and nights. It took me three weeks to recuperate."[17]

Dinky was "destroyed."

Mexico City, July 29, 1966: "An elephant being used in the filming here of a new 'Tarzan' television series went berserk today and killed a 30-year-old trainer. The elephant, after breaking from its cage, wrapped its trunk around the trainer when he tried to control it and then stomped him to death. The animal broke into a home, where it injured a woman and her 4-year-old son, before it was shot dead by a military cadet."[18]

On November 16, 1981, a few months after Bo Derek took the role, Enid Markey, the first Jane, died of a heart attack.

Johnny Weissmuller died on January 20, 1984. Johnny Jr. visited his seventy-nine-year-old father in a Mexico hospital shortly before his death:

> When we got to the hospital, we found two old Mexican women sleeping on the floor by Dad's bed. [. . .] The facilities were dirty, there was blood everywhere, and Dad just lay there, usually totally naked and exposed; doctors and nurses rarely came around to administer professional care. [. . . My] father had tubes in his belly and tubes in his throat and had not spoken an intelligible word during the last year or so of his life.

On Johnny Jr.'s next trip to Acapulco, he and his wife visited the site of his father's grave: "It was the most god-awful place I have ever seen. There were pigs and chickens and goats and cows running amok among piles of animal manure and human feces. The place was littered with rusty cans, broken bottles, and scraps of clothing hanging on bushes and weeds. I would not have buried a mongrel dog there. To cap it off, Dad's name was misspelled on his tiny gravestone, which was half buried in the ground. We had to brush the dirt off to read it."[19]

In May 1998, John Derek suffered a heart attack. After a couple of emergency surgeries, he was unconscious and on life support: "John would have been furious if he'd come to," writes Bo. "This wasn't our deal. He never wanted to be infirm or an invalid. Hell, he didn't want to get old.... I went to find the surgeon to order that life support be turned off immediately. It was actually very uneventful when it happened. Sean, Kerry, Layla, and I were there. He would have liked knowing that he died surrounded by beautiful women."[20]

The following month Maureen O'Sullivan died. She had always groused about being known only as, being identified solely with, Jane Parker. In her later years, however, she found a new sentimentalism for her immortalization as Jane. Her first husband, John Farrow, had worked as a scriptwriter on the first version of the film that would become, after much revision, *Tarzan Escapes* (1936). He died in 1963. O'Sullivan was (and is) survived by, among others, her daughter Mia Farrow and her adopted granddaughter Soon-Yi, who happens to have become the wife of her mother Mia's domestic partner of ten years, Woody Allen, so effectively the father during the formative years of his (Chinese) child-bride.

Steve Sipek, under the screen name Stephen Hawkes, played Tarzan in two Spanish films in the 1970s. In 1970, he and his Tarzan costar Kitty Swan—born Kirston Svanholm, and the actress behind the femme-Tarzan character Gungala—suffered severe burns during a torture scene in the filming of *Tarzan and the Rainbow*. Both received skin grafts and could not continue production for many months. The film eventually appeared in Spain in 1974.[21] In another film, *Blood Freak*, Sipek's character turned into a monster turkey.

While playing Tarzan, Sipek developed an affection for jungle animals and has since owned a number of them, including tigers, lions, and other jungle cats. "Trespassers will be eaten," a sign at his residence warns. One July day in 2004, his 600-pound tiger Bobo escaped—Sipek alleged someone must have released her. Florida wildlife officers found Bobo in Loxahatchee Groves outside West Palm Beach and prepared to subdue it with tranquilizers when, they reported, it charged an officer who shot and killed it in self-defense.

"Murder is the word," Sipek said. "They murdered a poor helpless animal that only looked ferocious, as any tiger would. But Bobo had a heart of gold."[22]

Herman Brix, Burroughs's choice to play Tarzan in his own production company against MGM's Weissmuller, in *The New Adventures of Tarzan* (1935) and its much shorter rehashing (with limited new footage) in *Tarzan and the Green Goddess* (1938), changed his name to Bruce Bennett to reinvent his career and leave Tarzan behind. He died on February 24, 2007, in Los Angeles; he was one hundred years old.

Ed Burroughs was in his late thirties, his youth well behind him and with two small children to raise, when he wrote the first Tarzan story. I was in my late thirties, my youth well behind me and with one small child to raise, when I began writing this Tarzan book. Shortly after my fortieth birthday, my (now) four-year-old daughter wrapped herself around my wrist after I sat on her bed to wake her: "Daddy, I don't want you to die."

~~~~~

G. Stanley Hall's turn-of-the-twentieth-century prescription for raising children and adolescents allowed them to satiate their natural creatureliness mostly secondhand in order for them to develop beyond it and transcend it through productive work, per Freudian sublimation. In the process of filling our lives with our culture, we transform the earth's physicality into objects of humanly constructed meaning and value. The individual project of communal participation beyond selfhood undergirds the communal project of culture's total warfare on nature itself, on the collective denial of death through the victory of our symbolic world over the animal of our nature. This symbolic world, this hyper-reality, in order to work to provide uncompromised value, must replace the primary world—the real one. Identifying with mythic figures, or otherwise investing ourselves in culture, be it high art or pop culture icons like Elvis and Tarzan, enacts this means to immortality.

David Abram's *The Spell of the Sensuous* charts humanity's fall into its current predicament by observing the progression of written language, from footprints and scratches to petroglyphs, pictograms, and ideograms, to alphabets. In the movement from image-based script to the phonetic alphabet, "the written character no longer refers us to any sensible phenomenon out in the world, or even to the name of such a phenomenon, . . . but solely to a gesture to be made by the human mouth. . . . [as] *the larger, more-than-human life-world is no longer a part of the semiotic, no longer a necessary part of the system."* If the original Semitic aleph-beth preserved some links to the observable world, such as the shape of Aleph resembling an ox's head— the Greek system "had no nongrammatalogical meaning whatsoever." The Greek name for a letter did not mean, for example, "ox," but "served only to designate the human-made letter itself."[23]

From Greek onward, writing became an entirely self-referential system both in terms of the alphabet and in terms of a new conception of selfhood. Such a system, severed from the phenomenal world, fostered abstraction. The birth of silent reading, of closed-mouth silent reading, sundered the last connection between written language and the physical world. There is a direct consequentiality from the self-referential alphabet to the hyper-reality, virtual living, and pop-culture incestuousness of our times. What could be less creaturely than surfing the Net, unmoving for hours on end? And it began with writing. It should not surprise us that Ferdinand de Saussure discovered the gap between linguistic signs and the signified object around the same time Sigmund Freund discovered the gap between the conscious and the unconscious, and around the same time that Western culture's abstraction of nature was finally on its way to daily realization for the majority of its citizens.

Around the same time, circa 1900, Tarzan the ape-creature, retreating from wildness inside his parents' cabin, finds their books: "In his hand was a primer opened at a picture of a little ape similar to himself. . . . Beneath the picture were three little bugs: BOY." Teaching himself to read and write takes years; in the process he learns literal selfhood. He can conceptualize, reflect upon, and question his own identity. He determines, first and foremost, that "He was a 'M-A-N,' they were 'A-P-E-S,' and the little apes which scurried through the forest top were 'M-O-N-K-E-Y-S.'"[24] Through literacy, through symbols, he conceptually separates himself from the animals around him— language separates the human from the feral, just as in Burroughs literacy demarks further gradations among humans. Young Tarzan has no idea that the written bugs are keys to pronunciation, to oral speech—he goes straight from animal grunting to reading as silent abstraction, skipping that middle stage in which the alphabet at least points to the physical reality of speech. He doesn't even know to pronounce them in his head.

Young Tarzan's books are his Tree of Knowledge, the irresistible temptation that will forever cast him out of his idyllic garden. He reads and, like

Adam, finds himself in want of clothes. And we admire him, as will Jane: "Never, she thought had such a man strode the earth since God created the first in his own image."[25] The Tarzan story is not a nostalgic return to the Garden of Eden, to nature and innocence, but an affirming allegorical flight from it. He begins to reject his natural world and yearn after the human one. He begins wondering how he should behave. He learns self-scrutiny, that most un-Tarzan-like trait. He is on his way to debilitating Prufrockian self-consciousness, Prufrock's "Dare I eat a peach?" having as its distant ancestor Tarzan's *Dare I eat a man?*—his first moment of self-doubt occurs after he has killed an African and realizes that he's hungry. (After the first book he returns to Africa and never again falters in his surety, as if we could eat of the Tree of Knowledge and miraculously restore our Edenic wholeness.)

His ape-creature tribe begins to bore and frustrate him. Their intelligence does not measure up to his, and they keep him away from his books. He spends more and more time in the cabin, less and less time with his ape-kind. Jane's later arrival and his following her to America are beside the point. His books primed him to expect her, and if she hadn't appeared, he would have found his way to civilization anyway. He needed to find himself, to use that worn modern phrase, among others. He had to look for meaning, value, and identity, in the symbolic, abstract world of civilization. The tooth-and-claw world of his childhood held no answers. If it could not solve the dilemma posed by his humanity and his creatureliness, perhaps civilization could.

Civilization. When we imagine Tarzan, we imagine him young and in the jungle, alone but for his ape-kind and the jungle cats and other beasts he battles. After Tarzan leaves Africa in the original book, after he and Jane marry, the entire Tarzan series falters. It becomes ridiculous. When a notable like Leslie Fiedler writes of "the immortal myth of the abandoned child who becomes Lord of the Jungle,"[26] he, like the rest of us, isn't thinking beyond the eleventh of the first book's twenty-eight chapters, much less the other twenty-three books.

Learning to read is Tarzan's ruination. It's the beginning of the end. It spits him out of the jungle. It sets him against himself, requiring Burroughs and his readers to accept Tarzan's farcical harmonizing of his beastliness and his gentility.

Tarzan's learning to read is also our ruination to the degree that his path from savage animal to civilized human traces humanity entire's. More pointedly, our act of reading and later watching Tarzan has ruined us. Tarzan became our escape from the very real struggle between civilization and nature. According to Perry Miller, this struggle, by the nineteenth century, had acquired a particularly American character as the country's last virgin regions found themselves tread upon: "Yet if history is so irresistibly carrying the defiling axe of civilization into our sublime wilderness, will it not be merely a matter of time—no matter how furiously . . . our poets and novelists, strive to fix the fleeting moment of primitive grandeur—before we too shall be cramped into mannerism, before our minds shall be debauched by artificial stimuli?" (Miller's vision of American's intellectual origin came to him on a trip to the Congo.)[27]

Tarzan artificially, virtually, and impossibly harmonized nature and civilization. He abstracted the confrontation by removing it from America and locating it in a fantasy of Africa, what Fiedler called "the imaginary womb of the Great Mother" that "civilization has in fact sullied and raped."[28] By having us imagine a pure natural world, Tarzan encouraged us to forget the sullying and raping. At a critical moment in America's relationship with nature, with all the wild spaces more or less tamed and the Industrial Revolution well underway, Tarzan allowed us to romanticize nature and the natural life from the comfort of the indoors, from our reading rooms and our movie theaters. He legitimatized the transference of our real relationship to a virtual one—one mediated through commercial culture, no less. Tarzan-in-the-city films and television shows failed because we have come to depend upon Tarzan's virtual junglescape.

Reading and watching Tarzan, we pretend the nature-civilization struggle continues even though the very act of reading and watching Tarzan signals civilization's victory. Reading and watching Tarzan we literally deny nature and our own creatureliness even while we pretend oppositely. Well-appointed tree houses embrace an achieved American suburban pastoral ideal, the illusion of a perfect balance: not too much nature in our manicured lawns, and not too much civilization in our distance from urban decadence. But this balance is illusion, of course. In civilization's eyes, there's always too much nature and never enough of itself.

And thus the suburbs spread.

～～～～

The regressive nature of the Tarzan fantasy, the denial of the natural angst-ridden mortal self and its paradoxical desire for death, becomes a collective death wish. This is the way the world ends, not with a bang, but an "um-gawa."

Maybe, though, there's hope. If Tarzan is dead to the popular imagination, perhaps his fate has followed from a collective realization that his absurd and impossible reconciliation of civilization with nature will not do. We know better. We have more or less come to terms with our selves. We are not children anymore, nor do we want to be.

In other words: If no one reads this book because no one cares about Tarzan anymore, that could be a good thing.

~~~~~

Can a myth as large as Tarzan be dismissed? Or are such seemingly dead myths inevitably and actively re-remembered by new generations? Tarzan's image and meaning have been in the public's hands for generations, and as any good Darwinian knows, survival depends upon random, adaptive morphing. On novelty. On change. As this book hopes to have done, however modestly, by refreshing our relationship with him.

Maybe, too, we can retell the ape-man's story. Maybe we can revitalize his old spirit in a way faithful to the original.

What else could capture the pure physicality of Tarzan's story than modern dance? What other medium could generate the sexual tension, the charge of bodies struggling with their desires but never realizing them, the intimacy and distance between the dancers as well as the dancers and the audience? What other art predicates itself upon its corporeal end and so invokes the nostalgia of the vanishing world and our perishing bodies?

No words at all. Ambient beach and jungle sounds round out an original score. No words because this Tarzan cannot speak any human language, because he can't understand what Jane and her party are saying, and because words finally interfere with our story. Tarzan is, as he should be, a sensory experience.

His parents are abandoned on the beach—she gives birth to Tarzan that very night. That night, the ape-creatures kill them, and Kala makes off with the baby. No bother about a cabin, about his learning to read. Later, he finds his father's knife buried in the sand. That's his only inheritance.

We watch him grow up and make his first kill. We watch him grieve while holding his dead ape-mother Kala. We watch him kill Kulonga, the native who killed Kala, and we understand why. But this Tarzan doesn't need to kill any other black Africans. He will watch them, from the trees, go about their lives. He will long to belong.

At the end of the first of two parts, Jane and her party arrive.

In the second part, Tarzan plays voyeur, eventually saving Jane from a rapacious bull ape only to fight his own desires for her while she struggles with her desires for him. All expressed through the power of movement.

As the end draws near, Tarzan's cousin Cecil finds Tarzan, exhausted after a fierce battle, sleeping near their beach camp. Cecil removes his own blouse to cover the ape-man, his rival for Jane's heart. It is the act of a perfect gentleman, an act only a civilized soul could perform. In the next scene, the final one, at the beach camp between the jungle and the ocean, Tarzan emerges from the jungle and, wearing Cecil's blouse, stands fully erect for the first time, Jane and bare-chested Cecil before him. Jane must choose.

This scene is silent.

She goes with Cecil, as she must. Her decision had always been whether to go native or live her proper life—Burroughs cheated when he made Tarzan both native and noble.

Turning her back on Tarzan, taking Cecil's hand, and clambering into the rowboat to make the ship, she has steeled herself and does not look back. The boat pulls away. Without ever leaving the jungle setting, the show ends just as Burroughs's 1912 story did: Jane gone with Cecil, and Tarzan left alone.

We become aware of movement in the jungle behind Tarzan. Something dark and sleek. A great jungle cat? A native woman (or boy)?

Then we hear the first human sound of the past two hours, when Tarzan beats his chest and cries the cry we all know, a cry we've never heard before. Pitch blackness hits us during the cry's last note. A few moments later, the house lights rise to an empty stage.

Was it the triumphant crowing of wildhood restored? Or the plaint of first love's—and last love's?—broken heart?

We'll never know.

NOTES

ONE. OUT TO SEA

1. Porges, *Edgar Rice Burroughs*, 389; Wood, "He Tarzan—You Fan," 48–52, 51.

2. Fenton, *Big Swingers*, 174.

3. Seventeen includes *Tarzan and the Trappers* (1958), a film patched together from three unaired episodes of a television pilot. Lesser quoted in Wood, "He Tarzan—You Fan," 50; and in Fenton, *Big Swingers*, 174.

4. Robert Lindsey, "Wily Tarzan Lives On, Dollarwise," *New York Times*, Aug. 29, 1975, 59.

5. Darwin, *Descent of Man*, 162.

6. Thoreau, "Walking," in Finch and Elder, *Norton Anthology of Nature Writing*, 180, 196, 197.

7. Ibid., 181.

8. "African American Perspectives."

9. Bederman, *Manliness and Civilization*, 223.

10. Burroughs, "Tarzan of the Apes," 355. I most often cite the original 1912 version (as "Tarzan"), though I sometimes cite the 1914 book edition of *Tarzan of the Apes* (as *Tarzan*) when the language is more revealing. The version in print today follows the 1963 Ballantine edition, which is slightly different still.

11. Burroughs in *Los Angeles Times* in 1922 (qtd. in Porges, *Edgar Rice Burroughs*, 368) and "Tarzan Theme," 29, though this very article elaborates at length on the Tarzan theme and its universal appeal.

12. Quoted in Porges, *Edgar Rice Burroughs*, 157.

13. Burroughs, *Return of Tarzan*, 8.

14. Burroughs, *Beasts of Tarzan*, 156.

15. Burroughs, *Tarzan and the Foreign Legion*, 48. See also 100–101.

16. Burroughs, *Tarzan and the Lion Man*, 189.

17. Ibid., 190–192.

18. Ibid., 9–10.

19. Ibid., 8.

20. All film quotations are the author's transcriptions.

21. Review of *Tarzan Escapes* in the *Film-Echo* (March 11, 1951), qtd. in Boller and Lesser, *Tarzan und Hollywood*, 62.

22. In Boller and Lesser, *Tarzan und Hollywood*, 88.

23. The term "damphool" in Porges, *Edgar Rice Burroughs*, 124, 148; "clown" in Taliaferro, *Tarzan Forever*, 15.

24. Though Elmo Lincoln, Johnny Weissmuller, Maureen O'Sullivan, and John Derek do.

25. Bo Derek, *Riding Lessons*, 131.

TWO. TARZAN THE APE-BOY

1. Harold R. Foster's original strip became a comic "book" that same year, *The Illustrated Tarzan Book* (Grosset and Dunlap, 1929), although many connoisseurs do not consider strip reprints in book form as comic books proper. According to a customer service representative at United Features Syndicate/United Media, "about 20 publications" currently purchase the rights to the Tarzan strip, though she had no information on how many actually publish it. George McWhorter, curator of the Burroughs Memorial Collection, reported knowing of no running of the daily strip since the *McLaughlin Messenger* of South Dakota in 1995, but the *Reading Eagle* in Pennsylvania still runs the Sunday strip (both are reprints of the Gray Morrow Tarzan). Edgar Rice Burroughs, Inc. mentioned that the strip is running in several papers, but they could only cite the *Reading Eagle* (personal emails, May 2006).

2. Mandel, "Tarzan of the Paperbacks," 11. Margaret Ronan adds that all fifteen suffered broken bones (*Practical English Magazine*, 78).

3. Fiedler, "Lord of the Absolute Elsewhere," 354; Perelman, "Cloudland Revisited," 18–21.

4. Perelman, "Cloudland Revisited," 18.

5. "Signal Presents 'Tarzan of the Apes,'" 25.

6. See Burroughs's letter of December 27, 1928, in Cohen, *Brother Men*, 136. Burroughs repeated this claim frequently (e.g., "Story of Tarzan").

7. See Burroughs in Cohen, *Brother Men*, 136.

8. Flanagan, "Why No Tarzan Comics?" 120. I have been unable to find the original article in the *Minneapolis Star and Tribune* or a full citation of it; I date it by Flanagan's quotation from Kevin B. Hancer: "It is interesting . . . to remember that just a few years ago an Ohio librarian claimed that Tarzan and Jane weren't married and she took the books off the shelves." That event occurred in 1964.

9. Burroughs, *Son of Tarzan*, 166, 168.

10. G. S. Hall, *Adolescence*, xi.

11. Ibid., vii, x.

12. Ibid., xiii, ix–x.

13. Burroughs, *Tarzan and the Foreign Legion*, 141–142.

14. Bederman, *Manliness and Civilization*, 223. See her chapter 3 on Hall.

15. Burroughs, "Tarzan of the Apes," 267.

16. See Fineberg, *Innocent Eye*. See also Goldwater, *Primitivism in Modern Art*.

17. G. S. Hall, *Adolescence*, 71–72.

18. According to the footnote that concludes the 1914 book version of *Tarzan of the Apes* (and all following book versions).

19. Trites, *Disturbing the Universe*, 11–12.

20. Quoted in Fenton, *Big Swingers*, 83.

21. Bertram Lewis gives this idea a Freudian twist by envisioning the blank screen as the mother's breast. See his "Sleep, the Mouth, and the Dream Screen" and "Inferences from the Dream Screen."

22. G. S. Hall, *Adolescence*, xi–xii.

23. U.S. Department of Commerce, *Historical Statistics of the United States*, 105–106.

24. See Holt, *Orphan Trains*.

25. See Griswold, *Audacious Kids*, 19.

26. See Levine, *Highbrow/Lowbrow*.

27. Karlin, introduction to *The Jungle Books* by Rudyard Kipling, 7.

28. See Taliaferro, *Tarzan Forever*, 30, 50, 52, 61; and Porges, *Edgar Rice Burroughs*, 17–18, 79–92.

29. Becker, *Denial of Death*, 3–5.

30. Ibid., 29.

31. Burroughs, "Tarzan Theme," 29–30.

32. Quoted in Porges, *Edgar Rice Burroughs*, 135–136.

33. Burroughs, "Tarzan of the Apes," 260.

34. Ibid., 330.

35. Ibid., 372.

36. See Rydell and Kroes, *Buffalo Bill in Bologna*, 3–4.

37. Eagleton, *Sweet Violence*, 232.

38. See Beer, *Forging the Missing Link* and *Arguing with the Past*. Sherlock Holmes pervades the secondary literature. Farmer puts them together in *Tarzan Alive* and *The Adventures of the Peerless Peer*; the fanzines reference Holmes more than any other non-Burroughs character; Burroughs mentions him in *The Son of Tarzan* (188).

39. Kipling's *Jungle Books* and the Romulus and Remus tale are the most mentioned sources, but Burroughs never admitted conscious borrowing. See the discussion of background sources in chapter 4 of this book as well as Porges, *Edgar Rice Burroughs*, 129–133, and Taliaferro, *Tarzan Forever*, 83–93. Neither mention Albert Robida's *The Monkey King*, partially translated from the French and published in *Puck* magazine in 1880 (www.erbzine.com/mag18/saturnin.htm). For possible source material for Kipling's *Jungle Books*, see Karlin's introduction, *Jungle Books*, 7–27.

40. Porges, *Edgar Rice Burroughs*, 656.

41. Her teacher is also an African American man; a tropical palm tree prominently ornaments the wall behind his desk. See chapters 4 and 6 for more subversions of Tarzan's whiteness and masculinity.

42. Trites, *Disturbing the Universe*, 1.

43. Becker, *Denial of Death*, 66.

44. Trites, *Disturbing the Universe*, x.

THREE. THE HOLLER HEARD 'ROUND THE WORLD

1. Porges, *Edgar Rice Burroughs*, 489.

2. Fenton, *Big Swingers*, 173.

3. Thursday, Sept. 15, 1949, p. 17. Reprinted in Rudolph, *My Father, Elmo Lincoln*, 125.

4. Weissmuller, *Tarzan, My Father*, 117–118. Fenton, *Big Swingers*, confirms the summary of the movies' success in almost identical language (172–173).

5. Wood, "He Tarzan—You Fan," 50.

6. Ibid., 48.

7. Duranty, "Russians Prefer 'Tarzan' to Marx," 23; Trumbull, "American Films Lead in Orient," 69.

8. Eshed, "Tarzan in Israel." This online essay is a short version of the special English-language introduction in the Violet Book edition of Eshed's *Tarzan in the Holy Land* (in Hebrew).

9. "U.S. in a Book War."

10. "10,000 Books Banned."

11. Pace, "Cairo Is Willing."

12. Crosby, "Tarzan—and Other Censored Tales."

13. Wood, "He Tarzan—You Fan," 50.

14. "Tarzan Is Back." By May another film, "Tarzan in the West," appeared in Russia—though I'm not sure to which American film this title refers (Salisbury, "Soviet Theatre Turns to Revivals"). According to a later article, the Moscow theaters were showing versions of the four films acquired in Berlin ("Pravda Scolds at Tarzan Films").

15. "Pravda Scolds at Tarzan Films."

16. "Tarzan Postcards"; "4 Columbia Students Tour Soviet"; Weissmuller, *Tarzan, My Father*, 117–118.

17. In Wagnleitner, *Coca-Colonization*, 230.

18. Fenton, *Big Swingers*, 174.

19. Wagnleitner, *Coca-Colonization*, 59.

20. Wagnleitner, "Propagating the American Dream," 71–72.

21. Wagnleitner, *Coca-Colonization*, 225.

22. Ibid., 57.

23. Trumbull, "American Films Lead in Orient."

24. "Young Marine Adopts."

25. Lopéz, "Are All Latins from Manhattan?" 69.

26. Navarro's homosexuality might also have attracted the district attorney's attention. "3 More Film Stars"; "Lupe Velez Obtains Divorce."

27. Wagnleitner, *Coca-Colonialization*, 236.

28. See Fein, "From Collaboration to Containment," 130–135.

29. Lopéz, "Are All Latins from Manhattan?" 70.

30. Boller and Lesser, *Tarzan und Hollywood*, 134.

31. Helm, "Too Many Cooks."

32. Barnes, "Theater."

33. Sheehan, *Bright Shining Lie*, 131.

34. Susan Jeffords's *Remasculanization of America* sees a renewed spirit of traditional masculinity informing the war and its literary representations.

35. Wagnleitner, *Coca-Colonization*, 131. The language is Wagnleitner's paraphrase of MPPDA president Will Hays—the same Hays of the Hays Code.

36. "History of Tarzan Part 7." The "ten percent" number also comes from this site, although Torgovnick gives a figure of "one out of every thirty paperbacks sold" (*Gone Primitive*, 42).

37. Fisher, "You can just bet."

38. Adaptation of *Untamed* in Gold Key's *Tarzan of The Apes* #163–164 (Jan. and Feb. 1967); *Invincible* in #182–183 (Feb. and April 1969); *Invincible* in #184–185 (June and July, 1969).

39. See Collins and Hagenauer, *Men's Adventure Magazines*; and Parfrey, *It's a Man's World*. On communists as cannibals, see Wagnleitner, *Coca-Colonization* (246–248).

40. Weege, "ALL THE WAY WITH L.B.J."

41. Sajak made the comment in response to one puzzle answer, "Tarzan and Jane Fonda." Stiger, "Tarzan and Jane FOnda" [sic].

42. Burroughs, *Beasts of Tarzan*, 5.

43. See Chrichton in Wagnleitner, *Coca-Colonization*, 248.

44. de Onis, "Havana Derides U.S." Cuba appears to have made this particular appropriation of Tarzan films at least four years earlier—see "Cuba Uses a Tarzan Film."

45. Fury, *Kings of the Jungle*, 198.

46. Set in Brazil, the film is geographically confused. Barcuna the villain is black, and the film includes animals like lions and hippos that don't belong in South

America. Such eco-confusion mars a number of the films, unintentionally repeating Burroughs's mistake of dropping tigers in Africa, and perhaps bespeaking the larger identity confusion—impossibility?—that is Tarzan.

47. "C.B.S. Drops Plan."

48. "Tarz an' the Apes!"

49. Curtis, "In Walkie-Talkie Code."

50. Ziegler, "Oh, great!" and Smaller, "Son, everyone went to college."

51. Fein, "From Collaboration to Containment," 131; "images, values, and sentiments" is Fein's paraphrase of the MPPDA document.

52. Maraniss, *They Marched into Sunlight*, 30.

53. Trumbull, "American Films Lead in Orient."

54. Weissmuller, *Tarzan, My Father*, 117–118.

55. Bass, "Spy Who Loved Us," 59.

56. Though in both mutinous crews in the first novel, we find a character more physically fit than the rest and of nobler spirit. Black Michael first, and then King, prove themselves to be gentlemen by sparing and equipping John and Alice Clayton, and then the Porter party, for jungle life. Black and King are noble savages; the first mutiny by a mutt crew against oppressive officers feels like a mini-American Revolution; and both events validate the possibility of Tarzan's noble actions despite his bestial upbringing. Yet the fate of these mutinous crews suggests that even these stalwart blue-collar men aren't noble enough; that American roughhewn manhood needs its dose of European breeding.

57. In *Tarzan's Secret Treasure* (1941), Weissmuller spoke "seventy-one lines" using "ninety-seven terms" for "a total of 231 words." In *Tarzan Finds a Son!* (1939), he spoke 118 words with a vocabulary "in the low seventies." In 1953 *Tarzan and the She-Devil* hit "an all-time low of 83 lines" for Tarzan, as producer Sol Lesser blamed the lackluster performance of the prior movie, *Tarzan's Savage Fury*, on Tarzan's logorrhea: "Tarzan spoke 137 lines in that one, . . . [n]early talked himself to death" (Wood, "He Tarzan—You Fan," 50). In *Tarzan's Revenge* (1938), he spoke four words: "Tarzan" twice, and "Eleanor" and "good" once each (Boller and Lesser, *Tarzan und Hollywood*, 66).

58. "Brazil Extends Ban." The article translates the Portuguese translation of the title as "Tarzan the Unconquerable," and it seriously misreads the story, in which the communists are the bad guys.

59. Meisler, "How Blacklisting Hurt Hollywood Children."

60. Buhle and Wagner, *Blacklisted*, 214; "Tarzan in Moscow."

61. An editor of a "pro-radical but noncommunistic Russian language daily in New York" admitted to changing the Tarzan comic strip by, for example, turning Tarzan's parents from lord and lady to a professor and his wife, removing a church wedding scene ("[m]ost of our readers being strongly anti-priest and anti-church"), and making

Russian villains into Russian Whites or Poles, such that "Edgar Rice Burroughs would not have recognized his own creation had it been translated from my version back to English" (Fenton, *Big Swingers*, 153–154).

62. Stokvis, *Cobra*, 324.

63. Lee, "Rumanians Enjoy Holiday."

64. Torgovnick, *Gone Primitive*, 8–9.

65. Newton, *Savage Girls and Wild Boys*, 205–206.

66. Wagnleitner, *Coca-Colonization*, 6–7.

67. Torgovnick, *Gone Primitive*, 57–58.

68. Jacobson, *Barbarian Virtues*, 5.

69. Stoler, *Carnal Knowledge and Imperial Power*, 6.

70. Ibid., 69–70.

71. Burroughs, "Tarzan of the Apes," 263.

72. Stoler, *Carnal Knowledge and Imperial Power*, 70.

73. Ibid., 1–2.

FOUR. NATIVE SON

1. *Oak Leaves* as quoted and summarized in Reynolds, *Young Hemingway*, 230–231. Hemingway's posthumously published *The Garden of Eden* evokes the repression-to-childhood "primitive" sexuality of miscegenation, gender play, and incest (and even cannibalism and the death wish) that this book observes with regard to Tarzan. On Hemingway's novel see Gubar, *Racechanges*, and Eby, *Hemingway's Fetishism*.

2. Burroughs, *Son of Tarzan*, 166.

3. Carl Hagenbeck, *Beasts and Men, Being Carl Hagenbeck's Experiences for Half a Century among Wild Animals* (London: Longmans, Green, 1909); first published as *Von Tieren und Menschen* (Berlin: Vita, Deutsches Verlaghaus, 1908). Burroughs's working title for *The Lad and the Lion*, his own faux-Tarzan bildungsroman first published in *All-Story Cavalier* (June 30 to July 14, 1917), was "Men and Beasts."

4. Burroughs knew of Galton at least by 1907, when researching fingerprinting (Porges, *Edgar Rice Burroughs*, 100). Galton had established the systematic use of fingerprints for establishing identity, a critical plot tool in "Tarzan of the Apes." Galton was also the Victorian who gave eugenics its name—Burroughs would himself make the case for eugenics during his reporting of the January 1928 trial of William Edward Hickman in Los Angeles (see Taliaferro, *Tarzan Forever*, 228–231). The first mention of Stanley in terms of Burroughs is a biographical profile, and the article's author makes the reference to Stanley presumably from a remark Burroughs made in their interview. But we don't know exactly what he said about Stanley. It's very possible that he was as dodgy as he was about Kipling and Romulus and Remus ("Edgar

Rice Burroughs, Inc.," *Writer's Digest*, August 1949). See Du Chaillu's encounter with a gorilla, a "hellish dream creature . . . of that hideous order, half-man half-beast" (quoted in Rothfels, *Savages and Beasts*, 2). Taliaferro wonders if Burroughs might have drawn from Jack London's novel *Before Adam*, which might have drawn from Livingstone's journals, and he also speculates about Buel and Du Chaillu (89–90). Atamian's *Origin of Tarzan* discusses Buel and Du Chaillu at length, though his is a spirited if not altogether convincing and sometimes rather odd argument.

5. Rothfels, *Savages and Beasts*, 190–191.

6. See "Study Chimpanzee's Brain," *New York Times*, May 28, 1921, 7; "Chimpanzee Perishes in 'Conquest' of Fire; Sets Himself Afire with Matches in Berlin," *New York Times*, March 17, 1927, 12.

7. Burroughs, *Son of Tarzan*, 167.

8. Burroughs, "Tarzan of the Apes," 297.

9. Qtd. in Geoffrey C. Ward, *Unforgivable Blackness*, 130.

10. Ibid., 133.

11. On Jeffries, see ibid., 133. On Burroughs's white-only development and Tarzan's message of the "superiority of the aristocratic white hero depend[ing] upon his ability to protect his freestanding, single-family house from homeless African savages," see Jurca, "Tarzan, Lord of the Suburbs."

12. *Boxing* magazine qtd. in Ward, *Unforgivable Blackness*, 164–165.

13. Qtd. in ibid., 197–198.

14. Gilmore, *Bad Nigger!* 59.

15. Ward, *Unforgivable Blackness*, 217.

16. Qtd. in ibid., 166.

17. Burroughs in Fury, *Kings of the Jungle*, 25–26.

18. Gilmore, *Bad Nigger!* 45.

19. Porges, *Edgar Rice Burroughs*, 124–125; on 1907, see 719 n. 3.

20. Taliaferro, *Tarzan Forever*, 60.

21. Burroughs, "Tarzan of the Apes," 322.

22. Ibid., 251.

23. Ibid., 336.

24. Ibid., 296.

25. See Schneider, "Tarzan the Censored."

26. Boller and Lesser, *Tarzan und Hollywood*, 82.

27. Derek, *Riding Lessons*, 152.

28. Ward, *Unforgivable Blackness*, 310–311.

29. Ibid., 313–314, 333. See also Gilmore, *Bad Nigger!* 118.

30. Gilmore, *Bad Nigger!* 107.

31. Ward, *Unforgivable Blackness*, 321–322.

32. Ibid., 345.

33. Gilmore, *Bad Nigger!* 119.

34. Nancy Cunard's collection of comments by French critics, qtd. in Lemke, *Primitive Modernist*, 106.

35. On American response to Baker, see ibid., 104–105.

36. See Gilmore, *Bad Nigger!* 103.

37. Burroughs, "Tarzan of the Apes," 323.

38. Gilmore, *Bad Nigger!* 37, 138. The congressman was leading the successful legislative effort to ban "the importation and interstate transportation of films or other pictorial representations of prizefighting," a law intended to prevent white and black America from seeing images of Jack Johnson's victories over white fighters (90).

39. Burroughs, *Tarzan of the Apes*, 111.

40. Tarzan the Orphan continues a tradition in American literature of orphans, *white* orphans, standing in for marginalized, scapegoated minorities: Native Americans, African Americans, immigrants, and Catholics. See Pazicky, *Cultural Orphans in America*.

41. Burroughs, "Tarzan of the Apes," 349.

42. Thomas Yeates, *Edgar Rice Burroughs' The Return of Tarzan #1* (Milwaukie, OR: Dark Horse Comics, April 11, 1997), 23.

43. Burroughs, "Tarzan of the Apes," 253.

44. See Burroughs, "Tarzan of the Apes," for the terms "brown" (302, 307), "indigenous" (311), and "tanned" (319).

45. Collins and Hagenauer, *Men's Adventure Magazines*, 165.

46. Burroughs, "Tarzan of the Apes," 321.

47. Lott, "White Like Me," 480; Evans, "'Racial Cross-Dressing,'" 396.

48. Valencius, *Health of the Country*, 232.

49. Chopin, *Awakening and Other Stories*, 176, 173.

50. A University of California professor explaining Johnson's victory over Jeffries, although attempting to buttress strict racial categorization, actually admitted racial slipperiness when he "declared that the victory affirmed his theory that blacks were not a separate race but simply 'tanned Caucasians'" (Gilmore, *Bad Nigger!* 46).

51. Burroughs, "Tarzan of the Apes," 350.

52. Ibid., 321, 325, 329.

53. "Tarzan Miscellania."

54. Bederman, *Manliness and Civilization*, 230.

55. See Andrews, introduction to *Autobiography of an Ex-Colored Man*, by Johnson.

56. Gubar, *Racechanges*, 75, 38.

57. Larsen, *Quicksand and Passing*, 144.

58. Dyer, *White*, 23.

59. Burroughs, "Tarzan of the Apes," 328.

60. Boller and Lesser, *Tarzan und Hollywood*, 33. The appearance of rapacious white ape-gorilla-creatures in films from the 1940s, such as *White Pongo* and *White Gorilla* in 1945, suggests an association with Nazi-Aryan brutishness. That White Pongo is thought to be the missing link adds another racist touch.

61. See M. Hall, "Wheeler and Woolsey."

62. Cox, *Tarzan Presley*, 298. Legal action from the Burroughs estate (ERB, Inc.) resulted in Cox and his publisher agreeing "not to authorise any copies to be exported [from New Zealand], and to change the names of the characters if the book is ever reprinted" (Price, "Tarzan Has Left the Building").

63. In Disney's 1967 *The Jungle Book*, an orangutan named King Louie (after that most famous black musician) sings in Louis Prima's "black" voice about wanting to become human.

64. The media associated Britney's behavior with mental instability, which it connected to her motherhood. On live television at the 2003 Grammy awards, Britney famously kissed with open mouth her pop mother figure, the very musculine Madonna. Britney wore frilly white; Madonna manly black pants.

65. Fenton, *Big Swingers*, 156.

66. Ullery, *Tarzan Novels*, 28.

67. *Tarzan the Magnificent* (1936–1937), quoted in Fenton, *Big Swingers*, 201.

68. Bogle, *Dorothy Dandridge*, 184.

69. Braudy, *From Chivalry to Terrorism*, 341.

70. Burroughs, "Tarzan of the Apes," 285.

71. Steve Neale's "Masculinity as Spectacle" as summarized in Tasker, *Spectacular Bodies*, 115.

72. Burroughs, *Tarzan of the Apes*, 138, 143. In the 1912 original, Burroughs had Tarzan kill a tiger, not indigenous to Africa, and for which he used a male pronoun.

73. Ibid., 278, 317.

74. Burroughs, *Tarzan of the Apes*, 48, 51.

FIVE. ENTER JANE

1. Farmer, *Tarzan Alive*, 79.

2. Boller and Lesser, *Tarzan und Hollywood*, 226–227.

3. Burroughs, "Tarzan of the Apes," 313, 320.

4. In Burroughs, "He removed his hunting knife from its sheath and handed it to her hilt first, again motioning her into the bower. The girl understood, and taking the

long knife she entered and lay down upon the soft grasses while Tarzan of the apes stretched himself upon the ground across the entrance" ("Tarzan of the Apes," 332).

5. Burroughs, "Tarzan of the Apes," 371.

6. Burroughs, *Tarzan of the Apes*, 258.

7. Burroughs, "Tarzan of the Apes," 372.

8. On this re-entrenchment, see Filene's chapter 5, "The Long Amnesia: Depression, War, and Domesticity," in *Him/Her/Self*, 158–190.

9. Qtd. in Reilly and Wallace, "Torrid 'Tarzan,'" 70.

10. Thus Jane appears in ten of the total twenty-four books. If we include the other three Burroughs Tarzan books—*Tarzan and the Tarzan Twins* (in which Tarzan is a minor character and Jane does not appear); *Tarzan: The Lost Adventure* (unfinished Burroughs manuscript completed by Joe R. Lansdale, and in which Jane does not appear), and *The Eternal Savage* (in which both Tarzan and Jane are only very minor characters)—Jane appears in eleven of twenty-seven.

11. In *Tarzan and His Mate*, Arlington and Holt tempt Jane back to civilization with such luxuries as pretty dresses. Tarzan arrives, inspects her in her dress and carries her off. Fury sees this scene as evidence that Tarzan "approves" of fancy clothes and perfume (*Kings of the Jungle*, 75), but I disagree. He inspects the dress skeptically, and we never see Jane in it again. It was seeing other men attempt to seduce his woman that got Tarzan worked up.

12. Ibid., 254.

13. Ibid., 255.

14. See Torgovnick, *Gone Primitive*, 67–89.

15. Griffin, preface, *Woman and Nature*, ix.

16. Griffin, *Woman and Nature*, 33. On the historical linking of white women with all blacks, see also Wiegman, chapter 2, "Sexing the Difference," *American Appetites*, 43–78.

17. Bederman, *Manliness and Civilization*, 33–38.

18. See also Carolyn Merchant, *The Death of Nature: Women, Ecology, and the Scientific Revolution* (San Francisco: Harper and Row, 1980). According to Annette Kolodny, newcomers perceived the North American continent as paradoxically a bountiful mother figure and a nubile if mysterious maid to be conquered, tamed, and subjugated. See Kolodny, *The Lay of the Land: Metaphor as Experience and History in American Life and Letters* (Chapel Hill: University of North Carolina Press, 1975). A contemporary perspective on such a gendered relationship finds both paradigms— take, take, take; or rape, rape, rape—as having contributed to the environmental mess in which we find ourselves today.

19. Ortner, "Female to Male," 73.

20. Griffin, *Woman and Nature*, 47.

21. See Baym, "Melodramas of Beset Manhood."

22. Burroughs, "Tarzan of the Apes," 250.

23. Ibid., 330; though Tarzan also mimics Jane's gesture, perhaps revealing his ape nature.

24. The term "femme-Tarzan" can be misleading, as the white jungle goddess motif can also be traced to MGM's film *Trader Horn* (1930), based loosely on a book of the same name and from which came much of the African footage and initial ideas for *Tarzan the Ape Man* (1932), as well as to H. Rider Haggard's 1887 novel *She* and indeed to Burrough's own La, who first appeared in his second Tarzan book, *The Return of Tarzan* (1913). Some of the films I've listed are clearly She-Tarzan films (e.g., *Savage Girl, Nabonga, Eve, Luana, Tarzana*), while others belong more generally to this muddled tradition of the white jungle woman.

25. Nason, "'Liane, Jungle Goddess.'"

26. Publicity sheet for *Tarzana the Wild Girl*, a presentation of First Leisure Entertainment Corp., released by Ellman Film Enterprises, Inc., 1972.

27. O'Sullivan in TNT, "MGM: When the Lion Roars" (1992), quoted in Fury, *Kings of the Jungle*, 75. The Legion of Decency's vow is quoted in Skinner, *Cross and the Cinema*, 37. Skinner mentions *Tarzan the Ape Man* once, in a paragraph that also cites the gender- and race-bending *Wonder Bar*, and Greta Garbo's *Queen Christina*, with its scene in which "the Swedish Monarch, dressed as a man, agreed to share a room for the evening with John Gilbert. She subsequently revealed her gender and spent an ecstatic night in his bed" (17).

28. Quoted in Weissmuller, *Tarzan*, 61–62.

29. Derek, *Riding Lessons*, 151.

30. Corliss, Brelis, and Dutka, "Tarzan Goes to Court."

31. Derek, *Riding Lessons*, 154.

32. Salmans, "HBO."

33. Derek, *Riding Lessons*, 155.

34. The fact that Bo's Jane becomes a piece of carved ivory links her with the elephants killed for their tusks, with the exploitative, rapacious aspect of Europe's nineteenth-century relationship with Africa. The value of an elephant or a woman comes from their commodification, per ecofeminism's foundational tenet, "that the ideologies that authorize injustices based on gender, race, and class are related to the ideologies that sanction the exploitation and degradation of the environment." Sturgeon, *Ecofeminist Natures*, 23. The entire climactic sequence resembles the ritual painting of ceremonial elephants Bo would watch from her Sri Lankan hotel room overlooking the temple gardens (Derek, *Riding Lessons*, 137).

35. Weissmuller, *Tarzan*, 106.

36. Qtd. in d'Aix, *Investigating Tarzan*. "Tarzanologist" is the documentary's term, not mine.

37. The forty-six films and the two television series listed in Fury's *Kings of the Jungle*, plus the telefilm *Tarzan's Return* (1996), *Tarzan and the Lost City* (1998), and the short-lived television series *Tarzan: The Epic Adventures* (UPN, 1996–1997) and *Tarzan* (WB, fall 2003).

38. On dictation in the 1920s, see Fenton, *Big Swingers*, 141; Porges, *Edgar Rice Burroughs*, 361–362, 477–478; Joan Burroughs in Fenton, *Big Swingers*, 142.

39. Fiedler, *Love and Death*, 30.

40. Ibid., 194, 209.

41. Ibid., 209.

42. Ibid., 209.

43. Ibid., 211.

44. Badderly, "Tarzan Polishes Grunts."

45. Johnny Weissmuller was married when MGM contracted him for the Tarzan role, but the contract stipulated that, in the interest of publicity, he and his wife divorce. Weissmuller initially refused, but after shooting the film and traveling to New York for the premier, he returned home to find that his wife, in his son's words, "was looking at divorce as a reasonable option," what with an enticement of $10,000 in compensation and the company's help in her career (Weissmuller, *Tarzan*, 56).

46. Filene, *Him/Her/Self*, 7–8. See also Welter, "Cult of True Womanhood."

47. On the shift from Fearsome God to Friendly Jesus, see Stephen Prothero, *American Jesus: How the Son of God Became a National Icon* (New York: Farrar, Straus and Giroux, 2003).

48. Fiedler, *Love and Death*, 79.

49. Burroughs, *Tarzan of the Apes*, 235, 243.

50. Fiedler, *Love and Death*, 80.

51. Sherwood Anderson, *Winesburg, Ohio* (New York: Bantam, 1995 [1919]), 108.

52. Katz, *Love Stories*, 249, 252. Katz here is specifically describing the transformed perspective of a writer using the pen name "Claude Hartland" for his 1901 memoir, though Hartland's radical revision of the relationship between the two kinds of love clearly, for Katz, matches and reflects the larger culture's revision.

53. Ibid., 73.

54. Becker, *Denial of Death*, 163, 162.

55. Griffin, *Woman and Nature*, 15. While the Annunciation suggests that Mary/women provide the body and God/men the spirit, her virginity links asexuality with divine creativity and immortality.

56. Burroughs, *Tarzan the Invincible*, qtd. in Fury, *Kings of the Jungle*, 31.

57. Dyer, *White*, 26.
58. Fiedler, "Lord of the Absolute Elsewhere," 354.
59. Burroughs, "Tarzan of the Apes," 325.
60. Burroughs, *Son of Tarzan*, 240–241.
61. Ibid., 239.
62. Ibid., 224.
63. The cover depicts either of the scenes just described. Dell's Tarzan comic book #109 (Nov.–Dec. 1958) had on the cover Tarzan actor Gordon Scott holding a knife with a handle that to many readers looked like a penis.

SIX. MONKEY BUSINESS

1. Farmer, *Feast Unknown*, 266–267.
2. See René Girard, *Deceit, Desire, and the Novel: Self and Other in Literary Structure*, trans. Yvonne Freccero (Baltimore: Johns Hopkins University Press, 1965); Girard, *Violence and the Sacred*, trans. Patrick Gregory (Baltimore: Johns Hopkins University Press, 1977); Eve Kosofsky Sedgwick, *Between Men: English Literature and Male Homosocial Desire*, with new preface by author (New York: Columbia University Press, 1985).
3. See *After Dark* 6, no. 3 (Sept. 1973). *Playgirl*, another "straight" magazine famous for its gay male audience, featured a "real life" Tarzan, John Ericson, in January 1974, as well as both title character actors of *Tarzan and the Jungle Boy* (1968): Tarzan Mike Henry in 1982 and jungle boy Steve Bond in October 1975. On Sandow: Kasson, *Houdini, Tarzan and the Perfect Man*, 67. On Bernarr Macfadden's magazine *Physical Culture*: Robb, *Strangers*, 134.
4. Kasson, *Houdini, Tarzan*, 33.
5. Creed, "Me Jane."
6. Wertham, *Seduction of the Innocent*, 188–189.
7. Bederman, *Manliness and Civilization*, 13.
8. See Katz, *Love Stories*, 53.
9. Letter of 1919, qtd. in Fury, *Kings of the Jungle*, 25–26.
10. Sheldon Lord, *The Third Way* (Boston: Beacon Press, 1962); P. J. Reed-Marr, *Women without Men* (New York: Fawcett, 1957); Delta Martin, *Twilight Girl* (San Francisco: Cleis Press, 1961); Carl Corley, *A Fool's Advice* (San Diego, Publishers Export, 1967). On lesbian pulp, see Keller, "'Was It Right.'"
11. Kasson, *Houdini, Tarzan*, 12. Kasson has borrowed the "age of the bachelor" from Howard P. Chudacoff, *The Age of the Bachelor: Creating an American Subculture* (Princeton, NJ: Princeton University Press, 1999).

12. Kasson, *Houdini, Tarzan*, 12–13. On wrestling (and photos of men wrestling naked) see Katz, *Love Stories*, 226–227.

13. Cohan, *Masked Men*, 203.

14. Bleys, *Geography of Perversion*, 84.

15. Puts, Jordan, and Breedlove, "O Brother." Arthur matters to the degree that the uterine environment matters. According to Porges, as a child Ed's "sensitive" disposition and an "impression of lightness—pale skin and golden-brown hair—conveyed also the image of delicate health that concerned his parents," and the loss of two infant brothers may have increased their protective attitude toward him (9, 14). I am tempted to wonder whether this delicacy, whether actual or impressed upon him, could have fostered anxiety about his gender identity.

16. See, for example, Fiedler, *Love and Death*, 134, or his description of Cooper's novels (201).

17. Ibid., 211.

18. Writing his book in the 1950s, Fiedler might have insisted upon the absence of the sexual relationship for the more practical, strategic reason that he did not want his work dismissed outright as the "gay" book. Indeed, his 1948 *Partisan Review* essay, which digested the book's basic argument, "provoke[d] a furor seldom associated before or since with an academic essay" (Harris, introduction to *Love and Death*, vi).

19. Fiedler's *Love and Death* does mention Tarzan: "Saul Bellow, composing a homoerotic *Tarzan of the Apes* in *Henderson the Rain King*, is back on the raft with Mark Twain" (13).

20. *The Jungle Twins* No. 1, Gold Key Comics, Western Publishing, April 1972, 3.

21. "Brothers of the Spear," *Edgar Rice Burroughs' TARZAN* 1 no. 30 (March 1952), Dell Comics. The story had its own comic book in the mid-1970s, until February 1976 (#17), with one belated final issue in 1982. See *Don Markstein's Toonopedia* Web site (2003–2005), http://www.toonopedia.com/brospear.htm.

22. One man with blond hair and one slightly darker-skinned man with brown hair form the title couple of "The Ambiguously Gay Duo" animated short series from NBC's *Saturday Night Live*. Robb argues for the homoerotic subtext of the Sherlock Holmes tales, even connecting Holmes's powers of observation with "the anthropological association of clairvoyance with homosexuality" (Robb, *Strangers*, 267). Burroughs's original novel gives us Tarzan and Paul D'Arnot as a detective pair solving the mystery of Tarzan's origins. For other Holmes-Tarzan associations, see chapter 2, note 38.

23. Ellison summarized in Cohen, "Tarzan the German-Eater," 158.

24. Fuchs, "Body Politic"; Tasker, *Spectacular Bodies*; Wiegman, *American Anatomies*, 117–118. See Wiegman's chapter revisiting Fiedler, "Canonical Architecture" (149–178),

a richly complex discussion, but for what I read as a mistaken attribution of sentimentality and romanticism in Fiedler for the interracial buddies.

25. Tasker does not connect the women's mastery of their physical bodies with their whiteness whereby the decade's white musculinity becomes an assertion of racial superiority after the prior two decades' clamoring for empowerment by the black man (as well as his occasional heroic film role). She does note that the decade's black female action characters "often function as 'exotic' creatures within the narrative." Grace Jones, the very model of black female musculinity, in *Conan the Destroyer* "is literally given a tail" (Tasker, *Spectacular Bodies*, 21). The two coeval equality movements for African Americans and white women, often read as synergistic, can be read sinisterly. Giving white women the vote (1920) and then access to professional power (1960s–70s) served as disempowering counters to black empowerment.

26. Katz, *Love Stories*, 62. For literary representations see Robb, *Strangers*, 215–216; and Packard, *Queer Cowboys*. Young Ed Burroughs spent a great deal of time in the West, working on his brothers' ranch and their river mining operation, and serving in 1896–1897 with the Seventh Cavalry at Fort Grant, Arizona Territory. "'The cavalryman,' recalled a former Union cavalryman, John McElroy, in a memoir published in 1879, 'always sleeps with a chum.'" And *chum*, according to Katz, "sometimes served double-duty . . . as a term for a sexual partner" (*Love Stories*, 138). Fiedler would have been pleased to learn that Burroughs "befriended one scout in particular," a Native American called Corporal Josh (Taliaferro, *Tarzan Forever*, 42).

27. Katz, *Love Stories*, 182.

28. Aldrich, *Colonialism and Homosexuality*, 5.

29. On the *vice aristocratique*, see Bleys, *Geography of Perversion*, 41, 63. Bleys discusses the "natural or decadent" question on 155, 186–192.

30. Katz, *Love Stories*, 48–49.

31. Burroughs, "Tarzan of the Apes," 319, 342.

32. Baraka qtd. in Wiegman, *American Anatomies*, 85.

33. Bleys, *Geography of Perversion*, 18.

34. Stoler, *Carnal Knowledge*, 2.

35. Bleys, *Geography of Perversion*, 84.

36. Ibid., 148. See Valencius, *Health of the Country*.

37. Qtd. in Bederman, *Manliness and Civilization*, 35.

38. Qtd. in ibid., 36.

39. Gubar, *Racechanges*, 204.

40. See Lemke, *Primitive Modernist*, 99, 106.

41. Gubar, *Racechanges*, 116, 121.

42. And sometimes still do. In the film *Thirteen* (2003), the homoerotic energy

between the two adolescent girls reaches its height in a transgressive hetero scene involving two African American male teens.

43. Diana Fuss qtd. in Gubar, *Racechanges*, 192.

44. Mumford, "Homosex Changes."

45. Bean, "Transgressing the Gender Divide," 245. On the homoeroticism and transvestism of minstrelsy, see also David R. Roediger, *The Wages of Whiteness: Race and the Making of the American Working Class* (London: Verso, 1991), 121.

46. Lott, *Love and Theft*, 120.

47. Blackface can also be read as appropriation of what white culture conceived of as African Americans' natural talent for mimicry and an assertion of superiority: blacks mimic being human and have little choice, whereas whites mimicking blacks is a game they choose. Tarzan, too, especially in Disney, is a good mimic.

48. "To black up was an act of wildness in the antebellum US. Psychoanalytically, the smearing of soot or blackening over the body represents the height of polymorphous perversity, an infantile playing with excrement or dirt. It is the polar opposite of the anal retentiveness usually associated with accumulating capitalist and Protestant cultures" (Roediger 118–119). Alexander Saxton discusses how blackface performances also participated in the ideology of the American frontier and nature in opposition to the northern American city. See Saxton, *The Rise and Fall of the White Republic: Class Politics and Mass Culture in Nineteenth-Century America* (London: Verso, 1990), 172–173.

49. Wiegman, *American Anatomies*, 82; Burroughs, "Tarzan of the Apes" 278. The adjective "hideous," added to the 1914 book (114), appeared as late as the 1990 Signet Classics edition but does not appear in the 2003 Modern Library edition.

50. See Daniel, *Lost Revolution*, 158–161.

51. Howard, *Men Like That*, 147. Howard also analyzes Carl Corley's gay pulp fiction from 1966 to 1971, much of which involves a Fiedlerian white and nonwhite pairing (or dark white, but never black), the darker partners "cast as desirable in their 'savage earthiness'" (214).

52. Katz, *Love Stories*, 64.

53. Ibid., 66.

54. Norris, *McTeague*, 40.

55. "According to the Kinsey report from 1948, about 17 percent of boys raised on farms had 'experienced orgasm as the product of animal contacts'" (qtd. in Rydström, *Sinners and Citizens*, 8).

56. Kasson, *Houdini, Tarzan*, 208–209. Rothfels describes a "gorilla fantasy" illustration in Du Chaillu, with "that something we are not supposed to see hidden by a judiciously placed branch" (Rothfels, *Savages and Beasts*, 3).

57. Bleys, *Geography of Perversion*, 116. See also 74, 151.

58. Katz, *Love Stories*, 71, 362 n. 47.

59. Burroughs, *Jungle Tales of Tarzan*, 1–2.

60. Ibid., 5, 17. Per Girard: Tarzan first discovers his desire for Teeka when he sees her snuggling with his rival and playmate Taug.

61. Burroughs, *Jungle Tales of Tarzan*, 27. "Pêro de Magalhães Gandavo observed in 1576 that Indian men indulged in sodomy 'as if they did not have the reason of men'" (Bleys, *Geography of Perversion*, 25).

62. Quoted by both Corlis, Brelis, and Dutka, "Tarzan Goes to Court"; and Reilly and Wallace, "Torrid 'Tarzan,'" 72.

63. Reilly and Wallace, "Torrid 'Tarzan,'" 70.

64. Robb, *Strangers*, 5; Wertham, *Seduction of the Innocent*, 178.

65. "Tarzan and Bo," *Playboy* (September 1981), 244, 246.

66. Tasker, *Spectacular Bodies*, 5.

67. Decker, "You're not supposed to smile."

68. Bleys, *Geography of Perversion*, 22, 24, 25, 27.

69. Katz, *Love Stories*, 74–76. That year Bram Stoker's *Dracula* appeared in *Lippincott's Magazine* (see 89).

70. Cohen astutely reads the cover in terms of international European politics.

71. The native companion tries to kill the pretty white man in their party, perhaps to remove the competition. He also gives his "lover" an emasculating leg wound.

72. Gubar, *Racechanges*, 82.

73. Burroughs, "Tarzan of the Apes," 280.

74. Burroughs, *Tarzan and the Ant Men*, 44.

75. Burroughs, *Jungle Tales of Tarzan*, 215.

76. Ibid., 223.

77. Ibid., 229–230.

78. Ibid., 230.

79. Ibid., 231.

80. Ibid., 233; Burroughs, *Tarzan of the Apes* 105–106; Fiedler, "Lord of the Absolute Elsewhere."

81. Burroughs, *Tarzan and the Ant Men*, 34, 46–47.

82. See also *Tarzan: Love, Lies, and the Lost City*, three issues, Malibu Comics (1992).

83. On the penetrated partner as the gay one, see also Howard, *Men Like That*, 121, 208. A passage on Carl Corley's male gay fiction is particularly apt here: "Lest they be feminized, white characters—no less frequently than non-black darker characters—act

as top to the narrator's bottom. And their strength and vigor are authenticated through an agrarian upbringing" (214).

84. Robb, *Strangers*, 246; Gubar, *Racechanges*, 182–183; Studlar, *In the Realm of Pleasure*, 32; Tasker, *Spectacular Bodies*, 39; Gubar, *Racechanges*, 199–200.

SEVEN. ALL IN THE FAMILY

1. Burroughs, *Son of Tarzan*, 171, 174.

2. Ibid., 175–177.

3. Ibid., 182.

4. On a steamship, no less—ships, those islands of men in tight holds, had a reputation for sexual activity between men. Jack's passing off Akut as his grandmother also echoes nineteenth-century male homosexual practice of men frequently referring to their male companions in kinship terms to disguise the nature of the relationship (see Katz, *Love Stories*, 170).

5. Burroughs, *Son of Tarzan*, 241.

6. Ibid., 223–224, 241. The sheik who kidnapped Meriem, the only father she knows, offers her to his brother. For Fiedler, when "the American writer does not make impotence his subject, he is left to choose between the two archetypes of innocent homosexuality and unconsummated incest: the love of comrades and that of brother and sister" (*Love and Death*, 348).

7. Twitchell, *Incest Theme*, xi, 18–19. Much of this is Twitchell's summary of Janice Radway. Kolodny's two metaphors for American's perception of the land, either as nurturing mother to provide or virgin earth to be sowed, conflicted: "In short . . . the new American continent had become the focus for both personalized and transpersonalized (or culturally shared) expressions of filial homage and erotic desire," with the incestuous implication of mixing these metaphors. Kolodny, *Lay of the Land*, 22.

8. Rank, *Incest Theme*, 369–370.

9. Burroughs once fancied writing "The Autobiography of Cain" as "a monkey-man story" revealing "the real facts which led up to the killing" of Abel: "I want to be irreverent," he wrote to Bob Davis, editor of *All-Story Cavalier*, "but I know you won't stand for it, so I'll just hover around the verge without offending anyone. . . . There are a number of things in that part of genesis which need explaining, and as Cain and I know all about them we'll clear that matter up a bit." To be fair, Burroughs specifies telling of Cain's "wanderings which led to the land of Nod, his finding and fighting for a mate there." Letter of January 24, 1916 (in Porges, *Edgar Rice Burroughs*, 277–278).

10. Creed, "Me Jane."

11. Qtd. in Kaplan, "Miscegenation Issue," 309.

12. Burroughs, "Tarzan of the Apes," 310, 330–331.

13. Farmer, "Extracts from the Memoirs," 39.

14. Ibid., 40.

15. Ibid., 41.

16. Though the Tarzan character seems to believe his "uncle" raped his mother and so became his actual father (making his mother's husband, his "father," his uncle), Farmer's novel suggests that she might have preferred sleeping with her husband's brother.

17. Burroughs, "Tarzan of the Apes," 323.

18. Ibid., 324.

19. Ibid., 300. He thinks this in the context of recognizing his cousin William Cecil as "very much as he had pictured his own people to be," and Burroughs later distinguishes "kind" from "race" in Clayton's regard for Jane as "not only of his own kind and race" (Burroughs, *Tarzan of the Apes*, 180, 199).

20. From that ambiguous (north or south?) border city Baltimore to be exact; though she self-identifies as southern (Burroughs, *Tarzan of the Apes*, 325).

21. One possible origin of the phrase is the marriage of William III of the Netherlands and Mary II of England, when English sailors complained about orders from their new king. William and Mary were first cousins. A character pretending to be Tarzan's first cousin uses the phrase in *Tarzan's Savage Fury*.

22. See Twitchell's discussion of fables involving animals and eating, as well as Dracula, as cautionary tales against incest (*Incest Theme*, chapter 2, 41–76).

23. Freud, *Three Essays*, 64.

24. Freud, *Future of an Illusion*, 17.

25. Freud, *Totem and Taboo*, 207.

26. Ibid., 234.

27. Ibid., 235–236.

28. Ibid., 231–232.

29. Per Girard, the sacrificial victim must resemble but not be a group member, in order to relieve rather than provoke internecine hostility. See *Violence and the Sacred*.

30. Burroughs, "Tarzan of the Apes," 269–271.

31. During the time the Dereks hatched the idea for the film, they saw a great deal of Ursula in Paris. The Dereks also shot much of the film in Sri Lanka because, according to John, "Ursula had shown me photos from two films she made in Sri Lanka," one of those films presumably *Cannibal God* (in Steranko, "Uncensored Bo," 22). The movies have other similarities, including a native woman who sleeps with

a white man and who is played by the same actress, spelled "Akushula Selayah" in *Tarzan* and "Akushla Sellajaah" in *Cannibal God*. The Dereks might have also been inspired by the ritual painting of elephants Bo witnessed (see chapter 5, note 34).

32. Reilly and Wallace, "Torrid 'Tarzan,'" 70.

33. Creed, "Me Jane."

34. In MGM's *Tarzan's Secret Treasure* (1941), the Irishman O'Doul is a clichéd working-class Irish drunk, but he also admires Tarzan's body in undeniably homoerotic eyefuls.

35. Freud, *Three Essays*, 64.

36. Paraphrase of Marie Bonaparte in Griffin, *Woman and Nature*, 47.

37. The Dereks seem to have scripted their movie off *Apocalypse Now*'s (1978) revision of the canonical African upriver journey novella *Heart of Darkness*, with Kurtz split into James Parker and the Ivory Chief and Harry Holt as the photographer played in Coppola's film by Dennis Hopper. Incidentally, the *Burroughs Newsbeat* fanzine once reported that "Lord Greystoke is the pseudonym Marlon Brando has frequently used to resister in hotels where he didn't want his identity known!" (*Newsbeat Omnibus*, 122). James Parker's self-destructive monomaniacal quest for elephant ivory recalls Harris's role chasing and hunting killer whales in *Orca* (1977), his first movie with Bo, itself an awkward amalgam of *Moby Dick*, *Jaws*, and *Last of the Mohicans* (with a boat named after Natty Bumpo and a Native American sidekick).

38. Apparently the Dereks' May–December relationship developed in parallel with the on-screen one between James and Jane, as Bo came into her own as the film's producer. "John now claims that even his paternal relationship with Bo has reversed," *People* magazine reported: "I've become totally dependent on her" (qtd. in Reilly and Wallace, "Torrid 'Tarzan,'" 74). Before the film begins, we see the production company's image: "Svengali Productions," but with Bo holding the strings to control the puppet John. Burroughs's second wife was not only young enough to be his daughter, she and his daughter Joan became close friends when they were new mothers. His second wife was also the former wife of his film production company partner, who left her for Ula Holt, the woman who played Tarzan's eye-candy partner "Ula" in *The New Adventures of Tarzan*.

39. Freud, *Civilization and Its Discontents*, 48.

40. She further binds Andress's character to her by placing an amulet around her neck in the scene in which she gives her the drug. By the end, nontransgressive heteronormative sexuality is restored: the native woman, the gay pair, and the brother are dead, and we have learned about the husband's earlier death—Andress's character did not commit adultery after all. She tosses away the amulet as she and the surviving white male hero, her lover, float downriver to safety.

41. The edition combines both of the twins' stories into one title: *Tarzan and the Tarzan Twins*. On the cover of the Dell Fast-Action Story book series adaptation, *Tarzan with the Tarzan Twins in the Jungle* (1938), Tarzan himself is slender with a pageboy haircut and rouged cheeks, looking very much the pretty boy as he affectionately embraces his somewhat distant cousins.

42. Katz, *Love Stories*, 236, 249; Howard, *Men Like That*, 42–43.

43. I am drawing on Georges Bataille's *Erotism: Death and Sensuality*, and Adam Phillips's explication of Freud in "The Death of Freud," *Darwin's Worms: On Life Stories and Death Stories.*

44. Becker, *Denial of Death*, 41. This Parker is also masochistic in his impossible-to-achieve desires, and "Because symbiotic remerge [with the mother] is a physical impossibility, death becomes the fantasy fulfillment to desire" (Studlar, *Realm of Pleasure*, 26).

EIGHT. ENDINGS

1. Marks, "Fumble in the Jungle"; Brantley, "Tarzan Arrives on Broadway."

2. Horgan, "Tarzan Trounced."

3. Qtd. in Rothfels, *Savages and Beasts*, 1.

4. Canby, "Screen: Jane since Tarzan." This paragraph draws from Becker, *Denial of Death.*

5. Lincoln qtd. in Vernell Coriell's "Elmo the Mighty," reprinted with permission from the Classic Film Collector as chapter 2 of Rudolph, *My Father, Elmo Lincoln*, 31.

6. Fury, *Kings of the Jungle*, 17.

7. Taliaferro, *Tarzan Forever*, 167.

8. Burroughs, *Tarzan and the Lion Man*, 26. See Taliaferro's debunking of the legend of Searle's death (*Tarzan Forever*, 166–168).

9. Fury, *Kings of the Jungle*, 35.

10. Van Hise, "Tarzan and His Mate (Revisited)," 39.

11. "Animals: Jiggs."

12. See Boller and Lesser, *Tarzan und Hollywood*, 152.

13. Fury, *Kings of the Jungle*, 118.

14. Rudolph, *My Father, Elmo Lincoln*, 126. Source of obit not provided.

15. Fenton, *Big Swingers*, 201.

16. Bogle, *Dorothy Dandridge*, 548.

17. Essoe, *Tarzan of the Movies*, 182.

18. "'Tarzan' Elephant Kills Trainer."

19. Weissmuller, *Tarzan, My Father*, 194, 198, 202. Johnny saw the grave again in

April 2001 and to his delight found it transformed into a "beautiful" plot. A red rose adorned the grave, placed by one of his father's many visitors (207, 209).

20. Derek, *Riding Lessons*, 212, 214.

21. The film was variously called "Tarzan, King of the Jungle" and "Tarzan and the Golden Grotto." Their other film was *Tarzan and the Brown Prince*, also known as "Tarzan and the Treasure of the Emerald Cave."

22. Roach, "Tarzan's Escaped Tiger Killed."

23. Abram, *Spell of the Sensuous*, 100–101, 102.

24. Burroughs, "Tarzan of the Apes," 267–268.

25. Burroughs, *Tarzan of the Apes*, 270.

26. Fiedler, "Lord of the Absolute Elsewhere," 354.

27. Miller, *Errand into the Wilderness*, 206, vii.

28. Fiedler, "Lord of the Absolute Elsewhere," 354.

BIBLIOGRAPHY

Abram, David. *The Spell of the Sensuous: Perception and Language in a More-Than-Human World.* New York: Vintage, 1997.

"African American Perspectives: Pamphlets of the Daniel A. P. Murray Collection, 1818–1907." American Memory Project, Library of Congress. http://memory.loc .gov/ammem/aap/.

d'Aix, Alain. *Investigating Tarzan.* Quebec, Canada: Digital Video, 1997. Color. 58 min.

Aldrich, Robert. *Colonialism and Homosexuality.* London: Routledge, 2003.

Andrews, William L. Introduction to *The Autobiography of an Ex-Colored Man,* by James Weldon Johnson. New York: Penguin, 1990. vii–xxvii.

"Animals: Jiggs." *Time,* March 14, 1938, 37.

Atamian, Sarkis. *The Origin of Tarzan: The Mystery of Tarzan's Creation Solved.* Anchorage: Publication Consultants, 1997.

"Award to Go to Maureen O'Sullivan." *New York Times,* Nov. 16, 1980, 69.

Badderly, Norman J. "Tarzan Polishes Grunts." Dispatch filed to *New Bedford Sunday Standard-Times* from Nairobi, Kenya, March 27, 1960. Seen on eBay.

Barnes, Clive. "Theater: Amsterdam Hit." *New York Times,* July 8, 1969, 36.

Bass, Thomas A. "The Spy Who Loved Us." *New Yorker,* May 23, 2005, 56–67.

Baym, Nina. "Melodramas of Beset Manhood: How Theories of American Fiction Exclude Women Authors." *American Quarterly* 33.2 (Summer 1981): 123–139. Reprinted in *Locating American Studies,* ed. Lucy Maddox. Baltimore: Johns Hopkins University Press, 1999. 215–231.

Bean, Annemarie. "Transgressing the Gender Divide: The Female Impersonator in Nineteenth-Century Blackface Minstrelsy." In *Inside the Minstrel Mask: Readings in Nineteenth-Century Blackface Minstrelsy,"* ed. Annemarie Bean, James V. Hatch, and Brooks McNamara. Hanover, NH: Wesleyan University Press, 1966. 245–256.

Becker, Ernest. *The Denial of Death.* New York: Free Press, 1997 (1973).

Bederman, Gail. *Manliness and Civilization: A Cultural History of Gender and Race in the United States, 1880–1917.* Chicago: University of Chicago Press, 1995.

Beer, Gillian. *Arguing with the Past: Essays in Narrative from Woolf to Sidney.* London: Routledge, 1989.

———. *Forging the Missing Link: Interdisciplinary Stories.* Cambridge: Cambridge University Press, 1992.

Bleys, Rudi C. *The Geography of Perversion: Male-to-Male Sexual Behavior Outside the West and the Ethnographic Imagination, 1750–1918.* New York: New York University Press, 1995.

Bogle, Donald. *Dorothy Dandridge: A Biography.* New York: Amistad, 1997.

Boller, Reiner, and Julian Lesser. *Tarzan und Hollywood: Von Johnny Weissmuller bis Gordon Scott—Die Klassichen Tarzan-Filme von Produzent Sol Lesser.* Unpublished trans. Matt Stinson. Berlin: Schwarzkopf and Schwarzkopf, 2004.

Brantley, Ben. "Tarzan Arrives on Broadway, Airborne." *New York Times,* May 11, 2006.

Braudy, Leo. *From Chivalry to Terrorism: War and the Changing Nature of Masculinity.* New York: Alfred A. Knopf, 2003.

"Brazil Extends Ban." *New York Times,* Dec. 15, 1937, 17.

"Brothers of the Spear." *Edgar Rice Burroughs' TARZAN* 1.30 (March 1952), Dell Comics.

Buhle, Paul, and Dave Wagner. *Blacklisted: The Film Lover's Guide to the Hollywood Blacklist.* New York: Palgrave Macmillan, 2003.

Burroughs, Edgar Rice. *The Beasts of Tarzan.* In *The Beasts of Tarzan/The Son of Tarzan.* New York: Del Rey, 1996. First published in *All-Story Cavalier Weekly Magazine,* May 16–June 13, 1914.

———. "How I Became an Author." *Chicago Examiner,* April 4, 1918. http://www .erbzine.com/mag16/1696.html.

———. *Jungle Tales of Tarzan.* New York: Grosset and Dunlap, 1919. Individual stories published in *Blue Book* Sept. 1916–Aug. 1917.

———. *The Return of Tarzan.* New York: Ballantine, 1963.

———. *The Son of Tarzan.* In *The Beasts of Tarzan/The Son of Tarzan.* New York: Del Rey, 1996. First published in *All-Story Cavalier,* Dec. 4–23, 1915.

———. "The Story of Tarzan." Long version, 1932 or 1933. http://www.erbzine.com/ mag2/0256.html.

———. *Tarzan and the Ant Men.* New York: Grosset and Dunlap, 1924. First published in *All-Story* Feb. 2–March 17, 1924.

———. *Tarzan and the Foreign Legion.* New York: Ballantine, 1964. First published 1947.

———. *Tarzan and the Lion Man.* New York: Ballantine, 1964. First published in *Liberty* Nov. 1933–Jan. 1934.

———. "Tarzan of the Apes." *All-Story Magazine,* Oct. 1912, 241–372. Facsimile ed., John Monster, 2001.

———. *Tarzan of the Apes.* New York: A. C. McClurg, 1914.

———. *Tarzan of the Apes.* Intro. John Taliaferro. New York: Modern Library, 2003.

———. "The Tarzan Theme." *Writer's Digest,* June 1932, 29–32.

Canby, Vincent. "Screen: Jane since Tarzan: From Limb to Limb." Review of *Jane Bleibt Jane* (Jane Is Jane Forever). *New York Times,* April 7, 1978, c7.

"C.B.S. Drops Plan for Tarzan Show." *New York Times,* March 25, 1964, 83.

Chopin, Kate. *The Awakening and Other Stories.* Ed. Nina Baym. Intro. Kaye Gibbons. New York: Modern Library, 2000.

Cohan, Steven. *Masked Men: Masculinity and the Movies in the Fifties.* Bloomington: Indiana University Press, 1997.

Cohen, Matt, ed. and intro. *Brother Men: The Correspondence of Edgar Rice Burroughs and Herbert T. Weston.* Durham, NC: Duke University Press, 2005.

———. "Tarzan the German-Eater." *Comparative American Studies* 4.2 (2006): 151–174.

Collins, Max Allan, and George Hagenauer. *Men's Adventure Magazines in Postwar America.* With essay by Steven Heller. London: Taschen, 2004.

Corliss, Richard, Dean Brelis, and Elaine Dutka. "Tarzan Goes to Court." *Time,* July 20, 1981, 70.

Cox, Nigel. *Tarzan Presley.* Wellington, New Zealand: Victoria University Press, 2004.

Creed, Barbara. "Me Jane: You Tarzan!—A Case of Mistaken Identity in Paradise." *Continuum: Australian Journal of Media and Culture* 1.1 (1987). http://wwwmcc .murdoch.edu.au/ReadingRoom/1.1/Creed.html.

Crosby, John. "Tarzan—and Other Censored Tales." *Los Angeles Times,* Dec. 29, 1968. Reprinted in *The Edgar Rice Burroughs Newsbeat Omnibus,* ed. James Van Hise. Yucca Valley, CA: Van Hise, 2005. 80.

"Cuba Uses a Tarzan Film for Anti-U.S. Propaganda." *New York Times,* Aug. 16, 1964, 42.

Curtis, Charlotte. "In Walkie-Talkie Code, Ford Is Tarzan and Mrs. Ford, Jane." *New York Times,* Aug. 17, 1976, 21.

Daniel, Pete. *Lost Revolution: The South in the 1950s.* Chapel Hill: University of North Carolina Press, 2000.

Darwin, Charles. Selections from *The Descent of Man, and Selection in Relation to Sex* (1871), in *The Norton Anthology of Nature Writing,* college ed., ed. Robert Finch and John Elder. New York: Norton, 2002. 151–163.

Decker, Richard. "You're not supposed to smile, Mr. Leary." Cartoon. *New Yorker,* Aug. 11, 1934, 12.

de Onis, Juan. "Havana Derides U.S. in a Psychedelic Exhibition." *New York Times,* Jan. 10, 1968, 3.

Derek, Bo, with Mark Seal. *Riding Lessons: Everything That Matters in Life I Learned from Horses.* New York: ReganBooks, 2002.

Duranty, Walter. "Russians Prefer 'Tarzan' to Marx." *New York Times,* April 17, 1924, 23.

Dyer, Richard. *White.* London: Routledge, 1997.

Eagleton, Terry. *Sweet Violence: The Idea of the Tragic.* Williston, VT: Blackwell, 2002.

Eby, Carl P. *Hemingway's Fetishism: Psychoanalysis and the Mirror of Manhood.* Albany: SUNY Press, 1999.

Eshed, Eli. "Tarzan in Israel" (1999), www.violetbooks.com/tarzan-israel.html.

Essoe, Gabe. *Tarzan of the Movies.* Secaucus, NJ: Citadel Press, 1968.

Evans, Nicholas M. "'Racial Cross-Dressing' in the Jazz Age: Cultural Therapy and

Its Discontents in Cabaret Nightlife." In *Hop on Pop: The Politics and Pleasures of Popular Culture*, ed. Henry Jenkins. Durham, NC: Duke University Press. 388–414.

Farmer, Philip José. "Extracts from the Memoirs of 'Lord Greystoke.'" In *Mother Was a Lovely Beast: A Feral Man Anthology*, ed. Philip José Farmer. Radnor, PA: Chilton, 1974. 26–75.

———. *A Feast Unknown.* New York: Playboy Press, 1969.

———. *Tarzan Alive: A Definitive Biography of Lord Greystoke*. New York: Popular Library, 1972.

Fein, Seth. "From Collaboration to Containment: Hollywood and the International Political Economy of Mexican Cinema after the Second World War." In *Mexico's Cinema: A Century of Film and Filmmakers*, ed. Joanne Hershfield and David R. Maciel. Wilmington, DE: Scholarly Resources, 1999. 130–135.

Fenton, Robert W. *The Big Swingers: A Biography*. Englewood Cliffs, NJ: Prentice-Hall, 1967.

Fiedler, Leslie. "Lord of the Absolute Elsewhere." *New York Times*, June 9, 1974, 354.

———. *Love and Death in the American Novel*. Normal, IL: Dalkey Archive Press, 1997 (1960).

Filene, Peter G. *Him/Her/Self: Gender Identities in Modern America*. 3rd ed. Foreword by Elaine Tyler May. Baltimore: Johns Hopkins University Press, 1998.

Fineberg, Jonathan. *The Innocent Eye: Children's Art and the Modern Artist*. Princeton, NJ: Princeton University Press, 1997.

Fisher, Ed. "You can just bet the C.I.A. is behind this!" Cartoon. *New Yorker*, Oct. 3, 1964, 57.

Flanagan, Barbara. "Why No Tarzan Comics?" *Minneapolis Star and Tribune*. Reprinted in *The Edgar Rice Burroughs Newsbeat Omnibus*, ed. James Van Hise. Yucca Valley, CA: Van Hise, 2005. 120.

"4 Columbia Students Tour Soviet." *New York Times*, Aug. 25, 1954, 7.

Freud, Sigmund. *Civilization and Its Discontents*. Standard ed. Trans. and ed. James Strachey; intro. Peter Gay. New York: Norton, 1961.

———. *The Future of an Illusion*. Trans. W. D. Robson-Scott. Ed. Ernest Jones. New York: Liveright, 1949.

———. *Three Essays on the Theory of Sexuality*. Intro. Steven Marcus; trans. and ed. James Strachey. Foreword by Nancy J. Chodorow. New York: Basic Books, 2000.

———. *Totem and Taboo: Resemblances between the Psychic Lives of Savages and Neurotics*. Trans. A. A. Brill. New York: Moffat, Yard, 1919.

Fuchs, Cynthia J. "The Body Politic." In *Screening the Male: Exploring Masculinities in Hollywood Cinema*, ed. Steven Cohan and Ina Rae Hark. London: Routledge, 1993. 194–210.

Fury, David. *Kings of the Jungle: An Illustrated Reference to "Tarzan" on Screen and Television*. Foreword by Maureen O'Sullivan. Jefferson, NC: McFarland, 1994.

Gilmore, Al-Tony. *Bad Nigger! The National Impact of Jack Johnson*. Port Washington, NY: Kennikat Press, 1975.

Goldwater, Robert. *Primitivism in Modern Art*. Enlarged ed. Cambridge, MA: Harvard University Press, 1986.

Griffin, Susan. *Woman and Nature: The Roaring inside Her*. San Francisco: Sierra Club Books, 2000 (1978).

Griswold, Jerry. *Audacious Kids: Coming of Age in America's Classic Children's Books*. New York: Oxford University Press, 1992.

Gubar, Susan. *Racechanges: White Skin, Black Face in American Culture*. New York: Oxford University Press, 1997.

Hall, G. Stanley. *Adolescence: Its Psychology and Its Relations to Physiology, Anthropology, Sociology, Sex, Crime, Religion, and Education*. 2 vols. New York: D. Appleton, 1904.

Hall, Mordant. "Bert Wheeler and Robert Woolsey on a Jaunt in African Jungles with Trained Lions." *New York Times*, April 24, 1933, 11.

Harris, Charles B. Introduction to *Love and Death in the American Novel* by Leslie Fiedler. Normal, IL: Dalkey Archive Press, 1997. v–xii.

Helm, Everett. "Too Many Cooks Make Operatic Hash." *New York Times*, July 13, 1969, D17.

"The History of Tarzan, Part 7: Into the 21st Century." www.tarzan.com/tarzan/tarz7 .html.

Holt, Marilyn Irvin. *The Orphan Trains: Placing Out in America*. Lincoln: University of Nebraska Press, 1992.

Horgan, Richard. "Tarzan Trounced." FilmStew.com (Jan. 7, 2004). http://www .filmstew.com/ShowArticle.aspx?ContentID=7640.

Howard, John. *Men Like That: A Southern Queer History*. Chicago: University of Chicago Press, 1999.

Jacobson, Matthew Frye. *Barbarian Virtues: The United States Encounters Foreign Peoples at Home and Abroad, 1876–1917*. New York: Hill and Wang, 2001.

Jeffords, Susan. *The Remasculanization of America: Gender and the Vietnam War*. Bloomington: Indiana University Press, 1989.

The Jungle Twins, no. 1. Gold Key Comics. New York: Western, April 1972.

Jurca, Catherine. "Tarzan, Lord of the Suburbs." *Modern Language Quarterly* 57.3 (Sept. 1996): 479–504.

Kaplan, Sidney. "The Miscegenation Issue in the Election of 1864." *Journal of Negro History* 34.3 (July 1949): 274–343.

Karlin, Daniel. Introduction to *The Jungle Books* by Rudyard Kipling. Ed. Daniel Karlin. New York: Penguin, 1987. 7–27.

Kasson, John F. *Houdini, Tarzan, and the Perfect Man: The White Male Body and the Challenge of Modernity*. New York: Hill and Wang, 2001.

Katz, Jonathan Ned. *Love Stories: Sex between Men before Homosexuality*. Chicago: University of Chicago Press, 2001.

Keller, Yvonne. "'Was It Right to Love Her Brother's Wife So Passionately?' Lesbian Pulp Novels and U.S. Lesbian Identity, 1950–1965." *American Quarterly* 57.2 (June 2005): 385–410.

Larsen, Nella. *Quicksand and Passing*. Ed. and intro. Deborah E. McDowell. New Brunswick, NJ: Rutgers University Press, 1986.

Lee, John M. "Rumanians Enjoy Holiday." *New York Times*, Aug. 25, 1968, 39.

Lemke, Sieglinde. *Primitive Modernist: Black Culture and the Origins of Transatlantic Modernism*. Oxford: Oxford University Press, 1998.

Levine, Lawrence. *Highbrow/Lowbrow: The Emergence of Cultural Hierarchy in America*. Cambridge, MA: Harvard University Press, 1988.

Lewis, Bertram. "Inferences from the Dream Screen." *International Journal of Psychoanalysis* 29 (1948): 224–230.

———. "Sleep, the Mouth, and the Dream Screen." *Psychoanalytic Quarterly* 15 (1946): 419–434.

Lindsey, Robert. "Wily Tarzan Lives On, Dollarwise." *New York Times*, Aug. 29, 1975, 59.

López, Ana M. "Are All Latins from Manhattan? Hollywood, Ethnography, and Cultural Colonialism." In *Mediating Two Worlds: Cinematic Encounters in the Americas*, ed. John King, Ana M. López, and Manuel Alvarado. London: BFI, 1993. 67–80.

Lott, Eric. *Love and Theft: Blackface Minstrelsy and the American Working Class*. New York: Oxford University Press, 1993.

———. "White Like Me: Racial Cross-Dressing and the Construction of American Whiteness." In *Cultures of United States Imperialism*, ed. Amy Kaplan and Donald E. Pease. Durham: Duke University Press, 1993. 474–556.

"Lupe Velez Obtains Los Angeles Divorce." *New York Times*, Aug. 16, 1938, 22.

Mandel, Paul. "Tarzan of the Paperbacks." *Life*, Nov. 1963, 11–12.

Maraniss, David. *They Marched into Sunlight: War and Peace, Vietnam and America, October 1967*. New York: Simon and Schuster, 2003.

Marks, Peter. "Fumble in the Jungle: Disney's Tame 'Tarzan.'" *Washington Post*, May 11, 2006, C01.

Meisler, Andy. "How Blacklisting Hurt Hollywood Children." *New York Times*, Aug. 31, 1995, C13, C16.

Miller, Perry. *Errand into the Wilderness*. Cambridge, MA: Harvard University Press, 1956.

Mumford, Kevin J. "Homosex Changes: Race, Cultural Geography, and the Emergence of the Gay." In *Locating American Studies: The Evolution of a Discipline*, ed. Lucy Maddox. Baltimore: Johns Hopkins University Press, 1999. 385–407. First published in *American Quarterly* 48.3 (Sept. 1996): 395–413.

Nason, Richard W. "'Liane, Jungle Goddess' Is Shown Here." *New York Times*, Feb. 23, 1959, 19.

Newton, Michael. *Savage Girls and Wild Boys: A History of Feral Children*. New York: Picador, 2004.

Nichols, Robert. "A Poet Dissects Our Movies." *New York Times*, Sept. 27, 1925, SMI.

Norris, Frank. *McTeague: A Story of San Francisco*. Intro. Eric Solomon. New York: Signet, 2003.

Ortner, Sherry. "Is Female to Male as Nature Is to Culture?" In *Women, Culture and Society*, ed. Michelle Rosaldo and Louise Lamphere. Stanford, CA: Stanford University Press, 1974. 67–87.

Pace, Eric. "Cairo Is Willing to Let Tarzan Films Return." *New York Times*, Nov. 24, 1968, 115.

Packard, Chris. *Queer Cowboys: And Other Erotic Male Friendships in Nineteenth Century American Literature*. New York: Palgrave Macmillan, 2005.

Parfrey, Adam. *It's a Man's World: Men's Adventure Magazines, the Postwar Pulps*. Los Angeles: Feral House, 2003.

Pazicky, Diana Loercher. *Cultural Orphans in America*. Jackson: University of Mississippi Press, 1998.

Perelman, S. J. "Cloudland Revisited: Rock-A-Bye, Viscount, in the Treetop." *New Yorker*, Dec. 23, 1950, 18–21.

Porges, Irwin. *Edgar Rice Burroughs: The Man Who Created Tarzan*. Provo, UT: Brigham Young University Press, 1975.

"Pravda Scolds at Tarzan Films; Says Roars Scare Farm Livestock." *New York Times*, Dec. 28, 1953, 2.

Price, Steven. "Tarzan Has Left the Building." *New Zealand Listener* 197.3375 (January 15–21, 2005). http://www.listener.co.nz/issue/3375/features/3163/tarzan_has_left_the_building,1.html.

Puts, David A., Cynthia L. Jordan, and S. Marc Breedlove. "O Brother, Where Art Thou? The Fraternal Birth-Order Effect on Male Sexual Orientation." *PNAS (Proceedings of the National Academy of Sciences of the United States of America)* 103.28 (July 11, 2006). http://www.pnas.org/cgi/content/extract/103/28/10531.

Rank, Otto. *The Incest Theme in Literature and Legend: Fundamentals of a Psychology of*

Literary Creation. Trans. Gregory C. Richter; intro. Peter Rudnytsky. Baltimore: Johns Hopkins University Press, 1993.

Reilly, Sue, and David Wallace. "A Torrid 'Tarzan' Has Bo Derek and Her Husband, John, Swinging from Legal Vines." *People Weekly,* July 27, 1981, 70–75.

Reynolds, Michael S. *The Young Hemingway.* New York: W. W. Norton, 1998.

Roach, John. "Tarzan's Escaped Tiger Killed." *National Geographic News,* July 14, 2004. http://news.nationalgeographic.com/news/2004/07/0714_040714_tarzantiger.html.

Robb, Graham. *Strangers: Homosexual Love in the Nineteenth Century.* New York: W. W. Norton, 2003.

Ronan, Margaret. "Meanwhile, Back in the Treetops . . ." *Practical English Magazine,* May 8, 1964. Reprinted in *The Edgar Rice Burroughs Newsbeat Omnibus,* ed. James Van Hise. Yucca Valley, CA: Van Hise, 2005. 78–79.

Rothfels, Nigel. *Savages and Beasts: The Birth of the Modern Zoo.* Baltimore: Johns Hopkins University Press, 2002.

Rubin, William, ed. *"Primitivism" in 20th Century Art: Affinity of the Tribal and the Modern.* 2 vols. New York: Museum of Modern Art, 1984.

Rudolph, Marci'a Lincoln. *My Father, Elmo Lincoln: The Original Tarzan.* Studio City, CA: Empire, 2001.

Rydell, Robert W., and Rob Kroes. *Buffalo Bill in Bologna: The Americanization of the World, 1869–1922.* Chicago: University of Chicago Press, 2005.

Rydström, Jens. *Sinners and Citizens: Bestiality and Homosexuality in Sweden, 1880–1950.* Chicago: University of Chicago Press, 2003.

Salisbury, Harrison E. "Soviet Theatre Turns to Revivals." *New York Times,* May 18, 1952, XI.

Salmans, Sandra. "HBO: Subscribers Up, Ratings Down." *New York Times,* Feb. 23, 1984, C22.

Schneider, Jerry L. "Tarzan the Censored." *ERBville: The Home of the Public Domain Stories of Edgar Rice Burroughs in PDF Format.* Site last updated May 21, 2003; article last updated 2000. http://www.angelfire.com/zine2/erbville/censored.pdf.

Sheehan, Neil. *A Bright Shining Lie: John Paul Vann and America in Vietnam.* New York: Vintage, 1988.

"Signal Presents 'Tarzan of the Apes.'" *Signal Dealer News* 1.2 (Aug. 1932). Reprinted in *The Edgar Rice Burroughs Newsbeat Omnibus,* ed. James Van Hise. Yucca Valley, CA: Van Hise, 2005. 25.

Skinner, James M. *The Cross and the Cinema: The Legion of Decency and the National Catholic Office for Motion Pictures, 1933–1970.* Westport, CT: Praeger, 1993.

Smaller, Barbara. "Son, everyone went to college in the sixties—there was a war going on." Cartoon. *New Yorker,* Oct. 11, 1999, 73.

Smith, Sally Bedell. "Battle Intensifying over Explicit Sex on Cable TV." *New York Times*, Oct. 3, 1983, A1, C22.

Stark, Steven D. "10 Years into the Stallone Era: What It, Uh, All Means." *New York Times*, Feb. 22, 1987, A1.

Steranko, "The Uncensored Bo." *Mediascene Prevue* 2.46 (Nov.–Dec. 1981): 22–28, 47, 63–65.

Stiger, Jim "Stigs." "Tarzan and Jane FOnda" [sic]. "Most Recent Website Updates," USMC Combat Helicopter Association website. Posted March 26, 2005. http://www.popasmoke.com/recent.html?subaction=showfull&id=1111893185&archive =&start_from=&ucat=7&.

Stoler, Ann Laura. *Carnal Knowledge and Imperial Power: Race and the Intimate in Colonial Rule*. Berkeley: University of California Press, 2002.

Stokvis, Willemijn. *Cobra: The Last Avant-Garde Movement of the Twentieth Century*. Willston, VT: Lund Humphries, 2004.

Studlar, Gaylyn. *In the Realm of Pleasure: Von Sternberg, Dietrich, and the Masochistic Aesthetic*. New York: Columbia University Press, 1988.

Sturgeon, Noël. *Ecofeminist Natures: Race, Gender, Feminist Theory, and Political Action*. New York: Routledge, 1997.

Taliaferro, John. *Tarzan Forever: The Life of Edgar Rice Burroughs, Creator of Tarzan*. New York: Scribner, 1999.

"Tarz an' the Apes!" *Spoof* 1.2 (Nov. 1972).

"Tarzan and Bo." *Playboy*, Sept. 1981, 146–161.

"'Tarzan' Elephant Kills Trainer." *New York Times*, July 30, 1966, 14.

"Tarzan in Moscow." *Time*, Aug. 14, 1950, 82.

"Tarzan Is Back—on Soviet Screen." *New York Times*, Feb. 21, 1952, 9.

"Tarzan Miscellania." *Edgar Rice Burroughs*. London: New English Library, 1975. 8. This publication is an oversized magazine.

"Tarzan Postcards Sold under Counter in Soviet." *New York Times*, May 15, 1954, 6.

Tasker, Yvonne. *Spectacular Bodies: Gender, Genre, and the Action Cinema*. London: Routledge, 1993.

"10,000 Books Banned by Hungarian Regime." *New York Times*, Feb. 9, 1951.

Thoreau, Henry David. "Walking,"in *The Norton Anthology of Nature Writing*, college ed., ed. Robert Finch and John Elder. New York: Norton, 2002. 180–204.

"3 More Film Stars Face 'Red' Inquiry." *New York Times*, Aug. 19, 1934, 6.

Torgovnick, Marianna. *Gone Primitive: Savage Intellects, Modern Lives*. Chicago: University of Chicago Press, 1990.

Trites, Roberta Seelinger. *Disturbing the Universe: Power and Repression in Adolescent Literature*. Iowa City: University of Iowa Press, 2000.

Trumbull, Robert. "American Films Lead in Orient." *New York Times*, April 13, 1947, 69.

Twitchell, James B. *The Incest Theme in Literature and Legend: Fundamentals of a Psychology of Literary Creation*. New York: Columbia University Press, 1987.

Ullery, David A. *The Tarzan Novels of Edgar Rice Burroughs*. Jefferson, NC: McFarland, 2001.

U.S. Department of Commerce. *Historical Statistics of the United States: Colonial Times to 1970, Part I*. Bicentennial ed. Washington, DC: U.S. Government Printing Office, 2005.

"U.S. in a Book War on Soviet in Israel." *New York Times*, Nov. 21, 1953, 3.

Valencius, Conevery Bolton. *The Health of the Country: How American Settlers Understood Themselves and Their Land*. New York: Basic Books, 2002.

Van Hise, James. "Tarzan and His Mate (Revisited)." *The Edgar Rice Burroughs Newsbeat Omnibus*. Yucca Valley, CA: Van Hise, 2005. 39–41.

Vidal, Gore. "Tarzan Revisited." *Esquire*, Oct. 1973, 281–283, 484, 486.

Wagnleitner, Reinhold. *Coca-Colonization and the Cold War: The Cultural Mission of the United States in Austria after the Second World War*. Trans. Diana M. Wolf. Chapel Hill: University of North Carolina Press, 1994.

———. "Propagating the American Dream: Cultural Politics as Means of Integration." *American Studies International* 24 (April 1986): 60–84.

Ward, Geoffrey C. *Unforgivable Blackness: The Rise and Fall of Jack Johnson*. New York: Knopf, 2004.

Weege, William. "ALL THE WAY WITH L.B.J." Poster. San Francisco: Happening Press, 1967. Dist. Print Ming of Berkeley, CA.

Weissmuller, Johnny, Jr., with William Reed and Craig Reed. *Tarzan, My Father*. Toronto: ECW Press, 2002.

Welter, Barbara. "The Cult of True Womanhood: 1820–1860." *American Quarterly* 18.2 pt. 1 (summer 1966): 151–174. Reprinted in *Locating American Studies: The Evolution of a Discipline*, ed. Lucy Maddox (Baltimore: Johns Hopkins University Press, 1999). 43–70.

Wertham, Fredric. *Seduction of the Innocent*. New York: Rinehart, 1953.

Wiegman, Robyn. *American Anatomies: Theorizing Race and Gender*. Durham, NC: Duke University Press, 1995.

Wood, Thomas. "He Tarzan—You Fan." *Collier's*, May 9, 1953, 48–52.

"Young Marine Adopts South Korean Orphan, Who Refuses Rice after Tasting G.I. Food." *New York Times*, Aug. 22, 1950, 5.

Ziegler, Jack. "Oh, great! Here comes the policeman of the world again." Cartoon. *New Yorker*, Oct. 11, 1999, 72.

INDEX

and eternal youth, 10, 19, 81, 112, 116, 157; and gender/sexual development, 25, 102–4, 112–17, 159. *See also* Boy (character); boy characters; incest; nostalgia: for youth; ontogeny-phylogeny; polymorphous perversity; regression

chimps, 5, 46, 56, 81. *See also* ape-creatures; Cheta (character)

Chopin, Kate, *The Awakening*, 71

Christianity, 87, 99, 114–15, 142, 160, 191n55; Christian imagery, 110, 136; and colonial racism, 122; and a post-God world, 23, 25, 29; Protestant culture and anal retentiveness, 195n48; referenced in political poster, 44; and use of Sampson allusion, 40. *See also* Adam and Eve; Cain and Abel

Chudacoff, Howard P., *The Age of the Bachelor*, 192n11

civilization versus nature, 2–4, 8, 16–17, 55, 67–68, 116–18, 174–76; and blackface, 195n48; and gender/sexuality, 72, 86–92, 95–96, 121, 125; and the incest taboo, 142–43, 150–61. *See also* animal-human question

class, 26–28, 30, 52, 89, 184n56; aristocratic, 9, 21, 26, 27–28, 53, 75; and cannibalism, 52, 132; and homosexuality, 121, 132; and incest, 145; and the novel, 29; working, associated with ape-creatures and "lower races," 52–53

Clayton, Alice (character), 65, 70, 85, 88, 184n56; similarity to Kala, 24, 89, 112

Clayton, Jack (character), 85, 96, 98, 114, 132. See also *The Son of Tarzan* (Burroughs); *The Son of Tarzan* (film)

Clayton, John (character), 26, 65, 79, 85, 88, 184n56; quoted, 33

Clayton, William Cecil (character), 18, 23, 27, 82, 159, 198n19; death of, 26–27; as effeminate, 72, 121

Close, Glenn, 145

Cobra art movement, 53

Coca-Cola, 2, 46

Cohan, Steven, 112

Cold War, 38–49. *See also* communism and Marxism

colonialism, 33–57, 71, 76–77, 118, 165; and the homosexuality-bestiality association, 119–25, 126–27; and incest, 147, 156

Columbian Exposition (Chicago World's Fair), 60, 87, 122–23, 125

comics: and Burroughs's death, 169; and Burroughs's product empire, 34; censored in Russia, 184n61; dark-skinned Tarzan in, 70; femme-Tarzans in, 90; and Frederic Wertham, 109, 130; incestuous homoeroticism in, 158–59; interracial homoeroticism in, 117–18, 125; in *Modern Times*, 110; and publishing history, 13, 43, 47–50, 180n1; sexually suggestive, 93, 127, 192n63, 196n82; in Vietnam, 50

commercialization, 5, 14, 34, 55

communism and Marxism, 35–44, 50–54; and cannibalism, 40, 43–44; and investigations of the film industry, 38, 39, 52. *See also* capitalism; Cold War; materialism

Conan the Destroyer (film), 194n25

Connery, Sean, 6

Conrad, Joseph, *Heart of Darkness*, 11, 155, 199n37

Cooper, James Fenimore, 97, 117, 193n16. *See also* Bumpo, Natty (character)

Corley, Carl, 195n51, 196n83

Cox, Nigel, *Tarzan Presley*, 74, 144, 188n62

Crabbe, Buster, 104

Crawford, Dan, 60

Creed, Barbara, 109, 142–43, 151

cultural icon, decline of Tarzan as, 11, 49–50, 163–67

cultural relativism. *See* language, literacy, and books: cultural instruction; socialization

Curious George (character), 127

Dandridge, Dorothy, 169. See also *Tarzan's Peril* (film)

Danilowatz, Josef, 131

Dark Horse comics, 49, 187n42

D'Arnot, Paul (character), 21, 29, 65, 67, 193n22

Darwin, Charles, 3–4, 14, 126; and adolescence and ontogeny-phylogeny, 16–17, 123; and detective fiction, 29, 174; and Freud, 123, 148; and the post-Darwin world, 25, 29, 126

"A Date with Your Family" (film), 4

death: collective wish for, 175–76; fear of, 24–25, 31, 87, 101, 148, 166–72. *See also* immortality; Parker, James (character): desires death

"The Death of Freud" (Phillips), 200n43

The Death of Nature (Merchant), 189n18

The Deer Hunter (film), 47

Derek, Bo, 170, 171; photograph of, 80. See also *Tarzan, the Ape Man* (1981 film)

Derek, John, 171, 180n24. See also *Tarzan, the Ape Man* (1981 film)

detective fiction, 29, 31, 74, 193n22

Diamonds of Kilimandjaro (film), 90, 104, 111

diaspora. *See* immigration

Dickens, Charles, 18, 23

Disney, 35, 48, 163, 188n63. *See also* entries for specific film titles

Disney, Walt, 35

Dracula (character), 198n22

Dracula (Stoker), 196n69

Du Chaillu, Paul, 60, 186n4, 195n56

Dum-Dum ritual, 65, 132, 149

Dyer, Richard, 73, 91

eBay, 108

Eby, Carl, 185n1

ecofeminism, 86–92, 99, 190n34

Edgar Rice Burroughs, Inc., 34, 83, 150, 169, 180n1, 188n62

education: self-education, 17, 22, 173–74; in the United States, 4, 15–21, 23

Eliot, T. S., 23; "The Love Song of J. Alfred Prufrock," 30–31, 174; *The Waste Land*, 34

Ellison, Julie, 118

Eminem, 74

Ericson, John, 192n3

The Eternal Lover (Burroughs), 98; as *The Eternal Savage* (book version of magazine story), 189n10

The Eternal Savage (Burroughs), 189n10

Europe, 196n70; and colonialism, 42, 45, 54–57; and Old World–New World dichotomy, 21–28, 45, 54–55, 67–68, 84; rip-offs from, 35–36; and sexuality, 121; Tarzan's dominance in, 34, 37, 39, 41, 53–54. *See also* Ireland and the Irish; Paris, France

Evans, Nicholas M., 70

existentialism. *See* narcissism; nature versus nurture: and self-determination

"Extracts from the Memoirs of 'Lord Greystoke'" (Farmer), 144

family life, 20, 53. *See also* fatherhood; incest; motherhood; suburbs; tree house

Fanon, Franz, 132

fans, xi, 15, 43, 70, 113–16; on the films, 10, 99, 148

Farmer, Philip José, 47; *The Adventures of the Peerless Peer*, 181n38; "Extracts from the Memoirs of 'Lord Greystoke,'" 144; *A Feast Unknown*, vii, 47, 107–8, 131, 144, 157; *Tarzan Alive*, 81, 181n38

Farrow, John, 171

Farrow, Mia, 171

fatherhood, 15–16, 85; Burroughs and, 172; colonialism as, 76–77, 156. *See also* incest; paternalism

faux-Tarzans and Tarzan rip-offs, 4, 47, 117, 125, 171; Burroughs's own, 185n3; international, 35–36, 50. *See also* femme-Tarzans; *Forbidden Jungle* (film); parodies; Werper, Barton

A Feast Unknown (Farmer), 47, 107–8, 131, 144, 157; quoted, vii
feminism, 83, 87, 100, 104, 110, 125, 194n25. See also black (nonwhite) womanhood; ecofeminism; misogyny; white womanhood
femme-Tarzans, 48, 90–92, 93, 104, 111, 171
Fenton, Robert, 1
Fiedler, Leslie, 97–100, 116–19; and Fiedlerian pairs, 132, 141, 158–59, 194n26, 195n51; quoted, vii, 5; on Tarzan, 14, 135, 174–75
Fielding, Henry, 23
films, 1, 19, 22, 99; critiques of, 6–11, 75, 95; and the Hollywood Walk of Fame, 9; production rate of, 47; and U.S. cultural imperialism, 33–55; and Weissmuller's marriage, 191n45. See also Hays Code; and entries for specific films
Fimmel, Travis, 111, 164
Forbidden Jungle (film), 56, 120, 158
Ford, Betty, 48
Ford, Gerald, 48
Foster, Harold R., 180n1
Fraser, Brendan, 165
Freud, Sigmund, 4, 135, 173, 200n43; The Future of an Illusion, 147–48; and misogyny, 154; and moviegoing, 181n21; and orality, 133, 136, 147, 152; and the primal horde, 147–50, 155–61; and primitivism, 124, 125, 157; and repression, 15, 151; and sublimation, 172; Totem and Taboo, 148. See also incest; polymorphous perversity; regression; repression
frontier. See West, the American: and the closing of the frontier; Westerns
Fuchs, Cynthia, 118
Fury, David, 46, 189n11, 191n37
The Future of an Illusion (Freud), 147–48

Galton, Francis, 60, 185n4
Garbo, Greta, 190n27
Gates, Allene, 35
gender. See black (nonwhite) manhood; black (nonwhite) womanhood; homosexuality and gender-bending; white manhood; white womanhood
George of the Jungle (animated television series), 47, 50, 165
Girard, René, 108, 116, 126, 129, 159–60, 196n60; and the sacrificial victim, 198n29
Golden Temple Amazons (film), 104
The Green Berets (film), 46–47, 55
Greene, Graham, The Quiet American, 42
Greystoke: The Legend of Tarzan (film), 9, 14, 48–49, 83, 133; and incest, 144–46; white manhood and sexuality in, 119, 120
Griffin, Susan, 86–88, 101
Griffith, Gordon, 19
Gubar, Susan, 72, 123–24, 132–33, 136; on Hemingway, 185n1

Hagenbeck, Carl, 60–61, 125; Beasts and Men, 60, 139
Haggard, H. Rider, She, 190n24
Hall, G. Stanley, 16–21, 30, 172
Harris, Richard, 80. See also Parker, James
Harris, Trudier, 124
Hawkes, Stephen. See Sipek, Steve
Hays Code, 73, 76, 92–93, 183n35
Heart of Darkness (Conrad), 11, 155, 199n37
Hemingway, Ernest, 3, 185n1
Henderson the Rain King (Bellow), 193n19
Henry, Mike, 19, 46–47, 51, 55, 170, 192n3
Her Jungle Love (film), 90, 168
"Hiawatha" (Longfellow), 70
Ho Chi Minh, 40, 51
holler of Tarzan, 7–8, 10, 36–37, 48
Hollywood. See films
Holmes, Sherlock, 181n38, 193n22. See also detective fiction
homosexuality and gender-bending, 68, 101, 107–37, 183n26, 188n64, 199n34; and race, 122, 194n42; relation to incest, 139–42, 144, 147, 154, 157–60. See also Baker, Josephine; black (nonwhite) manhood; black (nonwhite) womanhood; masculinity;

homosexuality and gender-bending *(continued)* polymorphic perversity; primitivism; white manhood; white womanhood

Howard, John, 159

"How I Became an Author" (Burroughs), quoted, 13

humor, 5–11. *See also* parodies

hybridity: animal-animal, 139; animal-human, 56–57, 75, 89. *See also* bestiality; Romulus and Remus

identity confusion, 6–7, 21–22, 27–31, 54. *See also* childhood and adolescence

immigration, 17, 21–22, 28, 30–31, 101, 110; and the cocktail, 75; and fictional orphans as surrogates, 187n40; and Hispanic Americans, 125

immortality, 19, 101, 154, 163, 172, 191n51. *See also* childhood and adolescence: and eternal youth; death: fear of

imperialism. *See* colonialism

incest, 137, 139–61; as aspect of primitivism, 142–43, 147–50, 154–61; and colonialism, 147, 156; father-daughter, 142–43, 146, 151–61; father-son, 146; and homosexuality, 121, 140–41, 158–60, 197n4; mother-son, 141–42, 144–45, 146–47, 152–61; sibling, 141–42, 145–47, 158–60. *See also* cannibalism; polymorphous perversity; primitivism; regression

industrialization, 20, 23, 31, 110, 175

insanity, 17–18, 53, 86, 89, 167, 188n64; and motherhood, 70, 85

international popularity of Tarzan, 1, 11, 34–41, 50–54, 116. *See also entries for specific regions*

Iraq War, 49

Ireland and the Irish, 21, 151, 155, 199n34

isolationism, 37–38, 48–49

Jack (character). *See* Clayton, Jack (character)

Jackson, Janet, 74

Jackson, Michael, 74

Jacobson, Matthew Fry, 55

Jai (character), 22, 55

Jane (character). *See* Porter/Parker, Jane (character)

Jane Is Jane Forever (film), 167

Jaws (film), 199n37

Jeffords, Susan, *The Remasculanization of America*, 183n34

Jeffries, Jeff, 62–64, 69

Johnson, Jack, 62–64, 66–69, 73

Johnson, James Weldon, 72

Johnson, Lyndon, 44

Jones, Grace, 194n25

Joyce, Brenda, 81

Joyce, James, 23; *Ulysses*, 34

The Jungle Book (animated film), 188n63

The Jungle Books (Kipling), 23, 56, 181n39, 185n4

Jungle Comics (comic), 93

Jungle Jim (character), 90

Jungle Lovers (film), 147

Jungle Master (rip-off film), 35

Jungle Stories (comic), 93

Jungle Tales of Tarzan (Burroughs), 127–28, 134–35

Jungle Twins (comic), 117, 158–59

Jungle War Stories (comic), 43, 47

Kahn, Gordon, 52

Kala (character), 23, 56, 85, 89, 128; and Alice, 24, 89, 112; death of, 24, 89; and incest, 143–44, 145, 149; photograph of, xiv

Karlin, Daniel, 23

Kaspa the Lion Man, 4

Kasson, John, 112

Katz, Jonathan Ned, 100–101, 119, 121, 125, 135, 159

Kennedy, John F., 55

Kerchak (character), 26, 78, 79, 89, 144
Kid in Africa (film), 15, 147
King of the Jungle (rip-off film), 35
Kingston, Natalie, 82, 146
Kipling, Rudyard: *The Jungle Books*, 23, 56, 181n39, 185n4; "The White Man's Burden," 64
Kolodny, Annette, *The Lay of the Land*, 189n18, 197n7
Korak the Killer (character). *See* Clayton, Jack (character)
Kulonga (character), 69, 89, 124, 132–33, 176–77

Lacassin, Francis, 96
The Lad and the Lion (Burroughs), 185n3
Lamour, Dorothy, 168
Lan, Ly, 50
language, literacy, and books, 21, 25, 89, 110–11, 172–75, 184n57; cultural instruction, 21, 27, 72; and gender/sexuality, 1, 6, 95, 110–11, 129; and overseas film markets, 53; and Tarzan as working-class signifier, 52; and white superiority, 65–66
Lansdale, Joe, 189n10
La of Opar (character), 75, 85, 89, 101–2, 190n24; and Tarzan's ritual sacrifice, 132, 135
Lara, Joe, 111
Larsen, Nella, *Passing*, 72
Larson, Wolf, 111
Latin America, 34, 39–41, 55, 68, 75–76; Tarzan banned in, 52; and the U.S.-Vietnam war, 45–46
Lawless, Lucy, 119
Law of the Jungle (film), 127
lawsuits, 66–67, 94, 187n38, 188n62. *See also* censorship and expurgation
The Lay of the Land (Kolodny), 189n18, 197n7
Leave It to Beaver (television series), 2
The Legend of Tarzan (animated television series), 49–50, 82

Lesser, Julian, 8
Lesser, Sol, 1, 8, 34–35, 37–38, 81, 184n57
Lewis, Bertram, 181n21
Liane, Jungle Goddess (film), 90–91
Lincoln, Elmo, 2, 4, 19, 66, 167, 168; death of, 169; Hollywood Walk of Fame star for, 180n24; photograph of, 12
The Lion King: The Broadway Musical (stage production), 163
Livingstone, David, 59, 186n4
London, Jack, 3, 62, 186n4
Longfellow, Henry Wadsworth, "Hiawatha," 70
Lott, Eric, 70, 124
"The Love Song of J. Alfred Prufrock" (Eliot), 30–31, 174
Luana (film), 90, 111, 190n24

Macfadden, Bernarr, *Physical Culture* magazine, 192n3
Madagascar (animated film), 137
Mad Magazine (comic), 47
Madonna, 188n64
Mahoney, Jock, 70
Markey, Enid, 81, 170
Marx, Karl, 53. *See also* communism and Marxism
masculinity. *See* black (nonwhite) manhood; white manhood
masochism, 87–88, 104, 135–37, 154, 200n44
materialism, 28, 51–52, 166. *See also* capitalism; communism and Marxism
McTeague (Norris), 126
McWhorter, George, xi, 180n1
Melville, Herman, *Moby Dick*, 117, 199n37
men's magazines, 43–44, 70, 93
Merchant, Carolyn, *The Death of Nature*, 189n18
Merrill, Frank, 82, 146
métis. *See* mixed-race characters and individuals
MGM, 49, 50–51, 77, 93–94, 98–99; and

MGM *(continued)*
death of Jane, 120; and legal issues
with *Tarzan, the Ape Man* (1981), 66,
77, 94, 129; replaced by RKO, 8, 37; and
Weissmuller's first marriage, 191n45
Middle East: and Tarzan, 1, 35–36; U.S. wars
in, 49–50
Miles, Vera, 97
Miller, Perry, 175
minstrelsy. *See* blackface and minstrelsy
miscegenation, 57–58, 68–79; as bestiality, 104, 127–28; and Hemingway, 185n1;
and incest, 138, 142–45, 151, 157. *See also*
bestiality; black (nonwhite) manhood;
black (nonwhite) womanhood; hybridity;
mixed-race characters and individuals; primitivism; white manhood; white
womanhood
misogyny, 85–87, 104, 116; and homosexuality, 158. *See also* Porter/Parker, Jane (character); rape
mixed-race characters and individuals, 40,
56–58, 70, 71, 76, 147; Tarzan as, 69, 122
Moby Dick (Melville), 117, 199n37
modernism, literary, 23, 33, 87; and the visual
arts, 17. *See also* Anderson, Sherwood; Eliot, T. S.; Hemingway, Ernest; Johnson,
James Weldon; Larsen, Nella
Modern Times (film), 110
Monkey Business (film), 81
The Monkey King (Robida), 181n39
monogenesis versus polygenesis, 71. *See also*
tropicalization
Monroe, Marilyn, 81
Moreland, Mantan, 127
Morgan: A Suitable Case for Treatment (film),
53
Morrow, Gray, 180n1
motherhood, 15, 24, 29, 56, 85, 99; and colonialism, 56, 76; and insanity, 70, 85,
188n64; and Jane's relationship with Tarzan, 19; as universal female instinct, 89,

112. *See also* Africa; Clayton, Alice (character); incest; Kala (character); Porter/
Parker, Jane (character)
moviegoing, 19, 109–10, 130, 175
Mowgli. See *The Jungle Books* (Kipling)
musculinity, 118–19, 188n64, 194n25

Nabonga (film), 90, 104, 127, 190n24
Nambia/"Africa" (character), 77, 156–60
narcissism, 23–24; existentialism as, 29; and
homosexuality and incest, 144, 157–60; of
U.S. culture, 49
nationalism, U.S., 31, 33; and Americanization of immigrants, 28; as Europeanization, 54; and identity anxiety, 28, 31; and
manhood, 119, 121. *See also* colonialism
Native Americans, 55, 60, 119, 187n40,
194n26, 199n37; Acquanetta's claim, 41;
chapter epigraph, 13; Tarzan as, 70
naturalism, 3, 26, 27
nature versus civilization. *See* civilization
versus nature
nature versus nurture, 21, 26–28, 160, 193n15;
and self-determination, 3, 21–25, 29–30
Nemone (character), 75, 85, 89
neocolonialism. *See* colonialism
neoconservativism, 49–50, 166
The New Adventures of Tarzan (film), 40, 96,
172, 199n38; photograph from, 106
New Yorker, 43, 49, 130
"The Nightmare" (Burroughs), 134–35
nonwhite manhood. *See* black (nonwhite)
manhood
Norris, Frank, *McTeague*, 126
nostalgia: for colonialism 45, 55; for pastoral
life, 18, 121, 174; for youth, 18–19, 25, 30,
166. *See also* childhood and adolescence;
regression

Oak Park, Ill. *See* Chicago, Ill.
O'Keefe, Miles, 93–95, 111, 129–30
ontogeny-phylogeny, 16–18, 56, 123, 174

Tarzan: The Lost Adventure (Burroughs and
Lansdale), 189n10
Tarzan the Magnificent (film), 99, 117
Tarzan the Mighty (film), 146
Tarzan the Terrible (Burroughs), 98
Tarzan the Tiger (film), 82, 146
Tarzan the Untamed (Burroughs), 43, 98,
183n38
Tarzan Triumphant (Burroughs), 43; quoted,
59
The Tarzan Twins (Burroughs), 15, 159,
189n10, 200n41
*The Tarzan Twins with Jad-bal-ja the Golden
Lion* (Burroughs), 15
Tarzoon: Shame of the Jungle (animated film
parody), 48
Tasker, Yvonne, 118, 130, 136
Taur the Mighty (rip-off film), 35
Taylor, Frederick Winslow, 20
television, 22, 47–50, 52, 125, 175, 191n37;
asexuality in, 96–97; Home Box Of-
fice (HBO), 94. See also *The Legend of
Tarzan* (animated television series);
Saturday Night Live (television series);
Tarzan (animated television series); *Tar-
zan* (television series); *Tarzan and Jane*
(animated film); *Tarzan in Manhattan*
(telefilm); *Xena: Warrior Princess* (televi-
sion series)
Temple, Shirley, 15
Terkoz (character): rapacious desire of,
68–71, 73, 127, 134, 145; Tarzan's victory
over, 25, 102–3, 131, 141, 149, 159
Thirteen (film), 194n42
Thoreau, Henry David, 3
Tom of Finland, 125, 131
Torgovnick, Marianna, 54–55, 87, 183n36
Totem and Taboo (Fréud), 148
Trader Horn (film), 190n24
Trader Hornee (film), 48
Treasure Island (Stevenson), 8
tree house, 2, 4, 8, 84, 93

Trites, Roberta Seelinger, 30–31
tropicalization, 122. See also monogenesis
and polygenesis
Tublat (character), 89, 144, 145, 149
Turner, Frederick Jackson, 119
Twain, Mark, 74, 117, 193n19
Twitchell, James B., 142, 198n22

Ulysses (Joyce), 34
United States. See colonialism; nationalism,
U.S.; U.S. government
universal appeal, 1, 9, 11, 29–30, 50, 179n11
urbanization and urban life, 3–4, 20–23, 28,
110, 112, 175. See also suburbs
urban settings. See *Tarzan* (television se-
ries); *Tarzan in Manhattan* (telefilm);
Tarzan's New York Adventure (film); *Wild
Child* (film)
U.S. government, 37–50
USSR (Union of Soviet Socialist Repub-
lics), 35–37, 52–53
Utley, Steven D., 98

Valencius, Conevery Bolton, 70–71
Van Hise, James, 168
Van Vechten, Carl, 136
Velez, Lupe, 39–40
Vietnam War, 40, 41–48, 50–52, 54, 55

Warner Brothers, 49. See also *Tarzan*
(television series); *Xena: Warrior Princess*
(television series)
The Waste Land (Eliot), 34
Wayne, John, 112. See also *The Green Berets*
(film)
Weege, William, 44
Weintraub, Sy, 99
Weissmuller, Elizabeth, 138
Weissmuller, Johnny: death of, 37, 51, 170;
on eBay, 108; immigrated, 19; as Jungle
Jim, 90; never says "Me Tarzan, you
Jane," 82; photograph of, 138, 162; physical